The ASSIST Program

Affective/Social Skills: Instructional Strategies and Techniques

Teaching Cooperation Skills

A Validated Washington State Innovative Education Program

Published by:

Sopris West, Inc., 1140 Boston Avenue, Longmont, CO 80501

© 1990, Pat Huggins, Program Developer
1991 Revisions

Assisted by Petra Hanson
Artwork by Ernie Hergenroeder

This manual contains student handouts and transparency masters. Permission is granted for teachers to reproduce these pages for use in their classrooms. All remaining parts of this manual are the property of the author and may not be reproduced in whole or in part, by mimeograph or any other means, without her expressed written permission.

ISBN #0-944584-18-7

Acknowledgments

I would like to express my appreciation to the following people for their part in the conception and development of the ASSIST Program: to Kateri Brow, Superintendent of Issaquah School District, for her support and guidance; to Chuck Blondino and Don Glabe, for their original ideas and hours of consulting time; to Petra Hansen, Judy Christensen, and Dr. John Hoff for their special help and unique contributions to the program; to Ralph Carlson and Steve Nelson for their commitment to a successful evaluation design and help with statistical analysis; to Hergie (Ernie Hergenroeder) for his permission to use his illustrations. A large share of thanks goes to the following teachers who piloted the ASSIST Program and, through their feedback, helped to make the curriculum more effective:

Issaquah School District
  Ruth Adamitz
  Terry Adams
  Delores Stewart
  Mary Stolze
  Jim Jorden
  Cathy Kirkman

North Kitsap School District
  Renee Fossom
  Becky Sibbet
  Pat Jones
  Carolyn Russell
  Shirley Parrot
  Karen Campbell

Shoreline School District
  Paula Jones

Bellevue School District
  Meryl Thomson

A special thanks to Neale Huggins for his support, advice, illustrations, and his effort to make this curriculum as visually attractive as possible.

The ASSIST Program includes many activities and ideas contributed by teachers over the course of several years. We would appreciate any information that would allow for correction of any errors or omissions in acknowledgment of ownership of materials.

Teaching Cooperation Skills

Table of Contents

Overview .... 1 - 3

Introduction .... 5 - 49

Section A: Lessons 51

   Lesson 1:   Learning to Work Together .... 53 - 57

      Students will learn
- what cooperation means.
- roles that can be assumed in a group.
- how to work with a partner on a learning task.

   Lesson 2:   Working in a Group .... 59 - 63

      Students will learn
- how to assume the roles of both participant and helper while engaging in a small group activity.
- how to assess their behavior while engaging in a small group activity.

   Lesson 3:   Learning How to Listen to Others .... 65 - 74

      Students will learn
- the skills of good listening so that they may participate more productively in cooperation activities.

   Lesson 4:   Encouraging Others to Share Their Ideas ... 75 - 81

      Students will learn
- how to encourage one another to participate during cooperation activities.
- how to develop actions and feelings that promote cooperation in small groups.

   Lesson 5:   Responding to Others in Group Discussion ... 83 - 89

      Students will learn
- the skills of linking, restating, and summarizing one another's contributions when engaged in cooperation activities.

Lesson 6: Cooperative Problem-Solving Through Brainstorming . . . 91 - 96

    Students will learn
        to work cooperatively to generate as many ideas as they can for solving a given problem situation.

Lesson 7: Cooperative Decision-Making Through Consensus . . . . .97 - 105

    Students will learn
        to cooperate by striving towards consensus regarding a given problem situation.

Lesson 8: Dealing With Conflict in Cooperation Groups . . . . 107 - 113

    Students will learn
        the skill for giving negative feedback.

        to adapt to the give-and-take of working with others.

Lesson 9: Learning to Negotiate and Compromise . . . . 115 - 120

    Students will learn
        the skills for negotiation and compromise so that they may more effectively resolve conflict situations that arise in cooperative learning.

Lesson 10: Working Cooperatively on a Long-Term Simulation Project . . . . 121 - 126

    Students will learn
        to negotiate.

        to reach consensus.

        to work cooperatively while implementing a simulated farming adventure.

Lesson 11: Section B: Using Cooperation Skills in Classroom Meetings and Discussions . . . . 127 - 134

    Students will learn
        to participate effectively in classroom meetings and discussions and will gain skill and confidence in expressing themselves.

Section B: Activities Designed To Promote Cooperation Skills: . . . . . . 135 - 266
    1. Cooperative Decision-Making Activities
    2. Cooperative Art Activities
    3. Cooperative Structure-Building Activities

        4. Cooperative Survival Simulation Activities
        5. Cooperative Puzzle-Solving Activities
        6. Cooperative Free-Time and Recess Activities

Section C: Working Cooperatively On Academic Tasks: . . . . 267 - 308
        1. Cooperating on Math Activities
        2. Cooperating on Language Arts Activities
        3. Cooperating on Social Studies Activities
        4. General Cooperation Strategies
        5. Interdisciplinary Activities

Bibliography . . . . 309 - 310

Appendix: Sentence Starters for Promoting Thinking

Overview

What is it?

ASSIST is an affective education program designed to increase students' growth in the areas of self-concept, interpersonal relationships, and emotional understanding. Numerous studies indicate the students' personal and social adjustment in the classroom has a direct relationship to academic performance. The curriculum teaches critical affective skills which can benefit students throughout their lives. The ASSIST program can be incorporated into an existing social studies, health, or language arts program, or it can stand alone as a curriculum for personal growth and interpersonal relations.

The ASSIST curriculum is the result of 1) an extensive review of child development theory and research, 2) a review of existing social/emotional education programs, and 3) the contributions of many teachers and students who participated in the development of the program. ASSIST incorporates concepts and procedures from social learning theory, from behavioristic and humanistic psychology, and from proven educational practices.

What's included?

The ASSIST lessons include

- an objective, materials, and a "To the Teacher" section which provides a theoretical background for lesson concepts;

- a "scripted" lesson that includes everything that should be said when teaching lesson concepts and skills;

- a series of transparency masters and student worksheet masters; and

- a variety of supplementary activities, many of which relate to basic subject areas and which provide opportunities for integration of lesson concepts.

The ASSIST curriculum is grouped into the following manuals:

Building Self Esteem in the Classroom - This manual (formerly Building Self Concept in the Classroom) includes a series of sequential lessons and activities designed to promote self awareness and self regard. Students learn to use the techniques of positive inner speech to build self esteem and to cope effectively with mistakes and putdowns. Also included in the manual is a workbook for both primary and intermediate students and a self esteem unit for middle school students.

Teaching Cooperation Skills - This manual includes a series of lessons and experiential activities designed to teach students the skills necessary for cooperative learning to take place. Lessons focus on the skills of self-management, listening and collaborative problem solving. Students learn to resolve conflicts through compromise and to strive for consensus. A wide variety of cooperative learning activities are included so that these skills can be applied and practiced.

Teaching Friendship Skills - The manual includes a series of lessons designed to teach the identified processes used by children who get along well with their peers. Students learn to listen to others, to empathize with and understand their point of view, and to make them feel valued. In addition, a wide variety of structured activities, games and worksheets enables all students to acquire and practice the friendship skills they need to be happy and successful both in school and throughout their lives.

Helping Kids Handle Anger - This manual includes lessons designed to enable students to acknowledge, accept, and constructively express their anger. Students learn 1) to use inner speech to inhibit aggressive behaviors, 2) to use thinking skills for choosing constructive behaviors when angry, 3) appropriate language to express anger, 4) a variety of techniques to release energy after anger arousal, and 5) ways to deal with the anger of others. Role play and puppets are utilized to encourage active and creative student involvement.

Creating a Caring Classroom - This manual (formerly Establishing a Positive Classroom Climate) includes a collection of strategies designed to promote mutual respect, trust, risk-taking and support in the classroom. Included are 1) get-acquainted activities, 2) classroom management procedures, 3) an affective behavior scale and behavior improvement strategies for students with special needs, 4) a relaxation training program, 5) a "Warm Fuzzy" unit, 6) a large collection of activities and ideas for building a cohesive and caring classroom community.

Teaching About Sexual Abuse - The lessons in this manual are designed to provide students with information about sexual abuse in a low-key, matter-of-fact way. Lessons focus on 1) children's right to reject inappropriate behavior, 2) assertiveness skills helpful in the prevention of sexual abuse, and 3) the establishment of family and community support systems. Preventative education is one of the keys to addressing this problem, which can affect children from all social and economic classes.

Each ASSIST lesson presents one or more concepts that are central to social/emotional health. Because of the timelessness and generality of most of these concepts, the same lessons can be taught to students in more than one grade. Each time students are exposed to the concepts in an ASSIST lesson, they are able to consider them from a new frame of reference and make new and more precise applications.

The activities that accompany the lessons are designed to

- help students "process" the ideas presented in the lessons;

- provide opportunities for students to practice the personal/social skills related to lesson concepts; and

- nudge students into higher levels of social reasoning and affective skills. The teaching and learning methods in the ASSIST program emphasize the use of direct instruction, circle discussion, role play, puppets, games, learning partners, small group activities, and student worksheets.

Does it work?

ASSIST was developed with Title IV-C Innovative Education Funds and was tested in second through sixth grade classrooms in four school districts. Statistically significant gains in self-concept and social skills occurred in eight out of nine assessments. As a result, ASSIST was validated in Washington State, designated cost-effective and exportable, and is now in the State's Bank of Proven Practices, a clearinghouse for quality education programs.

ASSIST manuals can be obtained from Sopris West, P.O. Box 1809, Longmont, Colorado 80502-1809, (303) 651-2829.

TEACHING COOPERATION SKILLS

Introduction

Full development of the personality in its most intellectual aspects is indissoluble from the whole group of emotional, ethical, or social relationships that make up school life.

-- Jean Piaget

The Benefits of Cooperative Learning

Cooperation is the most important and basic form of human interaction, and the skills of cooperating successfully are essential skills everyone needs to master. Because much of the work we do in life requires collaboration with others, learning to work in a group lays an important foundation for later life. In many classrooms, students work individually or with limited interaction with one another. If there are questions, it is usually the teacher who answers them. When completing assignments, there is little opportunity for helping and sharing with peers. While it is sometimes necessary for students to work independently, research supports the educational benefits of sharing, helping, and working in pairs or small groups in the classroom. Cooperative learning is the appropriate format for many instructional situations. It provides a learning environment that serves children's intellectual development. As explained by Piaget, interaction is one of the essential ingredients for learning; cooperative learning maximizes the interaction that occurs among students.

A key element in cooperative learning is that students get to exchange their thoughts about various subjects with each other. In discussion, they justify their viewpoints, validate facts, deal with contradictions, and at times alter their opinions. As a result of becoming aware of different points of view, students are encouraged to analyze their own ideas and to be objective in their thinking. This is when learning occurs.

When students have the skills to work together, the following can happen:

- Students become more comfortable with one another and less defensive.

- More ideas are shared and students are typically more open to what they learn from their peers.

- Directions and assistance can come not only from the teachers, but from other students as well.

- Factual material is better remembered because it is discussed with peers in cooperative groups.

- Students improve their ability to see a situation from someone else's point of view.

- An enthusiasm for learning tends to develop when students share information, generate ideas, and complete tasks together.

Opportunities to learn the skills for working cooperatively in small groups may be especially useful in the classrooms where special education students are "mainstreamed." If mainstreaming programs are to achieve their goals, then these students must become fully participating members of the classroom. Participating in small groups is less threatening than participating in the whole group and is a good way to help mainstreamed students become known and accepted. In addition, when students work together on academic tasks, there is often an unspoken camaraderie that develops and these good feelings frequently continue into other activities. Group cooperation activities are not a "cure-all" for solving problems posed by mainstreaming but they can be helpful ways to promote the successful adjustment of these students.

Numerous personal and social benefits can also occur with students in cooperative learning. Helping students develop the attitudes and skills to work cooperatively can also help those students who have friendship problems. Typically, classroom friendship patterns are difficult to change. Children who have a few close friends are often reluctant to make more friends, and those who have had little past success in making friends are afraid to extend themselves to others. They see any attempt to make new friends as a potential threat to an already low self-esteem. By involving students in cooperation activities and implementing some of the strategies which will be described shortly, it is possible to increase the opportunities for students with few or no friends to interact with others and to reveal their potential as rewarding friends. Frequent interaction is a prerequisite to friendship. Working together in small groups is one way to open up communication and help students to build new relationships.

Varied arrangements of students in groups help to avoid the formation of classroom cliques and the perpetuation of inaccurate stereotypes. Working together in small groups, then, is one way to open up communication and to help students build new relationships.

Risks of Competition

Cooperative learning requires a classroom setting that is safe enough for students to risk trying out their ideas--one where the emphasis isn't always on being right, but on exploring ideas together. It is interaction with others that distinguishes cooperative learning from competition and from individualized learning. It is true that competition provides incentive and can be a powerful tool for learning. A little competition is often a good thing. It keeps people on their toes and helps them do a better job. But competition is destructive when it results in the following:

- trying to build up the importance of one's own job and lessen the importance of others;
- refusing to extend whole-hearted cooperation which others need to do their jobs well;
- exploiting another's weakness;
- sniping, backbiting, and criticism; and
- holding back information.

Because of the danger of these things occurring when a competitive format is used, it is best to have small groups of students rather than individuals competing against one another. In this way cooperation and support within a group can also be maintained.

Teaching Students Cooperation Skills

Many teachers like the idea of students cooperating with one another and attempt to involve students in small group learning activities. What often happens, however, is that the noise level rises and the group format is perceived by students as "fun time." Teachers then feel that not enough is being accomplished to merit continuing the small group work. Yet, if students could work productively in small groups, many teachers would like their students to engage in cooperative learning. Directly teaching students how to work together in small groups will enable teachers to handle the problems that usually occur when they initiate small group projects in their classrooms.

The approach to teaching cooperation skills is very similar to other good teaching. Any teacher who can teach reading and math can also teach cooperation skills. As with academic subjects, the steps for teaching social skills involve

1. defining the behaviors to be taught;
2. assessing the student's proficiency;
3. teaching the needed skills through presentation of examples, requiring responses, and providing feedback;
4. evaluating results of teaching, re-teaching where necessary;
5. providing opportunities for practice, generalization, and maintenance over time; and
6. using positive reinforcement.

Learning to work together requires that students know how to express their ideas without interrupting, how to disagree, how to gather more information, how to comply, how to encourage others to speak, how to negotiate, and how to reach consensus.

While specific objectives for group cooperation will vary among teachers and students, the following objectives would be common ones:

- Students know that cooperation means working together to achieve a goal.

- Students know that cooperation is different from competition (working against others) or from working individually.

- Students can differentiate between cooperative and non-cooperative behaviors.

- Students can identify specific behaviors that should be changed for a productive cooperative activity to take place and can provide helpful comments.

- Students are able to assume a helpful role in a small group activity.

- Students know the skills of good listening and use these skills in groups.

- Students can answer questions for one another rather than always involving the teacher.

- Given a completed group task, students are able to assess their own behavior in a group, identify positive behaviors, and suggest alternatives to non-helpful behaviors.

The lessons in this manual lead students through the following stages to ensure they learn the skills necessary for cooperative learning.

- Students are helped to get a clear understanding of what cooperation is conceptually and behaviorally.
- Cooperative behaviors are identified, sequenced, and demonstrated.
- Students are involved in practice situations that require the use of cooperation skills, at first in teams of two, then in small groups.
- Students are given immediate specific feedback on how well they are performing each cooperation skill so that they can correct errors and identify progress. This feedback increases student motivation to learn and practice the skill.
- Students are provided with a wide variety of problem-solving activities that involve cooperation skills.
- Students collaborate in small groups on academic subjects, group research, and investigation.

When to Use Cooperative Learning

The conditions under which it is effective and desirable to use cooperative learning are almost too numerous to list:

- whenever you want to promote divergent thinking or creativity;
- when the academic task is complex;
- when problem-solving is desired;
- when you want a wide range of cognitive and affective outcomes;
- when the social development of students is a major instructional goal; and
- when you want students to perceive each other as the major resource and source of support.

Many teachers involve students in cooperative learning 60% to 70% of the time, utilizing individual and competitive learning formats the remainder of the time. Some organize the classroom into cooperative learning groups with students sitting permanently in small clusters or groups. Others have students work cooperatively only on certain days or at certain times each day.

It is not only academic activities that lend themselves to a cooperative format. Every classroom has many opportunities for students to work together. These could include working in pairs on typical classroom maintenance jobs, such as cleaning the boards or emptying the wastebasket. Some class activities lend themselves to an assembly line operation, for example, making class folders or booklets, collating, etc. Typical classroom craft activities could be done together on an assembly line basis. The point that should be stressed is that dividing up a task and working together is sometimes the most efficient and effective way to get a job done.

What Is the Most Appropriate Group Size?

Whenever you use cooperative activities, you will need to decide on the appropriate group size for the assignment. The best size of a group will vary according to the desired processes and outcomes of the assignment, the age of students, the division of labor, and the number of students in the class. Small groups of four to eight members have been used successfully for cooperative discussions. The group is small enough to allow everyone to take an active part in the discussion, yet large enough to provide the diversity of opinions, information, points of view, and background needed for effective problem-solving. In groups larger than 10, members may not have enough time to express themselves. In problem-solving activities, a group size that maximizes each member's participation is preferable, and this may mean using pairs or triads for tasks that require high involvement and are not easily broken down into a division of labor. For many cooperative activities, a group of four or five is optimum. No rule of thumb is possible in deciding what size group to utilize; it is necessary to experiment to determine what size works best for a particular purpose.

One strategy for ensuring total participation and the chance for each student to develop interaction skills is to start a cooperative activity in pairs. When students have arrived at an answer, instruct each pair to join with another pair and discuss the issue in this group of four until they arrive at an appropriate answer. Proceed to combine groups until the total class is meeting as one group. Although this takes some time to accomplish, the payoff in active participation and involvement may well be worth it, and it gives the teacher a chance to watch students in action in a variety of groups. This exercise may answer your questions about optimal group size with your class.

Teaching Cooperation Skills

How Do You Assign Students to Groups?

There are many ways to form cooperation groups. Ability grouping is not suited to cooperative learning. It is heterogeneity that pays off. In a cooperative structure, random assignment usually assures a good mixture of boys and girls, highly verbal and passive students, leaders and followers, and enthusiastic and reluctant learners.

Random assignment can be accomplished by using a count-off procedure, which divides the number of students in the class by the number of members you want in each group. The latter is the highest number to which the students should number-off. For example, if there are 28 students and you want groups of seven, instruct students to count off from one to seven. Then have all the number ones form a group, the twos another group, and so on.

Another quick way to divide students into groups involves using a **deck of playing cards**. Label each cluster of desks with the number of playing cards (Ace, 2, 3, etc.). Select the corresponding cards from the deck, shuffle, and distribute to students. Those who hold Aces go to the Ace table, and so forth. The randomness of this system helps deal with typical elementary school situations where boys say they don't want to work with girls and vice versa, or where cliques like to work together to the exclusion of others.

Sometimes, such as during the early part of the school year, you may wish to have students work with friends of their choice in order to ensure that they will feel comfortable in the group. This plan can be followed easily by asking students to find two (or five or ten) other students with whom to work. Be aware, however, that sometimes students may be reluctant to take the risk of choosing other members for fear of being turned down, or they may be hurt if they are not chosen.

An alternative method of grouping is the use of a sociometric device. Give each student a card and ask him/her to write his/her name in the upper left-hand corner and then to list two class members with whom he/she would like to work. Collect the cards and assign each student to a group in which there is at least one person he/she wants to work with, or in which one person has chosen him/her as someone to work with.

Interest grouping is another alternative that works well when there are a variety of tasks, ideas, or problems. Allowing students to select the topic they are most interested in will often increase the initial involvement in the task. Another grouping possibility is to use such criteria as when birthdays fall (autumn, winter, spring, or summer) or what color clothing people are wearing (all the blues together, etc.). You can probably devise other grouping arrangements.

A special grouping technique that is very effective in promoting both cooperation and self-esteem is "jig-saw" grouping. "Jig-saw" groups are formed in the following manner:

1. Look for an area in science, social studies, or math that has a number of separate learning segments. For example, in a study of Northwest Indians, there may be the components of historical background, family life, work roles, food, clothing, religious beliefs, arts, customs, etc.
2. Decide on the number of learning segments necessary for the unit or project.
3. Assign students to groups either homogeneously by skills you've observed (e.g., reading level) or randomly, whichever would promote efficiency in teaching a specific learning segment.
4. Teach each group its segment.
5. Assign each members of the "learning segment" groups to one "jig-saw" group. Once assigned to a "jig-saw" group, each member must teach the rest of the group his/her special segment or part of the lesson.
6. After "jig-saw" group members have learned one another's segments, the group should accomplish an assigned task which incorporates all the segments such as a video or radio program presentation, simulated newspaper or potlatch, or arts-and-crafts demonstrations.

A grouping for a Northwest Indian lesson for a class of 30 might look like this:

Learning Segment Groups
Customs
Food
Shelter
Arts
Rituals
CCCCCC
FFFFFF
SSSSSS
AAAAAA
RRRRRR
to
JIG-SAW GROUPS
(cooperative teaching/learning)
CFSAR
CFSAR
CFSAR
CFSAR
CFSAR
CRSAR

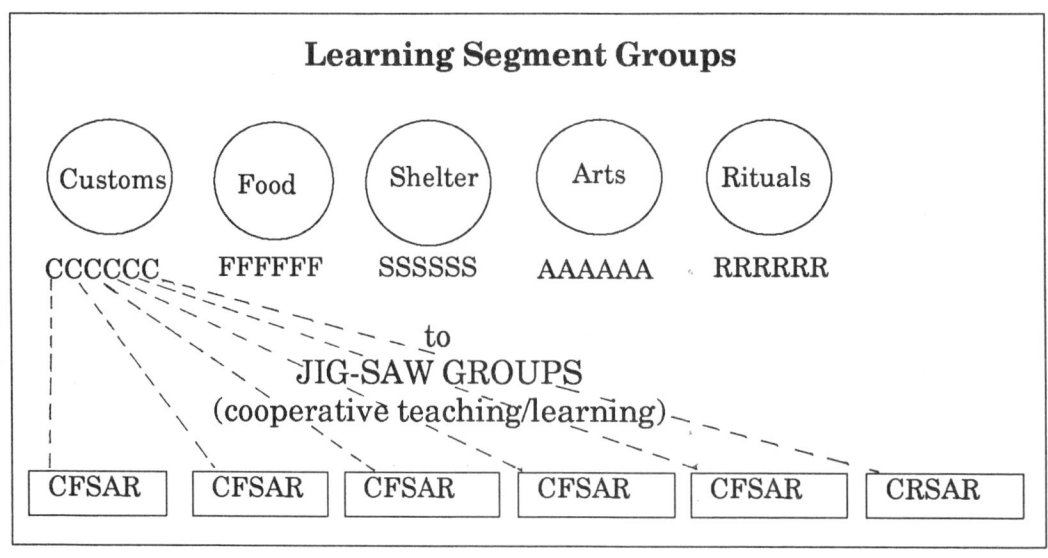

Explain to students that it's important that, over the course of the school year, each student have the opportunity to work with whoever is in their group. It's true that some groups work better together than others, but it's rare that a group finds it absolutely impossible to work together. If you have students sitting throughout the school day in cooperation groups, or clusters, they should work in that group for at least two weeks, preferably longer. When students are engaged in a specific cooperation activity, it is helpful to have them arrange their desk seating so that they can easily see and hear one another.

By using random, sociometric, and "jig-saw" groupings, and other strategies designed to increase cooperation, you can greatly enhance the effect of cooperation. You can also develop a positive social climate which supports cooperation, academic effort, and positive student self-concepts.

Building and Maintaining a Cooperative Attitude

Cooperation rests upon everyone's sharing resources, giving and receiving help, dividing the work, and contributing to group goals. A way to further these types of interactions is to present instructional goals and make it clear that during cooperative activities students should perceive each other as the primary resource for ideas and help. In order to get students into the habit of relying on one another, as well as to save needless repetition, many teachers establish the following rules:

1. Every student must be willing to help any group member who asks.
2. Students may ask for help from the teacher only when they cannot obtain the answer from anyone in the group, or only when everyone in the group has the same questions.

As often as they can, also remind and encourage students to

1. openly share their information, ideas, hunches, and reactions to group work;
2. share materials and resources;
3. express acceptance and support toward each other during cooperative activities; and
4. avoid nonsupportive behavior, such as ridicule and silence, that cuts off cooperation.

Each group member should be encouraged to experience a feeling of success when the group successfully completes an instruction activity. It is important to avoid comparisons among group members regarding the quality of their work, since such comparisons are likely to promote competition and undermine cooperation.

Classroom Management during Cooperative Learning Activities

Teacher praise for both appropriate behavior and effort is extremely important in shaping student behavior. Praise should be used frequently throughout any instructional process. When students are using the cooperation skills you have taught them, call attention to it. Point out appropriate group behavior as often as you can.

If you have a class where students are frequently disruptive, you may wish to try this procedure: Divide cooperative learning sessions into five-minute segments (increase this time as students become more and more successful). Establish a certain number of points that each group can earn for each five-minute segment, providing everyone has followed your rules for appropriate behavior during group work. Award or withhold points at the end of each block of time and explain clearly why the point was given or withheld. Establish some positive consequences for appropriate behavior and criteria for earning these consequences. For instance, if a certain number of points is gained, students may earn a free-time activity or game at the end of the working session. You may reward earned points with special privileges, or tangible items -- whatever you know students will work for.

When a particular student is engaging in inappropriate behavior, you may want to write the student's name on the board, placing a checkmark beside it every time the student is disruptive. One minute of the student's free time or recess can be deducted for every checkmark. If no names have been written on the board, the group gets an extra bonus point. This method utilizes peer pressure in a positive way. If a student consistently exhibits disruptive or noncompliant behavior, it is best to talk to him or her privately. Describe the behavior that is unacceptable to you and explain that you are counting on him or her to help you initiate group learning in the class. It may be necessary to also use brief time-outs for some students.

Setting up Group Contingencies to Promote Cooperative Achievement*

There may be times when you wish to reward groups for achievement and performance as well as behavior. There are three basic types of group contingencies that may be used to promote cooperative achievement. The first is the "average performance group contingency;" all members of a group are reinforced on the basis of the average performance of all the group members. Second, the group may be reinforced on the basis of the high performances in the group. Thus, the highest scores of one-quarter of the group may be used as a basis for determining reinforcements. This procedure is referred to as a "high performance group contingency." Finally, a group may be reinforced on the basis of the low performances in the group; the lowest scores of one-quarter of the group are used as a basis for determining reinforcements under a "low performance group contingency." Research on the use of these three types of group contingencies indicates that the most useful is the low performance group contingency. The performance of poor students is greatly raised, both through increased motivation to help their group and through tutoring by more able students. The performance of the more gifted students doesn't seem to be hampered by the use of this group contingency. The overall performance of the group tends to be higher when the "low performance group contingency" is used.

Some teachers have competition between groups. This should be used only occasionally, otherwise you will run into the same negative results that occur when individuals compete. It is far better to have groups compete with their own previous scores. When you do have groups compete with each other on a given assignment, here are a few strategies that can be used to reward high performing teams:

1. <u>Posted results:</u> A scoreboard that reports group improvement points and group standings. If you have space on your blackboard or scoreboard, it is also helpful to list the names of your top improvement point scorers.
2. <u>A newsletter</u> home after a competition.
3. <u>Time Off/On:</u> A reward for the winning group might be time off (extra time on the playground) or time-on (a computer or game area that you might have in your classroom).
4. <u>Special Place:</u> You may have a reward location in your classroom (a couch, a rug, etc.) where the winning group can sit for the week following their winning performance.

* D.W. Johnson, and F.P. Johnson, *Learning Together and Alone*, 1975, pp. 90-93.

5. <u>Special Privileges:</u> One teacher allowed her winning group to bring their stuffed animals to school for the week following their victory. Teachers also reward teams by letting them be first in line for a week.

6. <u>Stickers/Cartoons/Puzzles:</u> If you notice a group working very well together, you may want to reward them with a sticker or a cartoon. Verbal praise for cooperative behavior is always important too.

7. <u>School Recognition:</u> If you have a bulletin board in your office area that has space for student recognition, you may be able to put the name and picture of your "group of the week" in this highly visible space. Some teachers have bulletin boards outside their classroom which display a picture of the "group of the week."

8. <u>Polaroid Pictures:</u> The picture of the winning group could be displayed on your scoreboard each week.

9. <u>Traveling Trophy:</u> An object that is the Cooperative Group Trophy can sit on the winning group desks for a week.

10. <u>Bonus Points:</u> Many teachers give bonus and/or citizenship points for positive group behavior, extra credit assignments, following classroom rules.

Promoting Cooperative Behavior through Grading

Grading practices can also promote cooperation. Giving all members of a group the same grade based on the overall accomplishment of the group, rather than giving different grades to group members based on their differing contributions, has been shown to improve the quality of students' work. Often students who in the past have been nonperformers will begin working hard to avoid pulling down the group's average. You may wish to give each student two grades, an individual grade and a group grade, then average the two. Or you may wish to have each group member complete an assignment on the same or an individual topic, collect the papers, pull one from the stack, and use that as the group's grade on a given assignment.

Another option is to have only 1/3 of a student's grade depend on the group's work. Grading based on the accomplishment of the entire group rather than on individual performance is likely to produce anxiety in high-achieving students. For many, earning higher grades than other students has been their only way of achieving recognition and status. Alternative ways should be found for providing status and approval for these students while furthering the goals of the total group. For instance, they may gain recognition and admiration from the teacher and the group by taking leadership roles in their group, by making contributions to the group's progress, and by helping slower students improve their skills and thus raise the group's average grade. Changing a high-achieving student's relationship with others from competition to cooperation can have a profound and lasting positive effect. Some teachers base a student's grade partly on individual work and partly on the average of the grades of group members.

Debriefing Group Cooperation Activities

One of the best ways to help students learn to work together is to set aside time after a cooperation activity to allow students to reflect on the experience and to describe how they went about the task together. This provides an opportunity for students to review their own and others' behavior, and to assess whether it was cooperative or not. Assessing behavior is called sharing, critiquing, or debriefing. After a given task, students are provided with the opportunity to reflect on their performance. Often teachers omit these sharing sessions when they think the activity went well. Even on these occasions students need to hear all the things that did go well and to receive the reinforcement and support of the teacher. Debriefing provides an opportunity to praise the class for its participation and cooperation. It is always wise to budget time for a debriefing period.

Debriefing usually reveals some behaviors that hinder the progress of the group in completing the task. It provides an opportunity to offer suggestions for improving inappropriate behaviors. The emphasis is on how to improve the way the group works rather than on who did what. Students are not asked to judge the rightness or wrongness of what happened, but simply to take a good look at it and consider alternatives.

The time allotted to debriefing varies considerably. Sometimes debriefing can be done in a few minutes. At other times, debriefing may take 10 minutes or longer, especially if students have had difficulty working together on an activity.

Structured Experiences for Confronting Group Problems during Debriefing

During debriefing it will often be necessary to confront problems openly and focus on specific behaviors that are hindering the group progress. Since this may make students uncomfortable at first, it is best to start with procedures that are not too threatening and move gradually toward more open discussion. Anonymous observations are less threatening than reports from observers, and both of these procedures are less threatening than asking group members to speak directly to one another about the groups' problems.

Questionnaires

You can administer a questionnaire to the members of the group to gather data about the group's experience. You may wish to use one of the debriefing questionnaires provided here. Some of these forms are included again at the end of the lessons. Compile the results and summarize them for the class. Ask the group to discuss what conclusions they can draw from the results, posing questions such as the following:

- What can we learn about the way the group is functioning by looking at these results?
- What things seem to need improvement?
- How might we go about making the needed changes?

Primary/Intermediate Level   Page 19

Looking Back

How did things go? Choose one or more of the following to talk about.

I learned _____.

I was surprised _____.

There should have been more _____.

There should have been less_____.

I felt best when _____.

I wish that _____.

Next time _____.

My Group

When I am in a group, I _____
_____.

One thing I like to do in a group is _____
_____.

I like working in this group because _____
_____.

One thing I'd like to change about my group is _____
_____.

One person I enjoyed working with was _____ because _____
_____.

I felt I was part of my group because _____
_____.

I felt left out because _____
_____.

Group Climate Questionnaire

Below is a series of statements, each beginning "With this group I . . . ." Use the five-point scale provided below to indicate how you feel about each statement. Circle the word that most closely represents your response. There are no right or wrong answers. What is important is that you indicate honestly how you feel. Do not sign your name to this form.

With this group I . . .

1.	like letting others know my ideas.	Never	Seldom	Frequently	Always
2.	worry about my goofs or mistakes.	Never	Seldom	Frequently	Always
3.	feel comfortable.	Never	Seldom	Frequently	Always
4.	can let others know my feelings.	Never	Seldom	Frequently	Always
5.	talk to only a few members of the group.	Never	Seldom	Frequently	Always
6.	feel that others ignore me.	Never	Seldom	Frequently	Always
7.	feel that others care about me.	Never	Seldom	Frequently	Always
8.	feel that others do not listen to me.	Never	Seldom	Frequently	Always
9.	feel that others put down my ideas.	Never	Seldom	Frequently	Always
10.	feel that others make fun of me when I make mistakes.	Never	Seldom	Frequently	Always
11.	feel that others like me.	Never	Seldom	Frequently	Always
12.	usually have a chance to say all I want to in our group activities.	Never	Seldom	Frequently	Always
13.	help others express their ideas.	Never	Seldom	Frequently	Always
14.	am overly stubborn about my opinions.	Never	Seldom	Frequently	Always
15.	give in too quickly when I'm opposed.	Never	Seldom	Frequently	Always
16.	am too quiet.	Never	Seldom	Frequently	Always
17.	participate enough.	Never	Seldom	Frequently	Always
18.	am tolerant of opposite viewpoints.	Never	Seldom	Frequently	Always
19.	dominate the conversation.	Never	Seldom	Frequently	Always

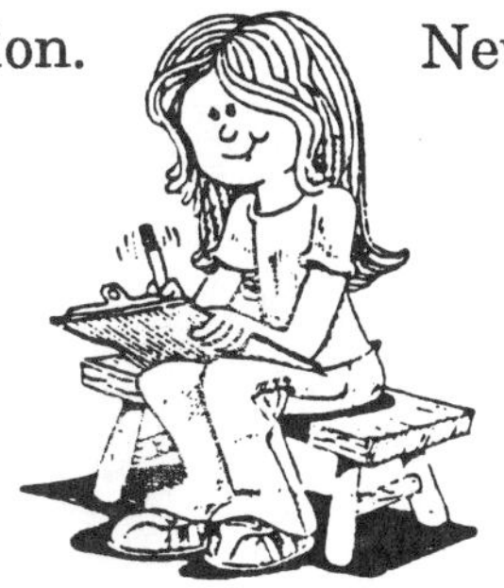

Self-report Cooperation Rating Scale*

Following are some questions about your behavior in the cooperative activity you have just completed. Answer each question as honestly as you can. There are no right or wrong answers.

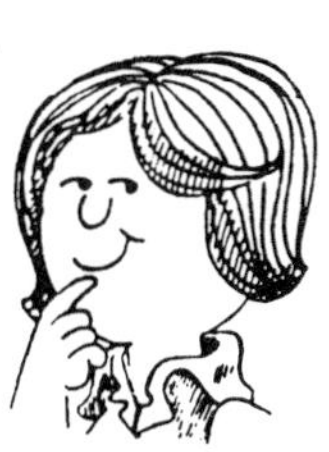

1.	I offer facts, give my opinion and ideas, and provide suggestions to help the group get the job done.	Never	Seldom	Frequently	Always
2.	I monopolize the discussion.	Never	Seldom	Frequently	Always
3.	I am polite; I do not interrupt unless it is necessary to do so.	Never	Seldom	Frequently	Always
4.	If I do not understand something, I courteously ask the speaker to explain.	Never	Seldom	Frequently	Always
5.	I share with the other group members any materials and books that I have in order to promote the success of all members and the group as a whole.	Never	Seldom	Frequently	Always
6.	I keep to the subject of a discussion.	Never	Seldom	Frequently	Always
7.	If the group needs to make a decision, I help make it.	Never	Seldom	Frequently	Always
8.	I help keep a discussion pleasant.	Never	Seldom	Frequently	Always
9.	I often summarize what other members have said before I respond or comment.	Never	Seldom	Frequently	Always
10.	I listen to what other group members have to say.	Never	Seldom	Frequently	Always
11.	I encourage all members to participate. I'm open to their ideas and friendly to them.	Never	Seldom	Frequently	Always
12.	I tell other group members that I appreciate their abilities or skills.	Never	Seldom	Frequently	Always
13.	I am happy when the teacher praises the work of one of the students in my group, since it means we are doing well.	Never	Seldom	Frequently	Always

To score this questionnaire, count "Never" as 1, "Seldom" as 2, "Frequently" as 3, and "Always" as 4.

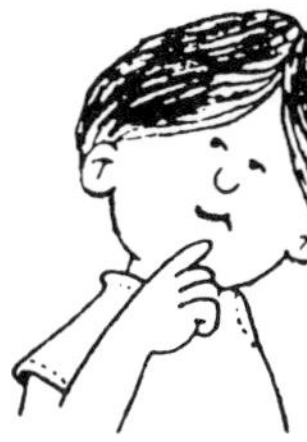

* D.W. Johnson and F.P. Johnson, *Learning Together and Alone*, 1975, p. 107.

Group Observation Forms

In addition to the debriefing questionnaires, another excellent way for the group to be provided with feedback regarding its performance is to have one or two members of the group, chosen either by you or by the group, sit outside the group as it works and observe the interaction. Their job is to watch and report their observations either to you or to the small or large group at the end of the task. The observers can be instructed to take notes on how the group could improve its functioning, or they can be assigned to look for specific things, such as the number of times students encourage others to talk, or instances in which members do not listen to one another.

Observers will function more beneficially if they receive instruction in good observation techniques.

- Observers are "silent members" of the group, attending to the process of the discussion, rather than the content. (They will find it difficult not to participate but can learn to restrain themselves.)

- Observers need to note specific behaviors (e.g., Jack started talking before someone was finished three times), rather than general (e.g., Jack interrupts people).

- When reporting observations, the observer needs to give feedback in a manner that does not embarrass or imply judgement. For example, although observation forms contain places for specific student names, it is preferable to omit them when orally reporting small group observations to the large group (e.g., One person did most of the talking in our group, rather than Kathy did most of the talking in our group). It is also good strategy to give negative feedback first, ending on a positive note with compliments.

Another way to utilize observers is to divide the class into two groups and have one group observe the other. Have the group members who will work sit in a circle, while the observers sit in a larger circle around them. Assign each person in the outer circle to observe one member of the inner circle. Have observers take notes on the behavior of their partners in the inner circle or use one of the observation forms provided at the end of this section. Afterwards, have the observers report their findings to their partners, adhering to the guidelines for giving feedback.

You can enable the group to observe itself by recording a cooperation activity on audio tape or video tape and then playing it back for students. Ask group members to identify the strengths and weaknesses of their work together.

Group Behavior Questionnaire

Answer all questions by naming members of the group. Base your answers on what occurred during the group activity. You can choose two students for each, if you want. You can use the same name more than once. Don't sign your name.

1. Which member of the group can most easily influence others to change their opinions?

2. Who is least able to influence others to change the group's opinions?

3. Who is most highly accepted by the group as a whole?

4. Who is most ready to protect and support members who are being criticized?

5. Who is most ready to get off the subject?

6. Who tried most to avoid fighting in the group?

7. Who tends not to get involved in active discussion when strong differences begin to appear?

8. Who has tried to help when others get in an argument?

9. Who has wanted the group to be friendly and comfortable?

10. Who has tried to do the most to keep the group on the ball?

11. Whom would you choose to work with on a project?

12. Who annoys you during class activities?

13. Are there some group members who do not seem to contribute toward the work of the group?

14. Who seems to be helping most in the group?

Group Observation Form

List the names of the group members down the left-hand side of the form. Each time a member seems to be doing one of the positive or negative things listed across the top, place a mark in the appropriate square.

NAME	Compliments Others	Organizes the Group	Summarizes Ideas	Encourages Others	Contributes Ideas	Puts Others Down	Gets off the Subject	Acts Silly	Wastes Time	Interrupts

Intermediate Level Page 33

Cooperation Ballot

Cooperation means getting along with yourself and with others.

I cast my Cooperation Vote for
_____
(most cooperative person in your group)

I am in _____ group.

Date _____

Cooperation Ballot

Cooperation means getting along with yourself and with others.

I cast my Cooperation Vote for
_____
(most cooperative person in your group)

I am in _____ group.

Date _____

Cooperation Ballot

Cooperation means getting along with yourself and with others.

I cast my Cooperation Vote for
_____
(most cooperative person in your group)

I am in _____ group.

Date _____

Cooperation Ballot

Cooperation means getting along with yourself and with others.

I cast my Cooperation Vote for
_____
(most cooperative person in your group)

I am in _____ group.

Date _____

Intermediate Level   Page 35

Individual Observation Form

Observer: _____

Person Being Observed: _____

This form is designed to record the behavior of one group member only. Put a check each time one of these positive or negative behaviors occurs.

Positive Behaviors

1.	Looks at the person talking	
2.	Asks questions to encourage others to speak	
3.	Invites others to give their opinions	
4.	Nods or uses facial expressions to show interest in others' ideas	
5.	Helps keep people on the topic	
6.	Expresses own ideas	

Negative Behaviors

1.	Acts silly	
2.	Doesn't look at the speaker	
3.	Doesn't participate	
4.	Interrupts	
5.	Gets off the subject	
6.	Talks too much	

Intermediate Level

Questions for Observers

1. Who is talking the most? _____
   _____

2. Who is talking the least? _____
   _____

3. What attempts do members make to encourage others to contribute? _____
   _____
   _____

4. What attempts do members make to link their contributions to previous contributions? _____
   _____

5. Do group members listen to one another? If not, jot down examples of when they don't. _____
   _____

6. What could members do to improve the way they are working together? _____
   _____
   _____
   _____

Things would go better next time if....

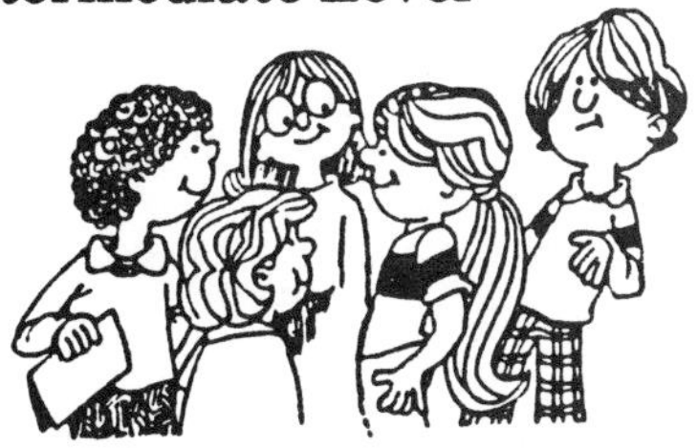

Group Behavior Tally Sheet

____
Observer

List the names of group members down the left-hand side of this form. Put a check in the appropriate box in Column A every time you observe a group member helping the group get the job done. Put a check in the appropriate box in Column B every time you observe group members not helping get the job done.

Things That Help a Group Get a Job Done

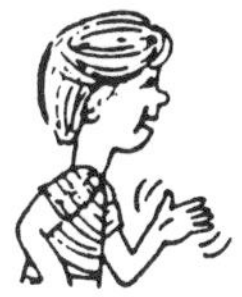

1. Listening to others
2. Giving ideas
3. Asking questions
4. Replying to ideas
5. Working well with others
6. Getting others involved
7. Keeping things under control
8. Keeping everyone on the subject
9. Summarizing what has been said
10. Encouraging and complimenting others

Things That Don't Help a Group Get a Job Done

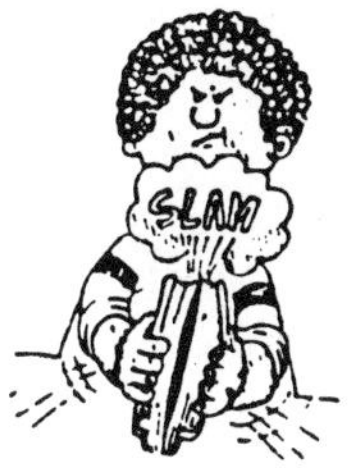
SLAM

1. Not listening
2. Interrupting
3. Acting silly
4. Fooling around
5. Putting others down
6. Letting others do all the work
7. Saying things that get the group off the topic
8. Refusing to consider other ideas
9. Acting bored

	A	B
Names of Group Members	Helped the Group Get the Job Done	Didn't Help the Group Get the Job Done
1.		
2.		
3.		
4.		
5.		
6.		
7.		
8.		

Analyzing Group Behavior

1. What was the atmosphere in which the group worked (happy, silly, angry, excited)?

2. How did the group reach decisions?

3. How did the group handle conflict (humor, sarcasm, open confrontation, shouting, withdrawing)?

4. To what extent were the members of the group involved in the task? Were there any procedures which helped get people involved?

5. How did the group decide who would speak and when?

6. How well did the group members listen to each other?

7. Were there any leaders? How did they get to be leaders?

8. How did the group assign jobs or responsibilities?

Debriefing Discussions

Once the group has become accustomed to examining its own behavior, it is possible simply to ask members to talk about how they are doing. Group members should be encouraged to identify problems when they occur and discuss them openly. When presenting your observations, you might keep these points in mind:

- Describe specific behavior rather than speaking in abstractions. For example, "Roger and Jean, you sat apart from the group and spoke only when someone else asked you a question" is better than "Roger, you and Jean weren't involved."

- Check the accuracy of your perceptions by asking whether the group members see their behavior as you did.

- Avoid words that imply a judgment. Don't say, "Today's discussion was not what I would have expected of you fifth graders. You were really acting immature." A better approach would be: "Throughout today's discussion, many of you interrupted the speaker. What effect do you think this had on the discussion?"

If a problem identified either by you or by the group concerns interpersonal conflict, the skills taught in Lesson 8, "Dealing With Conflict in Cooperation Groups," will enable students to deal with the conflict in a non-hostile manner during debriefing sessions.

The following are some questions that might be helpful during a debriefing discussion:

- Did your group members listen to one another?
- Did everyone in your group participate?
- In what part of the task were you most involved?
- What did each person do to help?
- How did you decide who would do what?
- What could group members do differently next time?
- What important things did you accomplish?
- Did group members encourage and compliment each other?
- Were you listened to when you spoke?
- Did anyone monopolize group discussion?

- Did group members share materials?
- Did some group members try to get others involved?
- What do you like best about your group product or decision?
- What do you like least about your group product or decision?
- Did you enjoy working together? Why?
- Was any time lost getting organized?
- When some of the group ideas needed to be written down, how did you decide who would do the writing?
- How did you pick the person who would tell the rest of the class what the group decided about an issue?
- How could you have improved your work as a group?

Another useful debriefing strategy is to have students respond orally to some of the sentence stems they may have previously responded to on paper. Some useful stems are:

- I liked it when . . .
- I appreciated . . .
- I didn't like it when . . .
- I felt that . . .
- I noticed . . .
- There should have been more . . .
- I felt best when . . .
- I felt worst when . . .
- I was surprised . . .
- I was confused . . .
- It would have been better . . .
- I get angry when . . .
- I wish that . . .

- Others didn't agree with me about . . .
- In this group I . . .
- When other people in this group are upset, I . . .
- Next time . . .

Debriefing can also include a review of the academic learning that takes place as a result of the cooperation activity. The following stems would be useful in reviewing any academic learning activity:

- I learned . . .
- I realized that . . .
- I discovered . . .
- I changed my opinion about . . .
- I'm beginning to wonder . . .

In the Appendix of this manual there is a set of signs/posters entitled "Sentence Starters for Promoting Thinking." These can be hung in a permanent place in the classroom. Their use is suggested at the end of each lesson in order to review, summarize, and process lesson concepts. They can also be used for debriefing any cooperation activities. Students can choose one or more sentence starters and complete them. Students' responses may be oral or written. These sentence starters are also appropriate for summarizing lessons in any academic subject area.

With groups that do well examining their own behavior, you might find the following procedure appropriate: Seat the group in a circle. Have everybody look around and then write down the name of the person in the group whose behavior they find the most puzzling, confusing, or surprising. Then give each member an opportunity to speak directly to that person and tell what is puzzling, confusing, or surprising about the person's behavior. Require the speaker to describe the behavior rather than judge it. The person addressed may either remain silent or respond by explaining the behavior described and the reasons for it. After the two persons interact briefly, proceed to the next group member. Once a particular problem within the group has been identified, there are several structured approaches to seeking a solution to the problem. Students can use the technique of brainstorming to come up with solutions to the problem. Lesson 6 in this manual is designed to teach students how to brainstorm.

Typical Group Behavior Problems

The following are some typical group behavioral problems and some specific suggestions you might implement for dealing with them:

- Students who talk too loud: Create a norm for using "quiet" voices by reminding students to use their "12-inch" voices when working together.

- Students who talk too frequently: During cooperation activities, give each student five objects, i.e., chips or cards. Ask students to place a chip in the center of the group each time they speak. When a student is out of chips, he/she cannot speak until the other students are also out of chips or have no more comments to make. At this point group members may reclaim their chips and continue the discussion/activity.

- Students who interrupt: use a make-believe microphone, a stick or a bean bag which is handed or tossed to a student to indicate that it is his/her turn to speak. Students may not speak unless they are holding the "microphone" or "talking sticks." Another alternative is to ask the interrupter to write a message on his/her hand as a reminder to wait until others are finished.

- A group that takes too long to get started: Set short time limits to heighten tension, which increases productivity.

- Students who either criticize others' contributions or simply never say anything encouraging or positive: At the beginning of a discussion/activity, give each participant three chips. During the activity, each student must make three positive or encouraging comments to others in the group. Whenever they do so, they must put a chip in the middle of the group. Encourage students to finish the activity with no chips.

- Students who consciously or unconsciously dominate discussions or activities: These students can be steered into an evaluative function where they will become aware of dominance and participation on the part of others. They can also be invited to record or to monitor discussions and group activities. Their real urge may be not to dominate, but only to gain some status that could be achieved in a number of other ways.

The Stop-Action Technique

"Stop-Action" is a technique of interrupting work on a task in order to examine the way the work is being done. It serves to correct the tendency to become too absorbed in what we are doing rather than in how we are doing it. Stop-Action helps students focus on cooperative behaviors they are practicing.

For instance, you may stop the groups when they have been working on a problem for approximately 10 minutes and ask them to analyze how they have been working. The following questions may be used to guide the discussion:

- a) Is everyone in the group participating?
- b) Whose ideas are being carried out?
- c) Have any ideas been ignored or rejected? Why?
- d) How are things being decided?

After reminding students of the cooperative behaviors you expect of them, the groups resume working.

Reporting on Small Group Work in the Large Classroom Group

Once you have had students working in small cooperation groups, you'll see how this learning structure greatly increases student participation. Students are able to talk more freely and more often in a small group. When small cooperation groups complete an assignment you will often want each group to report on what they have done to the rest of the class. Traditionally, this activity involves little student participation; one person from each group is designated as the group spokesperson and is the only one who speaks. There is seldom any interaction between groups using this reporting format.

The following procedures can increase student participation in large group reporting. Before you break students up in small cooperation groups, select one person from each group to be a beginning spokesperson or reporter. Then, explain that others in the group will also be expected to offer their comments concerning what the group has discussed or accomplished and it would be wise for everyone to pay close attention to what takes place. Students may even want to take some sort of notes. This encourages students to be attentive during group work as well as to participate in larger group discussion.

When small-group work is over, ask all of the groups to form one large circle. This way students can talk to each other and not just to the teacher. Small-group members should sit next to one another in the large circle so they will still feel a sense of group identity. Ask a group to volunteer to report first. The group spokesperson should be asked to begin the report on the group's work but he/she should encourage others in the group to add or correct what is said.

If the initial spokesperson seems to be delivering too much of the report, others in the group should be asked to continue. Once a second group member speaks, a third or fourth should be asked to give his/her opinion on the group's activity. Hopefully, the reporting will somewhat resemble a panel discussion.

In addition to encouraging reporting from many small-group members, you should encourage interaction between groups. Students should be told to feel free to react to reports after each is given, or to agree or disagree if all groups were working on the same assignment.

In addition, to report to the larger group, small-group members should feel free to ask other groups questions, especially if there are any problems assigned that they couldn't find solutions for in their own group. This encourages cooperation between groups.

A Final Note

Small-group cooperative learning involves significant changes in both teacher and student attitudes. Cooperative environments will not happen naturally in the classroom. There needs to be a commitment on the part of the teacher to develop cooperative skills. It is necessary to teach a sequence of lessons before students even attempt cooperative learning.

It takes time and practice for any new strategy to become a comfortable part of one's teaching repertoire. Teachers need to practice a new skill in context 5-20 times before it feels easy and natural. Inservice training and use of peer coaching in this area would be helpful.

If these steps are taken, cooperative learning can lead to marked academic gains and significant changes in classroom climate.

Many of the recommendations in this introduction have been adopted from Johnson and Johnson, *Learning Together and Alone:* Cooperation, Competition, and Individualization, 1975. Adapted by permission of Prentice-Hall, Inc., Englewood Cliffs, N.J.

Lessons

Section A

Learning To Work Together

Objective Students will learn what cooperation means, what roles can be assumed in a group, and how to work with a partner on a learning task.

Materials Transparency #1 - "Roles People Can Take in a Group"
Transparency #2 - "How To Be a Good Participant"
Handout #1 - "Ways We Cooperate in School"
Handout #2 - "Our Design"
Handout #3 - "Two Brains Are Better than One"

To the Teacher In order for students to work well together, it is helpful for them to see clearly the different ways they can function in a group. This lesson identifies three broad roles students can assume and some behavioral indicators of each role. After explaining these roles to students, it is suggested that students participate in one of the cooperation activities and then try to identify the role they assumed most of the time. This lesson is designed to teach cooperation skills and to give students practice in actively working together.

Lesson Presentation *In this lesson students will work in pairs. Paraphrase:* **Today we're going to take a close look at cooperation. To cooperate means**

- **to do something with someone else so that you help each other;**
- **it may be helping each other learn spelling words;**
- **it may be practicing throwing a ball to one another; or**
- **it may be putting on a play at home and agreeing on what parts you'll each have.**

We cooperate sometimes with one person and sometimes in groups. Sometimes we cooperate best when everyone is doing the same thing, as when we are in a tug-of-war game and our team members are pulling a rope against another team. Usually, though, when we're cooperating we help one another by doing different things. We cooperate every day in school.

Lesson 1

Handout #1 (or discussion)

I'd like you now to take a few minutes and think about how we cooperate when we do certain things. *Give students Handout #1, "Ways We Cooperate in School," or use some of the items on the handout for a group discussion. Say or paraphrase:* **In this lesson you'll learn some new ways to cooperate so we can begin to work in pairs and small groups in our classroom.**

Working in a group is like playing in a baseball game. Sometimes you're up to bat or you are pitching and the attention is on you. Sometimes you are sitting on a bench waiting for your turn and observing. Other times you help your team by being on the field and, even though the attention is not always on you, you're a very important part of the team.

Working in a cooperative group in your classroom is like playing on a team. There will be times when you are in the spotlight because you are sharing some good ideas or making helpful suggestions about what the group should do. There will be times when you will be helping the group by listening carefully to what others are saying. There will be times when you will be helping others or encouraging them to participate. A good team member realizes that everyone on his/her team is important and needed.

Let's talk about some ways we can work as a team. First we need to learn what we have to do to be cooperative. Here are some skills that we will be practicing. When people work together, they often do one or more of these three things:

Transp. #1/ (or handout)

Use Transparency #1 or handouts of "Roles People Can Take in a Group." Go through each role, giving examples which would be relevant to the students. For instance, you may say something like the following:

An observer usually sits quietly and looks at the persons who are trying to get the job done and listens to what they have to say. It's ok to be an observer sometimes. On a baseball team, it's important that team members who are waiting for a turn at bat watch what

the pitcher is doing and how the game is going. In a cooperation group, an observer helps the group by paying attention to what's happening and being ready to do what is necessary when the time comes.

Point to participant column and say: **A participant is also an observer some of the time. But a participant gives the group ideas on how to get the job done and works with others in the group to get the job completed. On a baseball team, it's important for players to give their ideas, and to play when they are needed. All of these things are important in working with other students in a cooperation group, too.**

Point to helper column and say: **A helper is sometimes an observer and sometimes a participant. But a helper does even more. A helper gets all the kids in the group working together so that everyone feels that they are important, that their ideas count, and that they are needed. A helper summarizes everyone's ideas, works out disagreements between group members, and tries to see that everyone is treated fairly. A helper is like the person on a baseball team who always tries to get the team to work well together.**

Explain to students that you would like them to practice doing the things listed in the first two columns (the observer and participant roles).

Handout #2

Divide the students into pairs and explain that you would like them to work together to create a colorful design. You may either give students the design, Handout #2 that follows this lesson, or have them make a design of their own. Explain to them that you would like them to plan together how they will color each section of the design and who will do what.

Transp. #2

At this point, show students Transparency #2, "How to be a Good Participant" and go over each behavior of a good participant. Either leave the transparency in view or give students a copy and ask them to use at least four or five of the sentence starters while doing the activity. When students have completed the activity, they should each sign his/her name on the design and hang it in a designated place.

Discuss with the entire class how it felt to do an art activity with a partner rather than alone. Ask students

- *which role they used most, observer or participant.*
- *how often they used the participant sentence starters*
- *if saying these things made doing a good design easier.*
- *if there were any conflicts, and if so, how they were resolved.*

Handout #3
Sup. Act.

After further practice working with a partner, you may wish to have students select one or more of the partner cooperation activities on Handout #3, "Two Brains Are Better Than One," or do the supplementary activity that follows this lesson.

Use the sentence starters in the Appendix to get a sense of students' thoughts and feelings about working cooperatively.

Ask students if they can think of things in school that would be more fun or easier to do with a partner or in a small group than to do alone.

List their suggestions on a chart. Add any activities you anticipate having students work on cooperatively. Explain that to work well together in any of these situations, they first need to become very good at certain cooperation skills, especially learning to listen to each other, to encourage each other to share ideas and feelings, and to respond to each others' comments. Explain that in the next lesson they will begin learning to listen well.

Finally, you may wish to display one or more of the following quotations in a permanent place in your classroom:

- *"No man is an island, entire of itself." (John Donne)*
- *"United we stand, divided we fall." (Aesop)*
- *"Two heads are better than one." (Heywood)*
- *"If we would seek for one word that describes society better than any other, the word is cooperation." (Montague)*

- *"Partners are powerful."*
- *"None of us is smarter than all of us."*
- *"If two heads are better than one, imagine how great three or four heads can be."*
- *"We sink or swim together."*

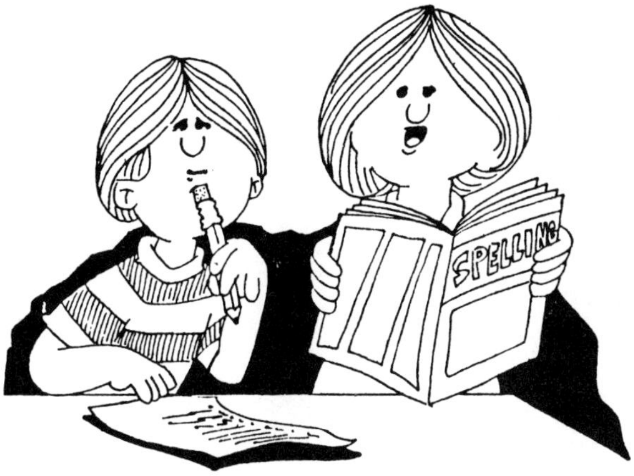
SPELLING

Lesson 1   Handout #1

Ways We Cooperate in School*

Use the space provided to explain why the following things require cooperation:

1. When we play games, we cooperate. How?
   _____
   _____

2. When class members do different things to build a bulletin board, we cooperate. How?
   _____
   _____

3. When we do the work the teacher assigns, we cooperate. How?
   _____
   _____

4. When we participate in a class discussion, we cooperate. How?
   _____
   _____

5. When we keep our classroom clean and organized, we cooperate. How?
   _____
   _____

6. When small groups of students do an experiment in science, we cooperate. How?
   _____
   _____

7. When we help break up fights between classmates, we cooperate. How?
   _____
   _____

8. When we have a class party, we cooperate. How? _____
   _____

* J.D. Casteel, *Learning to Think and Choose,* 1978, p. 133.

Roles People Can Take in a Group

Observer

1. Looks at and listens to others
2. Thinks about the job to be done

Participant

1. Looks at and listens to others
2. Thinks about the job to be done

PLUS

3. Gives ideas
4. Asks questions
5. Replies to ideas
6. Works well with others

Helper

1. Looks at and listens to others
2. Thinks about the job to be done
3. Gives ideas
4. Asks questions
5. Replies to ideas
6. Works well with others

PLUS

7. Gets others involved
8. Keeps things under control
9. Keeps everyone on the subject
10. Summarizes what has been said
11. Encourages and compliments others

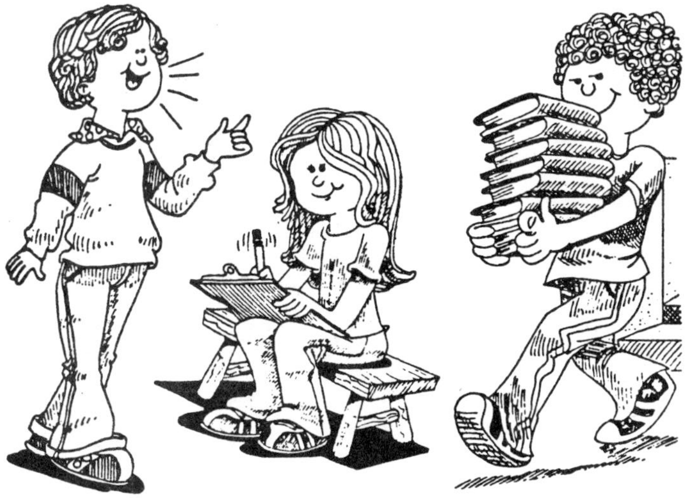

How To Be a Good Participant

Group participants do what observers do. They listen to others, but they also do more.

1. **Participants give ideas and information**

    I think ....

    Maybe ....

    My idea is ....

    We could ....

    A way to do this is ....

2. **Participants Ask Questions**

    What do you think about ... ?

    Would you like .... ?

    Who would like to .... ?

    What's the best way to ..... ?

    How should we .... ?

    Who knows .... ?

    When should we .... ?

    Do you mean that .... ?

3. **Participants reply to ideas**

    I like your idea because ....

    I disagree with your ideas because ....

    Yes, I agree because ....

4. **Participants work well with others**

    Let's do .... together.

    Can I help you .... ?

    Would you like to use ...... ?

    Let's share ....

    You could help me ....

Lesson 1 Handout #2

Our Design

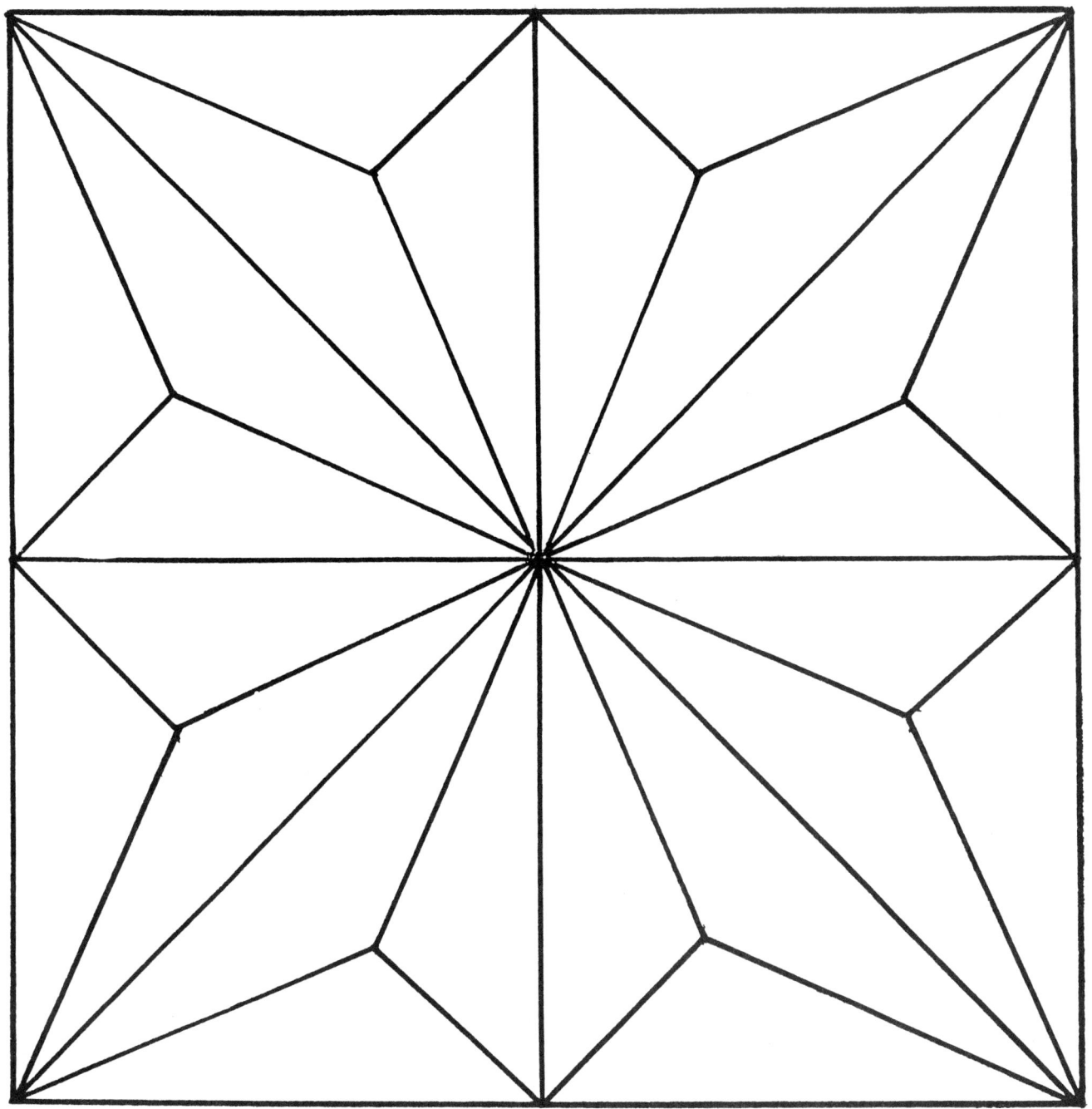

Lesson 1   Handout #3

Two Brains Are Better Than One

Look over the suggested activities below with your partner. Decide on one (or more) that you would like to do together. Have fun!

Our Favorite Foods

With your partner, create a menu that includes all of your favorite foods. Draw little pictures around the menu if you like.

Our Invention

You and your partner are to come up with an idea for a new invention. Try to make it something people would want. Write a detailed description of how it is built, what it does, and why people would like it. Also, provide a drawing of your invention.

Our Business

Pretend that you and your partner are opening a business. Design your own business cards, a sign, and an ad for the Yellow Pages. Be sure you give important information about what kind of business you have, your location, and any special things that would make your business a great success.

Together in a Time Machine

You both have a chance to be in an experiment with a time machine. This invention can transport you to any time, past or future, and any place you wish to visit. You can choose the date and place you will visit for 3 days. Write about where you will go and what you will experience.

The Perfect Life

Write a description of what you think would be the perfect life.

Thinking about the Future

Together make a list of five predictions you think might happen in the next 10 years.

Designing an Amusement Park

Managers of a kids' amusement park have asked you for ideas to add a whole new section to the park. What will the new area be called? What kinds of new rides will it have? What else will it have that kids like? Draw pictures and write a description of your ideas.

The Language of Whales

Let's say scientists have finally managed to decode the language of whales and they have discovered that whales may be more intelligent than people. What might they say to each other? What would you ask the whales? What lessons would they have to offer people?

(Adapted from B. Daniel & C. Daniel, *Strain Your Brain,* 1980.)

Planning a Wonderful Party

You and your partner get to plan a birthday party. You can spend $200 for food and other things you want for the party. Write a description of it. What food will you buy? what would the theme be? What games will you play? How many people will you invite? Where will you have the birthday party? What else would your party have?

A Better Body

Discuss together ways that the human body might be improved. Think of things other living things can do that humans can't. Think of things humans might be able to do better with some changes in their bodies. Draw a picture of your re-design and write an explanation of each change you've added.

Lesson 1 — Supplementary Activity

Our Different Ideas

Objective Students will work cooperatively to come up with solutions regarding certain situations.

Materials Handout

Procedure Ask students to get together with a partner and talk about what they would do regarding those situations described on the student handout. They are to first write down their own ideas, using bubbles A and B; then in bubble A & B write down the one idea they both agree on.

Supplementary Activity
Handout for "Our Different Ideas"

If you wanted to do something together on a Saturday, what would you pick?

Partner A:

Partner B:

A & B:

What's the best way to help someone who is new in school?

Partner A:

Partner B:

A & B:

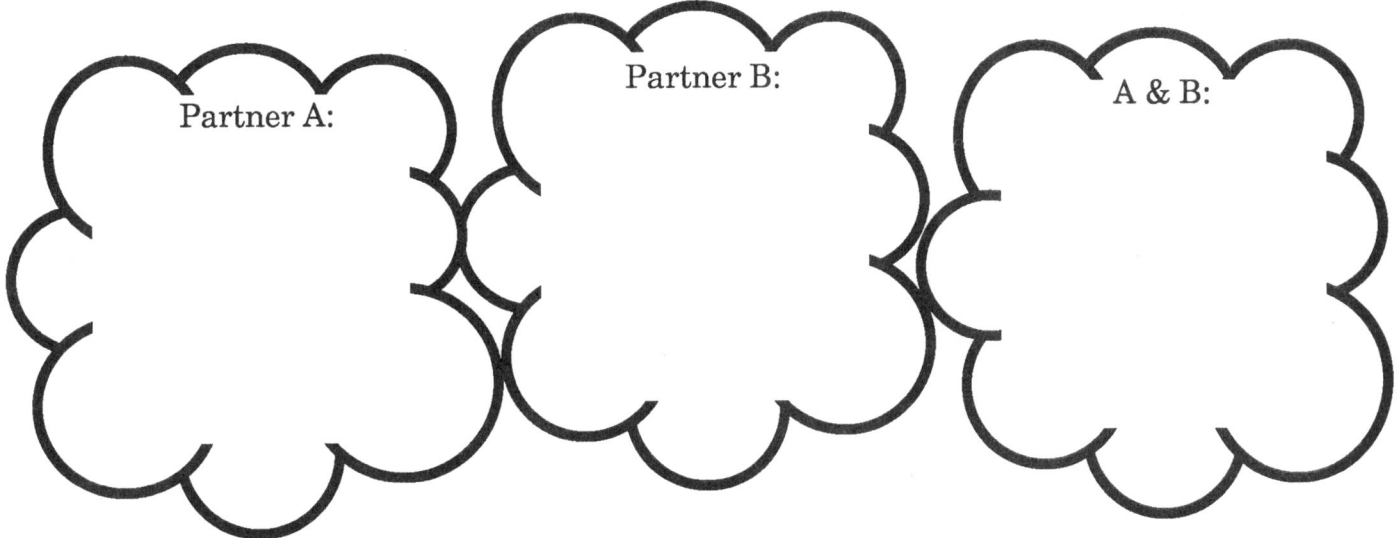

What activity can you think of that would be fun for the class to do together?

Partner A:

Partner B:

A & B:

Working in a Group

Objective Students will learn how to assume the roles of both participant and helper while engaging in a small-group activity.

Students will learn how to assess their behavior while engaging in a small group activity.

Materials Transparency #3 - "Roles People Can Take in a Group"
Transparency #4 - "How To Be a Good Participant"
Transparency #5 - "How To Be a Good Helper in a Group"
Handout #4 - "Summer Camp Symbols"
Handout #5 - "Looking Back"
Handout #6 - "My Group"
Handout #7 - "Describing Cooperation"
Miscellaneous - Sheets of paper and marking pens

To the Teacher In many classrooms there are no leaders other than the teacher, and students are unable to work on a common goal unless the teacher steps in to organize and help the group. Still other classes have a single student or a clique who dominates the class. When asked to choose a leader, students always choose one of their clique members. When one of these influential students is not in a small group, the group is unable to get organized and cooperatively complete an assigned task. Many students would like to organize or lead others effectively to get a job done, but don't know how to go about it.

This lesson teaches all students specific skills which will enable them to move in and out of a leadership role when working in a group. There is some evidence that the quality of student work is highest when helping or leadership roles are dispersed among as many students as possible. Encouraging and teaching all students how to be helpful to others enables them to feel influential and important in group cooperation projects or tasks.

In this lesson students work together on an activity in small groups. The emphasis is on participating.

Lesson Presentation

Today we are going to learn some more ways to work well together to get a job done. We've already learned some good ways to share ideas and information and to ask each other questions when we work together.

Transp. #3
Transp. #4

Review Listener and Participant behaviors on Transparencies #3 and #4.

By the end of this lesson you'll know how to be a helper in a group. Helpers do all the things a participant does. They listen, give ideas, ask questions, and work well with others. But helpers do more.

Transp. #5

Read items 7 to 11 in the third column of Transparency #3. Then show Transparency #5, "How to be a Good Helper in a Group." Go over the phrases that can be used for each behavior on Transparency #5. Ask students if they can think of more examples and add them to the list. Summarize by saying:

The thing to remember in cooperation is that you can do a good job only when you help others to do a good job, too. In almost every group there are going to be kids who will act in certain ways,

- some will talk a lot,
- some will be quiet,
- some will be very serious,
- some will fool around,
- some will try to take over,
- some won't get a chance,
- some will stick to the subject, and
- some will get off the subject.

A group needs help if they are to get anything done. A group needs someone

- to get quiet kids involved,
- to remind kids not to fool around,
- to make sure everyone stays on the subject, and
- to compliment kids who work hard.

If you remind each other in a nice way to do these things, you'll have a terrific group.

I'm going to ask you now to do a group activity where you can try out some of the cooperation behaviors that have been discussed. I would like you to practice as many cooperation behaviors as you can while you are doing the activity, but I'd like each of you to focus on one behavior in particular. I will give each of you a card that describes a single behavior.

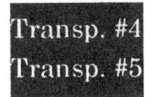

Make a copy of each of the masters for Transparency #4, "How to be a Good Participant," and #5, "How to be a Helper in a Group," then cut the different sections up to form "cards."

Say: **Use the sentence starters on your card as often as you can in a natural way while you are engaged in the cooperation activity. This doesn't mean you can only say the things that are on your card. Help your group in any way you can, but be sure to emphasize the behavior suggested on your card.**

Form small groups of three or four students, using one of the techniques suggested in the introduction of this manual for assigning students to groups, and distribute cards to each group. Make sure that each student in a group gets a different card and that there is a variety of cards in each group.

The activity I'd like you to do is to design a summer camp together. Think about what the camp should have to make it a terrific place to be.

Handout #4

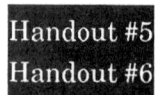

Give each group a large sheet of white paper, marking pens and a copy of the Handout #4, "Summer Camp Symbols." Explain:

I'd like you to come up with one drawing of a camp that everyone in your group likes. You can use any of the symbols on your handout that you like in your design. You don't have to use any you don't like. You can also make up five additional symbols. Discuss together what would make a great camp, the best place to put each thing, and who will draw what. Use quiet voices and remember to use the sentence starters on your card as you're working, as well as any other cooperation skills you can. When you're done with the activity I'm going to ask each of you to write and tell about how well you and your group operated.

After the groups have completed this activity, call students together and have them share their drawing with the other groups. The drawings can be displayed on a bulletin board.

Handout #5
Handout #6

Next ask students to fill out Handout #5, "Looking Back." You can collect them as they are finished and scan them so you can make some general statements regarding students' feelings about the activity. Don't use any names, just general comments. If you like, students can be working on student Handout #6, "My Group," as you prepare this summary.

Ask students for any verbal comments they wish to make about how things went during the activity and how each group went about getting the cooperative task done. Explain to students that in the next lesson they will be learning some more ways to make working together go smoothly and productively.

Working in a Group

Lesson 2
Page 63

Handout #7 *Handout #7, "Describing Cooperation," is a useful tool for helping students focus on the qualities of cooperative behavior. It can be used as a homework assignment.*

Sup. Act. *Before going to the next lesson use the supplementary activity, "Co-op Cards," that follows this lesson. This is a good way to give students additional practice in specific cooperative behaviors. You can involve students in one of the cooperation activities in Section B or C of this manual and have them play the "Co-op Cards" game as they do these activities. Another option for an activity is to have students work as they did in the "Design a Summer Camp" activity in this lesson, but this time have them design a zoo or an amusement park.*

Roles People Can Take in a Group

Observer

1. Looks at and listens to others
2. Thinks about the job to be done

Participant

1. Looks at and listens to others
2. Thinks about the job to be done

PLUS

3. Gives ideas
4. Asks questions
5. Replies to ideas
6. Works well with others

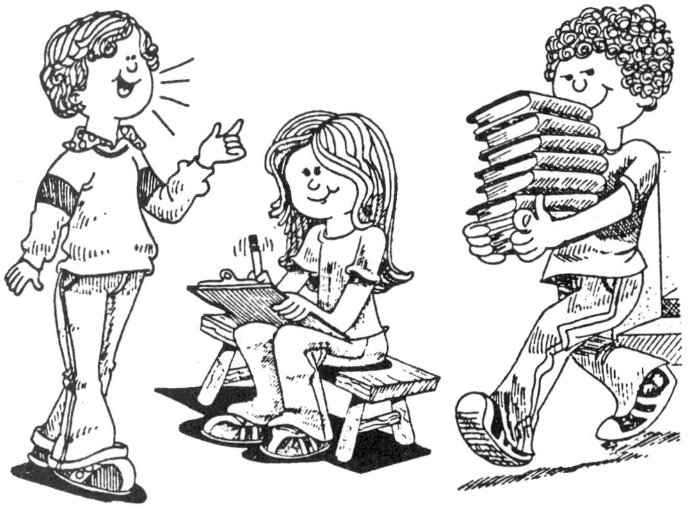

Helper

1. Looks at and listens to others
2. Thinks about the job to be done
3. Gives ideas
4. Asks questions
5. Replies to ideas
6. Works well with others

PLUS

7. Gets others involved
8. Keeps things under control
9. Keeps everyone on the subject
10. Summarizes what has been said
11. Encourages and compliments others

How To Be a Good Participant

Group participants do what observers do. They listen to others, but they also do more.

1. **Participants Give Ideas and Information**

    I think ....

    Maybe ....

    My idea is ....

    We could ....

    A way to do this is ....

2. **Participants ask Questions**

    What do you think about ... ?

    Would you like .... ?

    Who would like to .... ?

    What's the best way to ..... ?

    How should we .... ?

    Who knows .... ?

    When should we .... ?

    Do you mean that .... ?

3. **Participants Reply to Ideas**

    I like your idea because ....

    I disagree with your ideas because ....

    Yes, I agree because ....

4. **Participants Work Well With Others**

    Let's do .... together.

    Can I help you .... ?

    Would you like to use ...... ?

    Let's share ....

    You could help me ....

How To Be a Good Helper in a Group

Helpers or leaders do the things a participant does. They 1) give ideas, 2) ask questions, 3) reply to ideas, and 4) they work well with others. But they also do more:

1. **Helpers get others involved**

    How would you like to do it?
    Let's give _____ a chance to talk.
    Do you have any ideas?
    Would you like to use my . . . ?

2. **Helpers keep things on track**

    We're supposed to . . . .
    What we have to do is . . . . . .
    Let's talk about that later.
    I think we're getting off the subject.
    Let's get back to what we're supposed to do.
    Let's get going so we can get finished.
    Let's get organized.
    Let's divide up the jobs.

3. **Helpers keep things under control**

    Let's stop arguing.
    Let's get back to work.
    Hey, quiet down. I can't hear.
    Let's listen to what he/she has to say.
    Give _____ a chance.
    Hey, that's a "put-down."

4. **Helpers summarize**

    Most of us think . . . .
    It seems like most of us agree . . . .
    Sounds like most of us want to . . .
    Some of us want to . . . . ., but others want to . . . .

5. **Helpers encourage and compliment each other**

    Would you like me to help you . . . ?
    Would you like to use my . . . ?
    That's a good idea.
    That's great! That's really nice!

Summer Camp Symbols

Use these symbols and any five of your own you may wish to add:

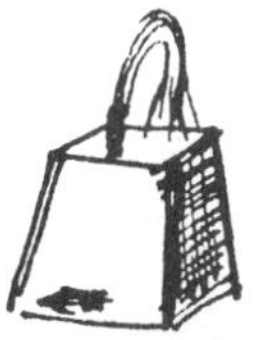
Water Fountain

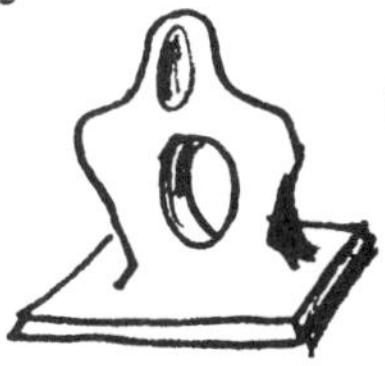
Sculpture

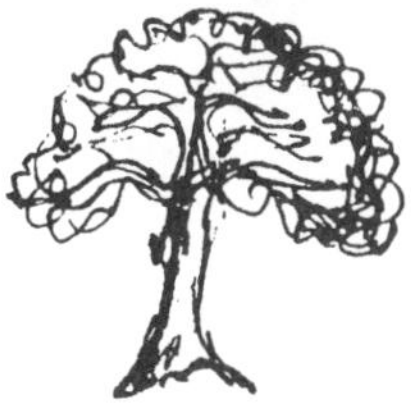
Tree

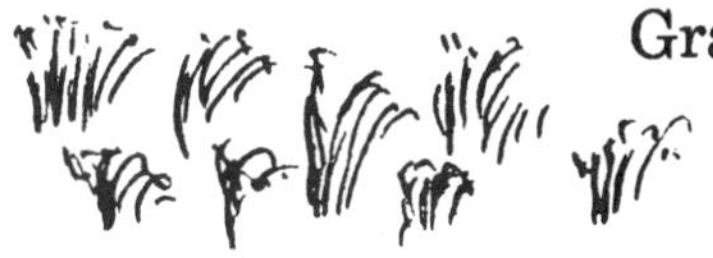
Grass

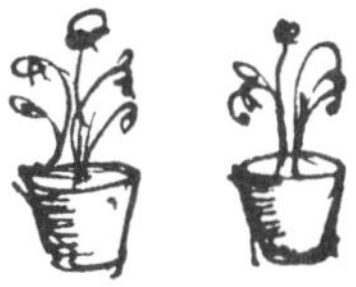
Garden

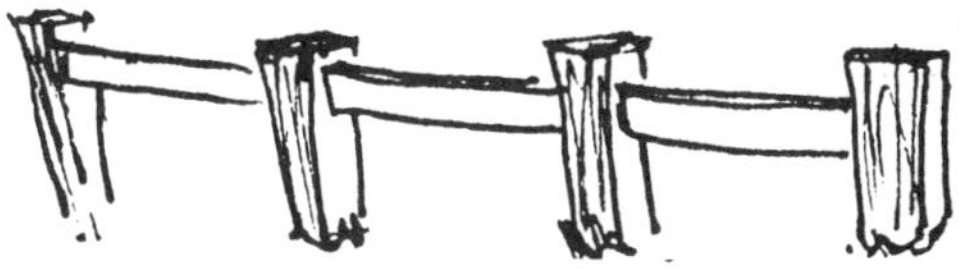
Fence

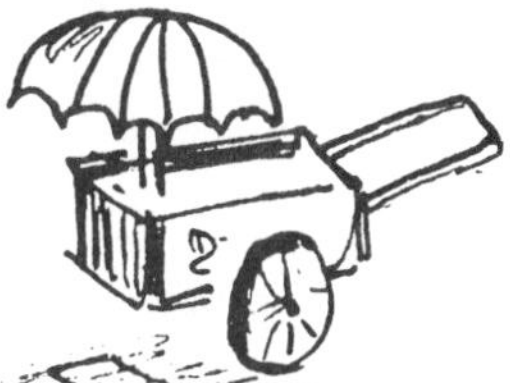
Food Stand

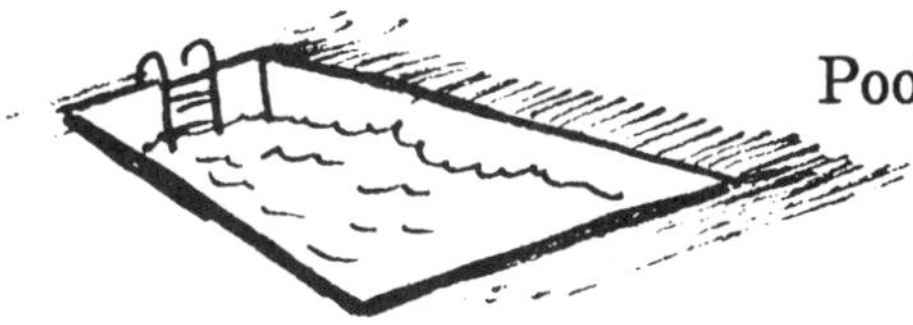
Pool

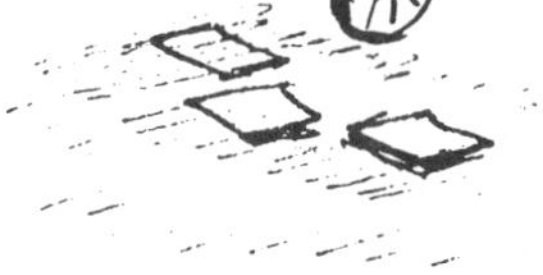
Path

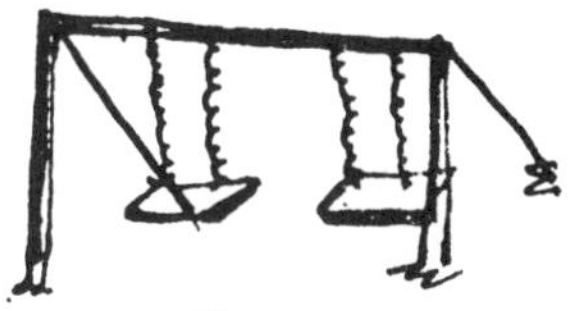
Swings

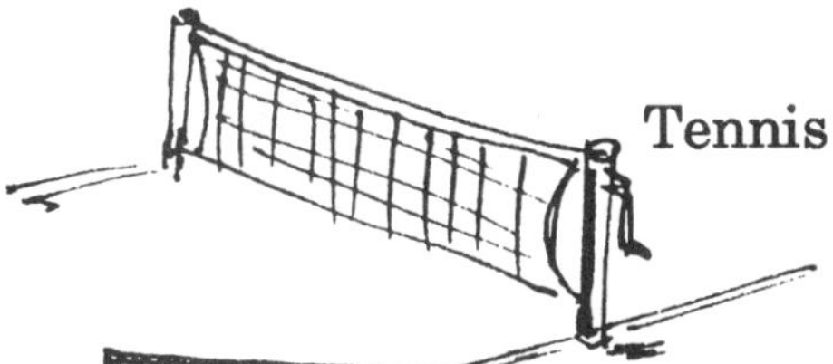
Tennis Court

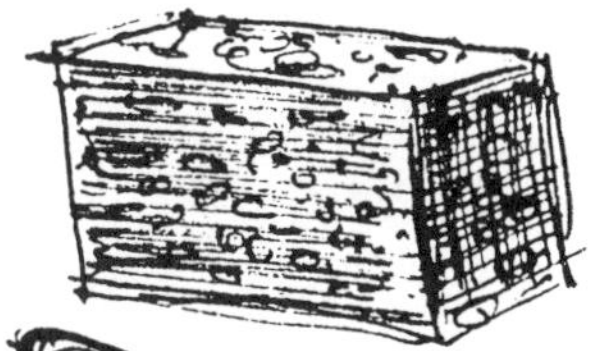
Concrete

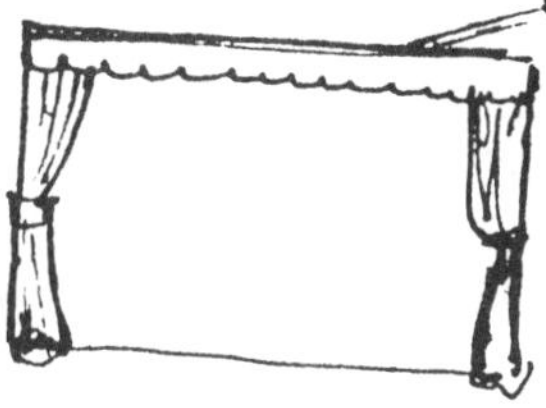
Stage

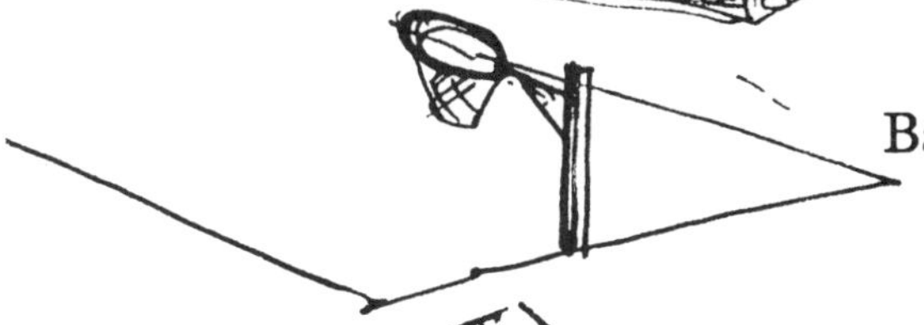
Basketball Court

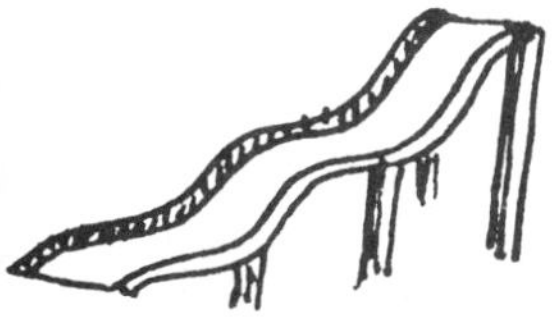
Slide

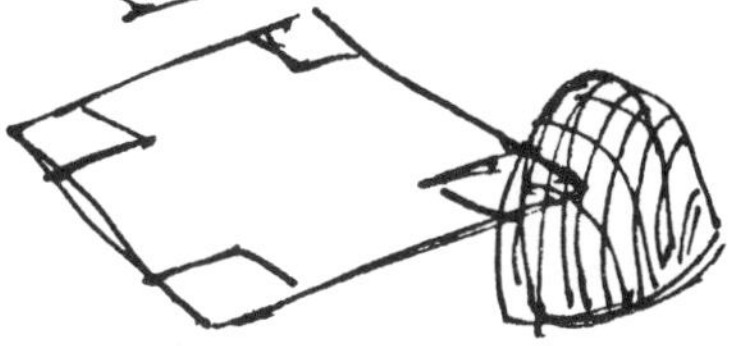
Baseball Field

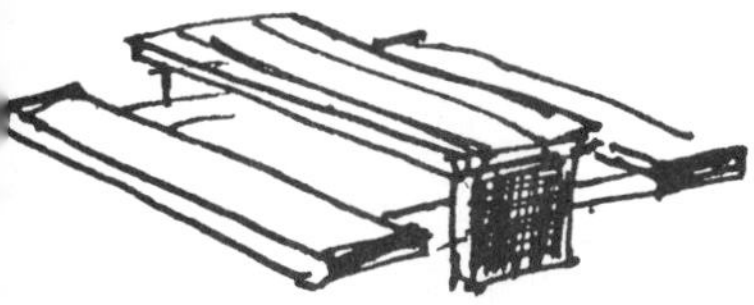
Picnic Area

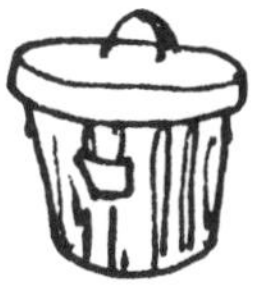
Trash Can

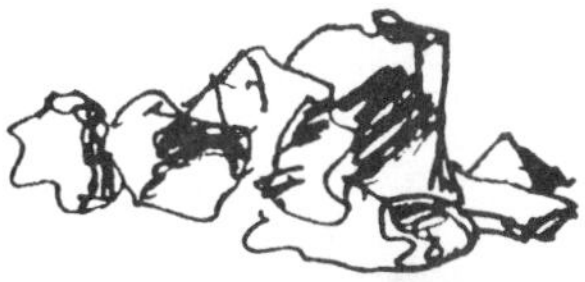
Rocks for Climbing

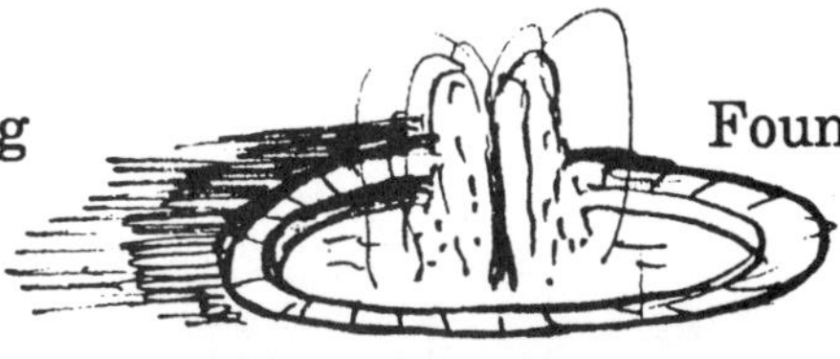
Fountain

Lesson 2 Handout #5

Looking Back

How did things go? Choose one or more of the following to talk about.

I learned _____.

I was surprised _____.

There should have been more _____.

There should have been less_____.

I felt best when _____.

I wish that _____.

Next time _____.

Lesson 2 Handout #6

My Group

When I am in a group, I _____
_____.

One thing I like to do in a group is _____
_____.

I like working in this group because _____
_____.

One thing I'd like to change about my group is _____
_____.

One person I enjoyed working with was _____ because _____
_____.

I felt I was part of my group because _____
_____.

I felt left out because _____
_____.

Lesson 2   Handout #7

Describing Cooperation

Cooperation is very important when people are working together. Think about characteristics that you would want a person you work with to have. Look over the list of words below.

confident	playful	truthful	eager
proud	silly	sloppy	lazy
kind	responsible	quiet	encouraging
bossy	thorough	neat	friendly
careful	enthusiastic	messy	efficient

1. Using words from this list or your own ideas, write four words that describe the kind of person you like to work with on a project.
   _____
   _____

2. Using the above list or your own ideas, write four words that describe the kind of helper you like to be.
   _____
   _____

3. Why do people cooperate? Check the ones you think are true.
   _____ They have to   _____ They're afraid
   _____ It feels good   _____ It prevents trouble
   _____ It brings attention,   _____ They get more of what
            recognition   they want
   _____ It helps make friends

4. Place these in order of amount of cooperation each demands. Number them from 1 to 6, #1 requiring the most cooperation and #6 requiring the least.

_______ building a house
_______ sailing a boat
_______ planting a garden
_______ raising a pet
_______ solving a problem
_______ deciding on watching a TV program

5. List at least five things in your family that require cooperation. When people don't cooperate, what happens?

____
____
____
____
____

6. Write a paragraph about one of the following statements:

- A friend of mine didn't cooperate with me
- Some of the things I don't understand about cooperation
- The things I don't like about cooperation
- The things I don't like about competition

____
____
____
____
____
____

7. Write a paragraph about a classroom project or assignment that you would enjoy working on with others and ways that you would cooperate.

____
____
____
____
____
____

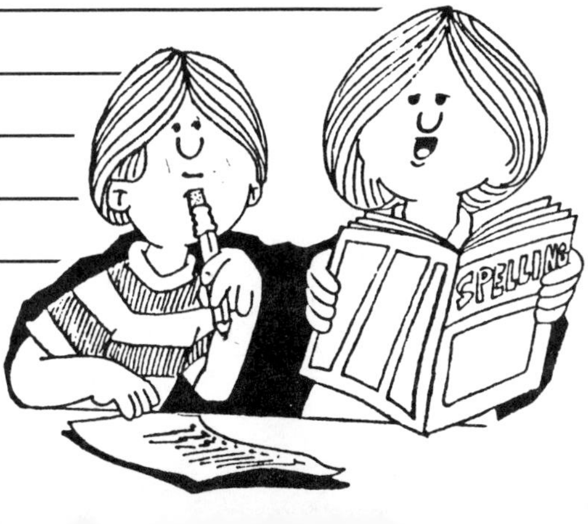
SPELLING

Lesson 2   Supplementary Activity

Co-op Cards

Objective Students will do helpful behaviors described on a card while participating in a cooperative activity.

Materials Packet of "Co-op Cards" for each group

Procedure Select a cooperation activity appropriate for your class from Section B or C in this manual. Introduce the activity to the class. Divide the class into groups of seven or eight students. Introduce the "Co-op Cards" game. Place a large deck of Co-op Cards in the middle of each group, face up. The deck should contain approximately 10 times as many cards as the number of students in the group. Stack the deck so that "Give Ideas," "Ask Questions," and "Encourage Others" cards are at the top, with most of the "Summarize" cards toward the end.

Explain the rules of the game.

1. The object is to take as many cards as possible.
2. To take a card, students must do what the top card indicates, as they participate in the activity. They should use one or more of the sentence starters on the card. As soon as a student has done so, he/she may take the top card.
3. Cards must be taken in order.
4. Students may, of course, do any of the Participant and Helper jobs at any time, but they may not take a card for them unless the job they do and the top card match.

After the cooperation activity is completed, you might ask the following:

- What cards were the hardest to do? Why?
- Who got the most cards?
- Who got the most "Give Ideas" cards?
- Who got the most "Ask Questions" cards?
- Who got the most "Encourage Others" cards?

Lesson 2 Supplementary Activity
Materials for "Co-op Cards"

Co-Op Cards

Give Ideas Card	**Ask Questions Card**
I think	What do you think about ...?
Maybe	Would you like ....?
My idea is	Who would like to ....?
We could	What's the best way to .....?
A way to do this is	How should we ....?
	Do you have any ideas .....?
Encourage Card	**Summarize Card**
That's a good idea.	Most of us think ....
That makes sense.	It seems like most of us ....
I like your suggestions.	Sounds like most of us want to ....
That's it! That's really nice!	Some of us want to ...., but others want to ....

Learning How to Listen to Others

Objective — Students will learn the skills of good listening so that they may participate more productively in cooperative activities.

Materials
- Handout #8 - "Are You a Good Listener?"
- Handout #9 - "Interruption Script"
- Handout #10 - "Non-Listening Behaviors"
- Handout #11 - "Who Gets the Trip?"

To The Teacher — Most cooperative learning activities require students either in pairs or in a group to arrive at a decision, an answer, or a solution to a problem. In order to do this, students have to listen carefully to other group members to see whether their ideas fit and the extent to which they agree or disagree with previous speakers. Then, when they enter the discussion, they can indicate the relationship between their ideas and the contributions of others. In other words, students need to learn to listen.

However, teaching students good listening skills is not an easy task. After years of listening and responding only to the teacher, it takes time and practice for them to learn to listen to one another.

The following lesson is designed to begin the work of training students in the art of listening. The lesson focuses on some of the key behaviors of both good and poor listeners. Students practice these behaviors in pairs. In subsequent cooperative activities, these behaviors can be referred to again and again as students gradually learn to quiet their minds and listen to everyone in the group who takes a turn to speak.

Lesson Presentation — **Would you be surprised if I told you that one of the hardest things to do is to really listen to someone? Well, it's true! Really listening is a very difficult thing to do, because most of us like to talk more than we like to listen. It takes a lot of self-control to be quiet when someone is talking and to think about what they are saying instead of thinking about what we are going to say next. It's especially hard to listen to someone else when we have something important to say.**

Handout #8 — **We're going to try some activities today that should help us be good listeners. First I would like you to quickly complete the form**

"Are You a Good Listener?" *Give Handout #8 to students.* **You don't need to put your name on it. It's just for your own information.** *Give a few minutes for students to complete handout.*

One reason it is so important to listen to someone who is talking is because it feels so terrible not to be listened to. To show you what I mean, let's focus on one non-listening behavior, interrupting.

[Handout #9]

At this point select a student who reads well and with good expression to do a short role play with you. Give the student Handout #9, "Interruption Script," found at the end of this lesson. Take the part of the interrupter yourself, interrupting the student every time he/she tries to say something.

After the script has been read, thank the student for helping and ask the following questions:

- **Who ended up saying the most?**
- **Did I even understand what _____ was saying?**
- **How do you think _____ felt when I interrupted him/her?**
- **How do you feel when someone keeps interrupting you?**

Discuss as a class how frustrating it is to be interrupted. Help the students to realize, through discussion, that when they interrupt someone, the person they interrupted probably feels just as frustrated as they do when it happens to them. Discuss also how futile it seems to try to continue a conversation when interruptions occur. Note whether students interrupt each other in the class discussion.

Explain to students that there are other ways to be a poor listener besides interrupting. Ask for a volunteer to tell you something and explain that you are going to be as terrible a listener as you can.

[Model Role Play]

Suggest a specific topic that you think a student would be eager to talk about. While the student is trying to talk to you, model as many inap-

propriate listening behaviors as you can. You may wish to include some of the following:

- *not looking at the speaker*
- *turning your body away from the speaker*
- *laughing inappropriately*
- *putting the student down*

saying things like:

- *"You think that's great? Only a dope would like that! You should hear what I did..."*
- *monopolizing the conversation yourself*
- *looking bored*
- *saying "yeah, yeah, yeah" as if you want the speaker to hurry*
- *playing with papers or other things*
- *looking through things in your briefcase or on your desk*
- *shifting your weight from one foot to the other*
- *fidgeting*
- *cleaning your fingernails, etc.*

After the role play has proceeded for a few minutes, stop the action and ask the speaker how he/she felt. Even though this is a role-play situation, the student is likely to have had some negative feelings during the role play. Give the student a chance to tell about his or her feelings, then ask the class to name the behaviors that they saw you, the listener, doing. As they name them, write them on the board or chart. Point out particularly these inappropriate behaviors:

- *interrupting;*
- *lack of eye contact;*
- *thinking that what you said was more important than what the speaker had to say; and*
- *doing other things.*

Now, tell students that you would like each of them to experience just how awful it feels to try to tell someone something when they are not listening.

Divide students into pairs and tell them they are each to take a turn as a non-listener and then as a listener. First, have them decide who will be A and who will be B. Then explain that for two minutes, beginning at the signal, A will talk to B, telling B about one of the following topics:

- *The best movie I ever saw*
- *Something that really bugs me*
- *Something that I would really like to do*
- *The best present I have ever received*

While A is talking, B is to imitate all the non-listening behaviors that you modeled earlier, adding any others he or she can think of. The noise in the room will increase a great deal and students will talk louder and louder because of their frustration at not being listened to. At the signal ending the 2 minutes, a 1 minute period will begin. During this time, A tells B how he or she felt when B wouldn't listen.

Then, at the signal, they will switch roles and B will try to talk to A about the topic of his or her choice and A will show non-listening behavior.

At the end of two minutes, have students return again to the larger group and discuss how it felt to be ignored or not listened to when they were trying to tell someone something. Point out that they were exaggerating the practice of not listening, but that sometimes people really do these things.

Model

Explain to students that you are now going to show them all the things that people do when they are really listening to someone who is speaking to them. Ask the students to watch you like a detective and try to notice every single thing you do to show the speaker that you are really interested in what is being said. Again, ask for a volunteer to talk to you about a subject in which he or she is quite interested. While the student is speaking, model the following behaviors in a genuine manner:

- *Turn your body towards the speaker*
- *Look into the speaker's eyes*

- *Do not interrupt*
- *Have an interested expression on your face*
- *Smile when appropriate*
- *Nod your head slightly when appropriate*
- *Hold your hands still and avoid fidgeting*
- *If appropriate, ask questions such as, "Then what did you do?" or "What else happened?"*

After you have modeled listening behavior, ask students to tell you all the behaviors they noticed that showed you were really listening. List these on a chart so that the list can remain up for awhile. Title the chart "Listening Behaviors."

Now explain to students the reasons for some of your listening behaviors by saying or paraphrasing the following:

A lot of what people try to express or get across to us can be understood by the expression on their faces and the way they move their hands and bodies as they are speaking. This is why we look at someone when he/she talks to us. It helps us understand what they are trying to tell us. We communicate with a lot more than words.

Another reason it's helpful to look at someone when he/she is talking to us is because it helps us keep our mind on what he/she is saying. It also is a way of showing that we are listening to him/her.

You may wish to explain that you're not implying that students "stare" at the person they are listening to and that most people feel awkward staring into someone's eyes. An alternative is to avoid continual staring by looking away from time to time. Also, when looking at the person, students can concentrate their vision on the spot just between the bridge of the nose and the corner of the right eye.

Say or paraphrase: **Frequently a listener's body will be inclined toward the person if he/she is really listening.**

A good listener doesn't interrupt, but might occasionally add comments or ask questions to understand better what the speaker means.

Model | **So, a good listener uses body postures and other behaviors that demonstrate interest in what the speaker says. Let's say that a student comes to me to ask for help with a difficult school subject. If I want to really listen to that student, I might show him that I am paying attention by looking at him and possibly by leaning forward a little. While he is talking, I wouldn't interrupt.** *(Demonstrate)*

I would not look bored or try to do some work at the same time I am listening to this student. If I needed to know a little more about the problem after he has finished talking, I would ask him a couple of questions.

At this point you might want to explain to students that you don't always have the luxury of offering them all these listening behaviors. Because you as the teacher have the responsibility to teach all the students in the class, and have so much to do, sometimes it is necessary for you to be doing other things while they are speaking to you. Ask them to understand your predicament. Let them know that if it is important to them to have your full attention, they should tell you and you will try to give it to them.

Look at the list of good listening behaviors on the board. Think about the ones you already do well. Decide which ones you could do better. Now you're going to have a chance to practice these behaviors.

The next step is to have students practice speaking and listening with one another. Ask students to form pairs and sit facing each other. Again, have students decide who will be A and who will be B. Then explain that for two minutes, beginning at the signal, A will speak on one of the topics suggested earlier. B's task is to listen as attentively as possible, helping A by nodding or smiling now and then, but not talking. At the end of the 2 minutes, announce that the listener has 2 minutes to tell back to the speaker as much as possible of what he or she has said. After that, allow a minute for the two to share with each other any feelings they may have as a speaker or listener.

Next, the exercise is repeated with the first listener doing the talking. This should be followed by a short discussion by the whole class regarding the exercise. You might ask questions like the following:

- *Were you really listened to?*
- *Did your partner really hear you?*
- *Did you listen to him/her?*
- *Did you really share your feelings or did you screen them before talking about them?*

A Synopsis

Round 1

One minute	**A** speaks on topic; **B** demonstrates poor listening skills.
One minute	**A** tells **B** how that felt.
One minute	**B** speaks on topic; **A** demonstrates poor listening skills.
One minute	**B** tells **A** how that felt.

Round 2

One minute	**A** speaks on topic; **B** demonstrates good listening skills and summarizes what **A** said.
One minute	**A** tells **B** how that felt.
One minute	**B** speaks on topic; **A** demonstrates good listening skills and summarizes what **B** said.
One minute	**B** tells **A** how that felt.

Explain to students that good listening is really a hard thing to do, and that they should not be discouraged when they find this out. Say or paraphrase the following:

Some people are just plain boring and take a long time to say things or repeat themselves. Even if a person does speak quickly and clearly, our brain is still always able to think faster than a person can talk, and we often have to wait for their next thought. So listening is often going to be hard work.

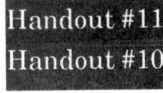

If you have time, you may also want to try the following activity to raise students' awareness regarding typical non-listening behaviors. Use either Handout #11, "Who Gets the Trip?" or select a cooperation activity that involves group discussion from the activity section of this book. Take the Handout #10, "Non-listening Behaviors." Cut up the non-listening behaviors in strips and fold them over once. Divide students into small groups. Ask students to draw one of the strips, but not to show others the strip they drew. Explain that they are to practice the non-listening behaviors as often as they can while they are involved in the group discussion. Urge students to try to complete the group activity in spite of the non-listening behaviors.

At the end of the activity, group members are to guess which non-listening behavior each person was practicing and tell which non-listening behaviors caused them the most frustration as they tried to speak. Have students review again the behaviors on the chart you made earlier entitled "Listening Behaviors" and contrast them with the non-listening behaviors they just experienced. You may want students to try the activity again, this time using all the listening behaviors suggested in this lesson.

Summarize the lesson by using the "Sentence Starters for Promoting Thinking" in the Appendix to encourage students to share some of the thoughts they had during the lesson and to help them evaluate and reflect on lesson concepts. For example,

- *"I liked..."*
- *"I didn't like..."*
- *"I'm still confused about..."*
- *"This might be helpful when..."*

Preview the next lesson by explaining to students that not only will they practice listening again, they will also learn ways to encourage others to talk. Then, when they are working in a group, they will be able to hear the ideas of people who are quiet by nature.

Are You a Good Listener?

	Usually	Occasionally	Seldom
1. Do you look at the speaker?	3	2	1
2. Do you watch the expression on the speaker's face?	3	2	1
3. Do you think about what the speaker is saying and not just about what you're going to say next?	3	2	1
4. Do you put yourself in the speaker's shoes and understand how the speaker feels?	3	2	1
5. Do you encourage the speaker to talk?	3	2	1
6. Do you let the speaker finish what he/she is trying to say, even though you understand what he/she means?	3	2	1
7. Do you question the speaker in order to get him/her to explain his/her ideas more fully?	3	2	1
8. Do you smile and nod your head to show interest in what the speaker is saying?	3	2	1
9. Do you listen even if you do not like the person who is talking?	3	2	1
10. Do you ignore distractions about you?	3	2	1
11. Do you decide some of the speaker's ideas are dumb before he/she finishes speaking?	3	2	1

TOTAL SCORE

If your score is 30 or better, you are a Good Listener.
If your score is 20-29, you are an Average Listener.
If your score is below 20, you are a Poor Listener.

Lesson 3 — Handout #9

Interruption Script

Speaker: Guess what! I learned how to divide fractions today!

Interrupter: I learned how to do that last week. The thing that's really hard is formulas.

Speaker: Oh, really? I was so happy when I finally learned how to . . .

Interrupter: Formulas are very hard, interesting though. Once you understand the formula you are working on it's fun. The most interesting formula for me is the way you find out the diameter of a circle.

Speaker: Oh? I haven't gotten to formulas yet. When I learned to multiply fractions, I felt the same way; I . . .

Interrupter: Multiplying fractions is easy. I can teach you how.

Speaker: I already know how. What was hard for me was understanding how to divide them. I just . . .

Interrupter: My big sister is taking trigonometry. If you think fractions are complicated, you should see her trigonometry book. There are more numbers and little symbols in there! It really looks hard.

Speaker: I guess that's just as hard for her as fractions are to us. My cousin is . . .

Interrupter: Naw. Trigonometry isn't hard for her. She enjoys it. I'll tell her to help you with your fractions. She can teach you how to multiply and divide them.

Speaker: But I already . . .

Interrupter: Hey, I have to go now. See you later.

Non-Listening Behaviors

- Changing the subject
- Trying to make a joke out of something the person says

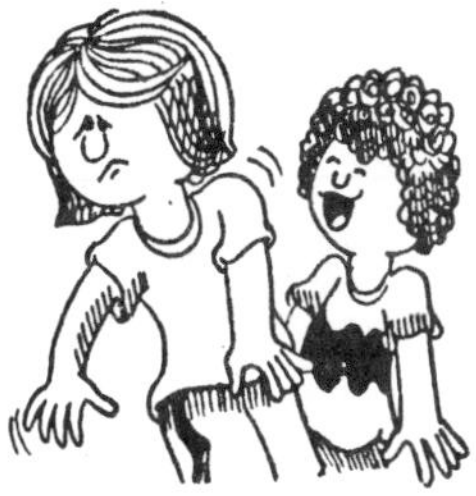

- Giving advice
- Ignoring or fidgeting
- Continually agreeing or disagreeing
- Not looking at the speaker
- Turning your body away from the speaker

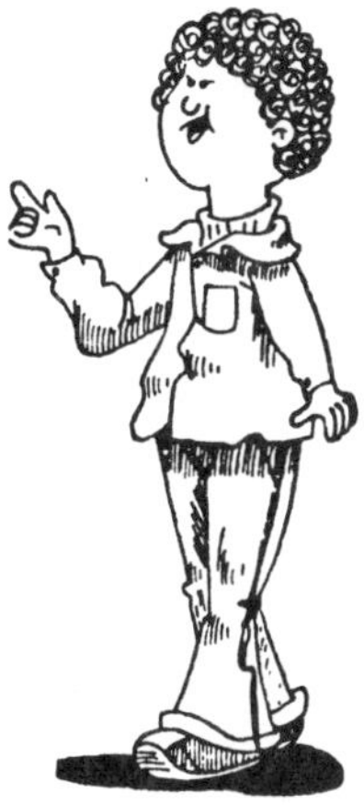

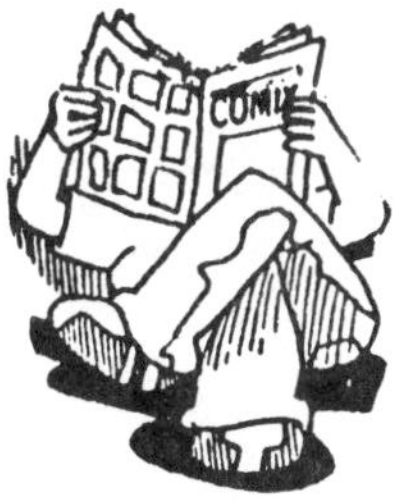

- Laughing inappropriately
- Interrupting by saying things like "You think that's great, you should hear what I did," or "That reminds me of the time I . . ."
- Looking bored

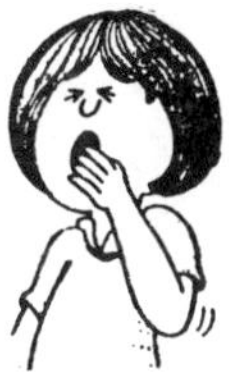

- Saying "Yeah, Yeah, Yeah" as if you want the speaker to hurry
- Playing with papers or other things

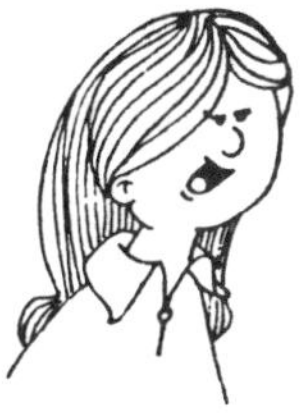

Lesson 3   Handout #11

Who Gets the Trip?

A family of four is fighting over the winnings of a raffle ticket. Here are the facts: The son, age 11, had the idea to buy the ticket. The daughter, age 8, gave her brother the money to buy the ticket. The father received the phone call announcing that their ticket had won the trip and then dug through the trash to retrieve the ticket. The mother drove across town in less than 10 minutes (the deadline for driving to the radio station to claim the prize). The prize is an all-expense paid trip for one person to Hawaii.

Discuss as a group who should get to take the trip.

Encouraging Others to Share Their Ideas

Objective Students will learn how to encourage one another to participate during cooperation activities.

Students will learn to develop actions and feelings that promote cooperation in small groups.

Materials Handout #12 - "Individual Observation Form"
Handout #13 - "Solutions to Susan's Dilemma"
Miscellaneous - Chalk board or chart paper and markers

To the Teacher In most classrooms the teacher fills almost all the leadership functions: setting goals, calling on people to contribute, drawing conclusions, and evaluating performance. Students are expected to interact directly with the teacher, so that when an opportunity does arise for students to work together, most don't know how to respond to others in a helpful way. Problems encountered in group interactions are generally ignored or handled by the teacher.

If students are to grow up learning how to solve problems in cooperation with other people, they should begin by learning to do this in the classroom. The purpose of this lesson is to provide opportunities for students to practice listening carefully to one another, to utilize the leadership skill of encouraging people to contribute, to draw out shy group members, and to evaluate performance.

Shifting from traditional teacher-centered activities to group-centered activities can be difficult for both teacher and students. Very few classes are able to undertake activities of this type without some problems at the beginning. Students will need guidance in practicing necessary group-centered skills, but if students are patiently helped to develop these skills, cooperative activities like the ones in this lesson will become more and more satisfying and successful.

In this lesson, students will practice "encouraging skills" in a "fish bowl" activity where half of the class observes the other half during a group discussion. Later the group trades places. It would be best if observers remained anonymous at this point, so write each observed student's name on the discussion groups' Handout #12, "Individual Observation Form," and pass them out randomly to the observers. Ask the observers not to say whom they are observing.

Lesson Presentation

Review with students the value of working cooperatively in a group to solve problems. Review the value of really listening to one another's ideas and some of the things people do when they are really listening.

Say: **Today there is another cooperation skill I would like to teach you. This is the skill of encouraging everyone in the group to share their ideas and thoughts regarding the problem to be solved. Help me make a list of some ways we can encourage each other to share ideas.** *List students' suggestions on the board or chartpaper. If students don't mention the following, include these:*

- *Looking at the speaker*
- *Nodding now and then to show you are listening*
- *Being quiet during pauses rather than rushing to respond*
- *Asking questions to make sure you understand*
- *Asking questions that cause the speaker to explain in more detail*
- *Making sure everyone has had a chance to share*
- *Summarizing the speaker's remarks from time to time to show you understand.*

Some encouraging phrases might be,

- *What is your opinion?*
- *Do you have any ideas?*
- *What are you thinking?*
- *Does anybody else have an idea?*
- *Does anybody disagree?*
- *Could you explain what you mean?*
- *What would you like us to do?*
- *How should we word this?*
- *What do you like about this?*
- *What don't you like about this?*
- *That makes sense.*
- *I like what you want to do.*
- *That's an interesting way of looking at it.*
- *That's a good point!*

Encouraging Others to Share Their Ideas — Lesson 4, Page 77

Discuss with the class how these behaviors differ from the way people in a group usually act. Leave this list in a place where students can refer to it during the following activity.

Divide the class into pairs and have the partners sit facing each other. Have them decide who will be A and who will be B. (Sometimes having the tallest or shortest be "A" saves time.) Explain that the A's will be the Speakers and the B's will be the Encouragers. The Speakers will give a detailed response to one of the following questions (or a question of your choice):

- *If you were the President, what things would you do to make the United States a better place in which to live?*
- *Suppose you could change our school. What improvements would you make?*

The Encourager should use the ideas on the board to respond in a way that draws the Speaker out. Encouragers are to see if they can keep the Speakers talking for 2 minutes. After 2 minutes, call time and say or paraphrase,

- **If you were the Speaker, did you feel the Encourager was genuinely interested in hearing what you had to say?**
- **What did the Encourager do that made you want to continue talking?**
- **What did the Encourager do that discouraged you from talking more?**
- **Did the Encourager ever interrupt you?**
- **What techniques seemed to be useful in encouraging the Speaker to keep talking?**

Have the partners change roles and repeat the activity.

Next, tell students that you would now like them to practice listening skills and encouraging skills. Explain that a person who wishes to contribute should be the focus of everyone's attention and listening members should refrain from arguing, being inattentive, failing to look at the Speaker, or otherwise shifting the focus away from the Speaker.

Explain: **I'm going to give some of you a problem that I'd like you to discuss and, in addition to solving the problem, I'd like you to use as many listening and encouraging behaviors as you can. To do the job well, each person in the discussion group must share his/her ideas about the problem, because everyone's opinion counts. When a member of the group speaks, he/she should be the focus of everyone's attention and the rest of the group should not argue, be inattentive, look away from the Speaker, or do anything to take the attention away from the Speaker. When the Speaker is finished, another member can become the Speaker and the group members should listen carefully to that person.**

Suggest to students that before beginning this task, it would be beneficial to discuss some typical problems that have to be worked out in group discussions. Ask students the following questions and help them establish the procedures they will use should any of these situations arise.

- **What if you have an idea that you'd like to share, but the minute one person stops talking, another person starts and you don't know how to get others to listen to you?**
- **Will raising hands work? If so, who would call on those with their hands raised?**
- **What if a few kids do all the talking? How can a group get them to give others a chance to speak?**
- **What if some members of the group agree on an idea, but others disagree?**
- **Who decides what the group answer to a problem will be?**
- **What if everybody agrees except one person?**
- **If some of the group ideas need to be written down, how will you decide who will do the writing?**
- **What do you do about kids who aren't helping the group or are annoying other people?**
- **How do you pick the person who is going to tell the rest of the class what the group has decided about an issue?**

Handout #12 *At this point, explain to students that you are now going to divide them into two groups: those who will participate in the discussion and those who will observe them. Have the Participants sit in a semicircle in the front of the room so that the Observers can see everyone. Give each of the Observers Handout #12, "Individual Observation Form." Go over the items on the rating scale with the entire class. Then explain that observers are to observe the person whose name is written on their forms during the discussion and that you would like them to use the group discussion Rating Scale to rate that person's skills in listening and encouraging.*

Read students the following problem situation:*

> **Dora, a friend of Susan's, has been delivering papers for a local newspaper. From time to time Susan has helped her with her route, folding papers and delivering them to the customers. Dora always paid Susan when she was her substitute and promised her friend that she would recommend her to the district manager when she decided to give up her route. When the time came, Dora kept her word and helped Susan get the paper route. Dora was to train her friend for a period of time until she was able to learn the route, how to collect, and keep records. For the last few weeks Susan was rolling the papers, placing them in plastic bags, carrying and delivering them to the customers, and helping Dora collect. She knows Dora is training her to be able to do a good job, but lately Susan has become increasingly unhappy. She feels that she is doing all the work, but Dora is getting all the pay. She feels this is unfair and she should do something about it.**

Handout #13 *Now give students in the discussion group Handout #13, "Solutions to Susan's Dilemma," and review the list of possible solutions to Susan's problem. Ask students to discuss one by one the merits of these solutions and, after that, to generate other possible solutions.*

* J.D. Casteel, *Learning to Think and Choose*, 1978, p. 142.

While students are involved in discussion, circulate quietly among the Observers to make sure that they are recording both positive and negative behaviors.

After about 5 to 8 minutes, ask the group to summarize and try to agree on a solution. While they are doing this, collect the Group Discussion Rating Scales from the Observers and quickly review them. See if you can determine whether, on the whole, there were more positive than negative behaviors noted by the Observers.

Then ask those students in the discussion group what conclusions they came up with regarding the problem they were given and help them summarize their discussion.

Ask students in the discussion group these questions:

- **Was it harder to listen in a group discussion than in the discussion with a partner? Why?**
- **How did your behavior in this group discussion differ from your usual behavior in group discussions?**
- **What are the advantages (or disadvantages) of stopping yourself from interrupting a speaker in order to say what you want to say?**

Share with the class your general impression of how they did according to the information on the observation forms and whether they exhibited more positive than negative behaviors. If you think it would be productive, give each group member his/her observation form, explaining that this is a general feedback device on his/her listening behavior that may be useful. Explain that it takes a while to learn to be a good observer and that it is a difficult task, so they may not completely agree with what's on their forms.

If you have time, reverse the group roles, letting the former observers discuss the problem while the former discussion group members observe.

Discuss with students how they can put into practice in future class discussions the procedures for encouraging a speaker. Say: **In any class discussion, whenever one of you has something to contribute, that person should be the focus of our attention, as in the activity you just did, and all other members of the class should act as encouragers until that person has finished saying what he or she wants to say.**

Use the "Sentence Starters for Promoting Thinking" in the Appendix to help students process lesson concepts and think about transfer to real-life situations. For example,

- *"I've got it! It means . . ."*
- *"I could use this when . . ."*
- *"What I need to know is . . ."*
- *"This could be helpful when . . ."*

Suggest that students try using some of the encouraging statements they have learned when they go home with their family and friends.

Finally, tell students that next time they will learn a cooperation skill which is harder than encouraging someone.

Individual Observation Form

Observer: ______________________________

Person Being Observed: ______________________

This form is designed to record the behavior of one group member only. Put a check each time one of these positive or negative behaviors occurs.

Positive Behaviors

1. Looks at the person talking	
2. Asks questions to encourage others to speak	
3. Invites others to give their opinion	
4. Nods or uses facial expressions to show interest in others' ideas	
5. Helps keep people on the topic	
6. Expresses own ideas	

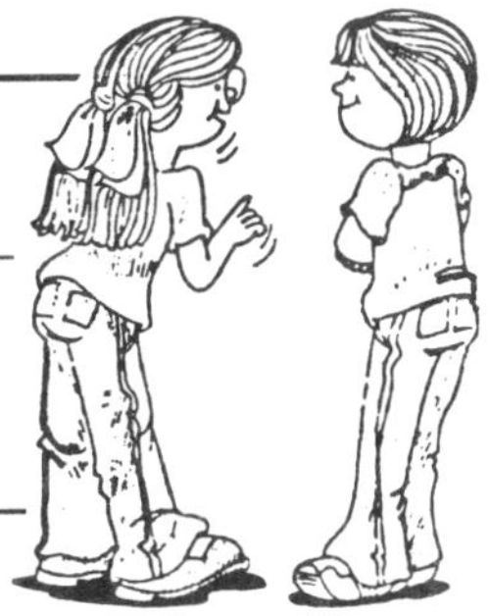

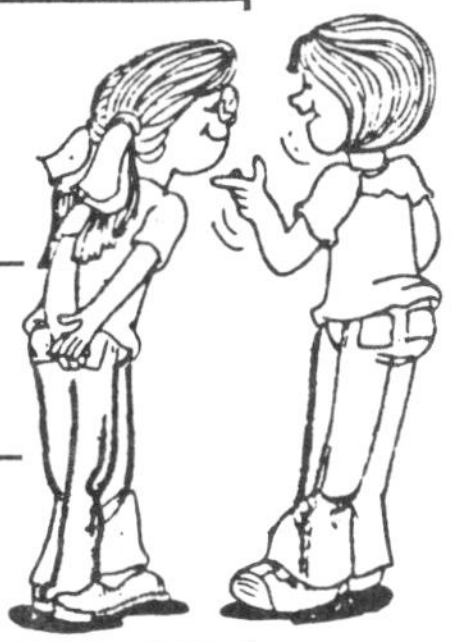

Negative Behaviors

1. Acts silly	
2. Doesn't look at the speaker	
3. Doesn't participate	
4. Interrupts	
5. Gets off the subject	
6. Talks too much	

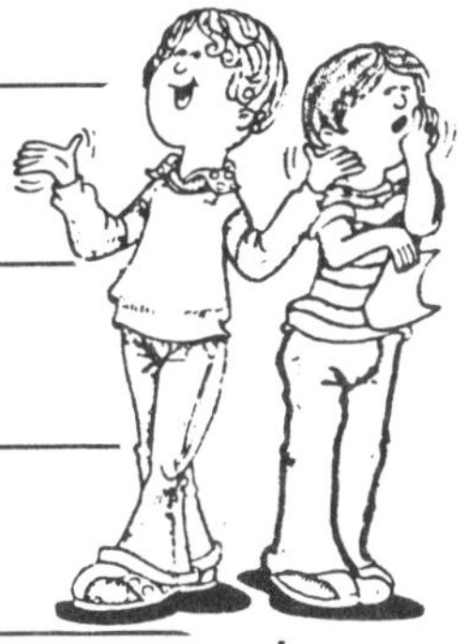

Solutions to Susan's Dilemma*

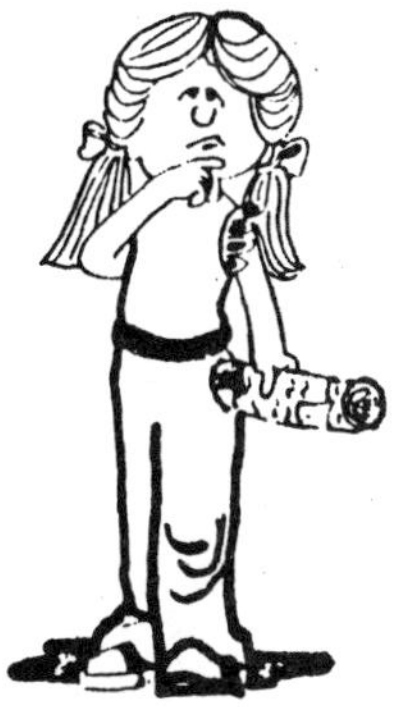

Good Bad

____ ____ Susan could save some of her schoolwork and do it at home. She could tell Dora she would love to help her with the papers, but she is too far behind in her schoolwork.

____ ____ Susan could ask her mother to tell Dora that she must help her with housework.

____ ____ Susan could tell Dora she has learned all she needs to know and will not help her again unless she agrees to pay her.

____ ____ Susan can continue to do Dora's work for her but tell her she is being unfair.

____ ____ Susan can tell Dora's parents what she is doing. They might make Dora treat her fairly.

____ ____ Susan could tell Dora that she's furious about the way she has been treated and demand to be paid for the work she has already done.

____ ____ Susan could tell Dora it's been great working for her but she hopes she can find somebody else that's as stupid as she has been to take over from now on.

____ ____ Susan can tell Dora's best friends how Dora is behaving. They will shame her into treating her fairly.

____ ____ Susan could buy Dora a gift thanking her for her training and tell her she is ready to begin work.

____ ____ Susan could write to Ann Landers about her problem, hoping that Dora will read it.

____ ____ Susan could call the district manager and report Dora.

____ ____ Susan could tell Dora she is finished with her training for the paper route and will not help Dora anymore.

____ ____ Susan can continue doing Dora's work but make a few careless mistakes. The customers may complain and Dora will lose bonus money.

____ ____ Susan could tell her parents what is happening.

* J.D. Casteel, *Learning to Think and Choose,* 1978.

Responding to Others in Group Discussion

Objective Students will learn the skills of linking, restating, and summarizing one another's contributions when engaged in cooperation activities.

Materials Handout #14 - "Listening Observation Form"

To the Teacher If students are to work together in a truly mature and productive manner, deliberate training must be given to improve the way students listen and respond to one another in group discussion. Most students use the time when other students are talking to daydream or rehearse a reply. Often students are merely interested in giving their own opinion in the hope of offering a more spectacular idea than anyone else is able to. Most cooperative learning activities, however, require the group to arrive at a decision on a solution to a problem. In order to do this, members must make connections between the ideas presented and link their contributions rather than just adding unrelated ideas to the heap for others to hear and then ignore.

In order to interrelate ideas, students must listen carefully to other members to see whether their ideas fit together in any way and the extent to which they agree or disagree with previous speakers. Then, when they enter the discussion, they can indicate the relationship between their ideas and the contributions of others.

The skill of responding to others' opinions and feelings before stating our own is not only an important ingredient for cooperative learning activities, but an invaluable skill for personal growth. Learning how to really listen and respond to what a person is saying and to the feelings implicit in their statements is an extremely important social skill. The skills students receive through the activities in this lesson can also serve to enhance their personal relationships throughout their lives.

The following lesson is designed to provide activities that will train students to respond to one another. First of all, a demonstration of poor and good listening and of responding to others is given. Then students practice responding in triads, and finally students practice these skills in a large group discussion. It would be helpful if they could sit in a circle or semi-circle for this.

Lesson Presentation *Review with students the value of listening to one another and encouraging everyone to contribute their ideas when working cooperatively. Write the word "responding" on the chalkboard. Ask if anyone would like to give an* *account of their use of encouraging skills outside the classroom. Explain that today you would like to focus on the cooperation skill of responding to what someone else has said. Say or paraphrase,*

Often in a group discussion, people don't really think about what the speaker is saying, but just sit there waiting for a chance to say their own ideas. It's difficult to think about and respond to what someone has said and connect it with what you want to say. Let's do an activity where we have to listen as well as make our ideas fit with what someone says.

Explain that you would like students to create a story together by each contributing one line. Start out by having one student begin telling a made-up story, giving only the first sentence or begin the story by supplying the first sentence yourself. Then go from student to student, asking them to add one new sentence to the story. Encourage students to preserve the continuity of the story and try to make it sound as much as possible as if one person had made it up. After students have finished, say,

We did this activity to practice linking ideas. It was important that you listen carefully to the previous speaker in order to follow the direction the story was taking.

If a group is trying to solve a problem together, they can do a much better job if they listen carefully to each other to see whether their ideas fit together and how much they either agree or disagree with what is being said.

Even before this is done, however, a speaker needs to know that he or she has been heard and understood. We can let the speaker know this by quickly summarizing what we think is the main idea the other person is trying to get across. This gives the person a chance to explain further if they feel he/she hasn't been understood by us.

Responding to Others in Group Discussion

Lesson 5
Page 85

At this point, demonstrate both skill and lack of skill in responding to what others say. Ask a student to volunteer to be the Speaker and you be the Listener. Have the Speaker talk about a fairly significant personal issue or controversial topic. For example, "Should there be a time limit set on how long students your age are allowed to use the phone? Why or why not?" or "Something that happened to me lately."

Model

Demonstrate poor listening first by doing such things as interrupting, strongly disagreeing, giving advice or judging what the person says, making suggestions, etc. You might preface your statements by some of the following phrases:

- *That's a dumb thing to say!*
- *Nobody thinks that way.*
- *You should . . .*
- *It would be better if you . . .*
- *What I think is . . .*
- *My idea is . . .*
- *That reminds me of the time I . . .*
- *You're totally wrong!*
- *That's crazy!*
- *That's wierd!*

Have either the same student or another student speak again on an issue significant to him/her. Demonstrate the appropriate listening skill of responding by the use of such phrases as the following:

- *Can you tell me more about why you feel or think that way?*
- *Do you mean that . . . ?*
- *It seems like you feel that . . .*
- *You'd like people to . . .*
- *It sounds like you . . .*
- *Are you saying that . . .*
- *So your idea is . . .*
- *So your opinion is . . .*
- *So you basically think that . . .*

- *Your main feeling is that . . .*
- *Could you explain that some more?*

Write these phrases on the chalkboard or on a chart for students to refer to as they now practice restating and summarizing one another's ideas.

Divide the class into groups of three. Designate one person in each group as the Speaker, another as the Listener, and the third as the Observer. Give the Speaker a controversial topic to talk about. For instance, "Do kids really need to go to school? Why or why not?" The job of the Speakers is to express their thoughts and feelings about the subject. The Listeners are to practice responding skills. The Observers are not to participate in the discussion, but to observe whether listeners are using any of the principles of good listening, particularly the responding skills that have just been discussed and demonstrated.

Handout #14 *Give Students a copy of Handout #14, "Listening Observation Form." Go over the contents of the form with all students, then have the Speakers and Listeners set their forms aside for later use. Tell the Speakers to begin. After 3 or 4 minutes, call time and have the Observers tell the Listeners how many times they observed them exercising the principles of good listening and responding. Have the same groups of three change roles within the group and repeat the same procedure.*

Another way to teach responding skills is to have students engage in a group discussion where each student can contribute only by responding in some way to the previous speaker. In other words, rather than simply stating their own position, they must comment on or add to the previous contribution. Require students to look at the last contributor as they link their comments to what has been said previously.

Read the following problem situation to students:

Leah's Difficult Decision*

Although Leah loved sports, especially basketball, she was not a very good athlete. She didn't run fast, didn't have quick reflexes, and didn't shoot baskets very well. When she was finally old enough to play on the school team, she sat on the bench most of the time and watched others play. When summer came, Leah decided she would really work hard at basketball. She practiced bouncing, passing, shooting baskets, running sideways and backwards. She was getting much better.

When school started again, Leah tried out for the seventh grade basketball team. She was sure she would make the first string this time. Unfortunately, the other girls trying out had also improved. The coach came and talked to Leah. He said he realized that she had worked very hard to improve as much as she had, but that she probably wouldn't get to play very much during the coming season. The coach wanted to keep her on the team, however, even though he would understand if she preferred to quit. The decision was up to her.

---

* J.D. Casteel, *Learning to Think and Choose,* 1978, p. 66.

Begin the discussion by doing the following:

1. *Call on a student to give his or her opinion regarding the discussion issue.*

2. *Ask for a volunteer either to*
   a) *use open-ended questions to encourage the Speaker to elaborate, or*
   b) *summarize or restate the Speaker's remarks to show he or she understood.*
   c) *Then have the volunteer add any new ideas he/she may have.*

3. *When the second speaker is finished, call for another volunteer to respond to either the first or second speaker by looking directly at one of them and commenting on that person's remarks before adding new ideas.*

Continue this procedure until you think that students can respond to the previous speaker's remarks before adding their contributions without your prompting.

Encourage students to try as a group to reach agreement about what Leah should do about her problem, and while they do this to also focus on practicing the listening skill of responding to one another in group discussion.

Sup. Act. *You may also wish to use the supplementary discussion activity, "A Difficult Situation," that follows this lesson to provide more practice in responding skills. Remind students to use this skill throughout the day during academic discussion as well as at home.*

Use the "Sentence Starters for Promoting Thinking" in the Appendix to help students summarize and process what they have learned in this lesson and to deal with any remaining questions or confusion. For example,

- *"I realized that . . . ,"*
- *"The main idea seems to be . . . ,"*

- *"This could be helpful when...,"*
- *"I was surprised...," or*
- *"I'm still confused about..."*

Explain that in the next lesson students will learn a fun way to work together to come up with lots of creative solutions to problems.

Listening Observation Form

Observer: ______________________________

Person Being Observed: ______________________________

This form is designed to record the behavior of one person only. Put a check each time one of these positive listening behaviors occurs. Be particularly on the lookout for behaviors #4 and #5.

Positive Behaviors

1. Looked at the person talking	
2. Nodded or used facial expressions to show interest in the speaker's ideas	
3. Asked questions to encourage the speaker to go on	
4. Restated what the speaker said	
5. Summarized what the speaker said	

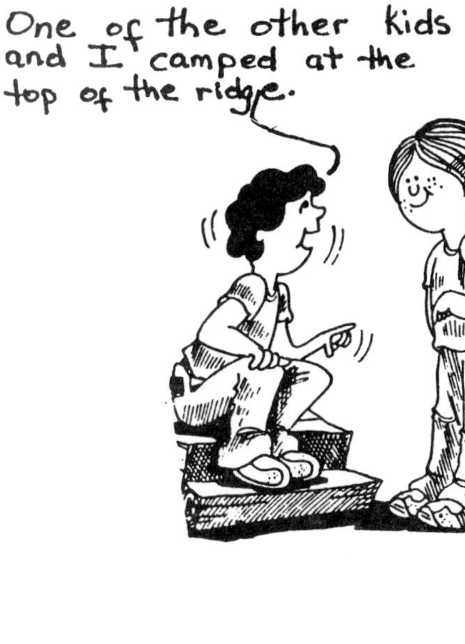
One of the other kids and I camped at the top of the ridge.

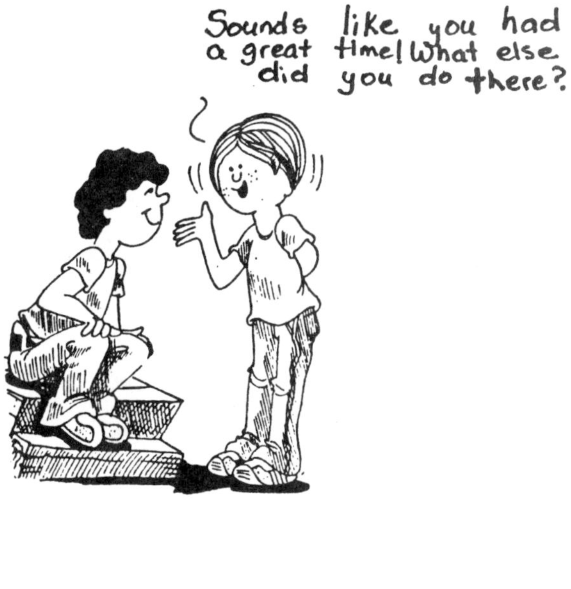
Sounds like you had a great time! What else did you do there?

Lesson 5   Supplementary Activity

A Difficult Situation

Objective   Students will work cooperatively to rank-order characters in a conflict situation.

Materials   Handout "A Difficult Situation"

Procedure   Read the following conflict situation to students and ask them to rank-order the characters from the one they sympathize with the most to the one they sympathize with the least (1 = Sympathize with the most, 5 = Sympathize with the least).

Lesson 5

Supplementary Activity
Handout for "A Difficult Situation"

A Difficult Situation

Jane was always an A student. She never had to study very hard. She seemed to be able to remember and understand new things very easily. Jane's best friend was Toni. Toni had always found school work harder.

They were both in the same Math class and there was a very important test coming up in Miss Smith's class. Everyone was getting more and more concerned about this test. The people who got over 90% were going to be in a special TV show.

Toni asked Jane to help her study but Jane wasn't planning on putting in much study time, so she wasn't very helpful. Toni went to another friend, Jeff. Jeff told her to get lost because he was too busy. Toni was close to tears. She went to Miss Smith for extra help. Miss Smith said that she felt Toni would not be able to achieve the necessary 90%.

Toni was very upset and depressed. Jane noticed how upset her friend was so she offered some last minute help. Toni flatly refused it. Jane felt awful.

During the test Jane got a note passed to her from Chris. The note came from Toni asking for some answers. Jane debated whether or not to respond. Finally she did and Miss Smith caught her with the note and tore up her test. Toni said nothing.

Jane was no longer eligible for the TV show but Toni got a 91% to everyone's amazement. Toni accepted the role on the TV show.

Now rank order the characters from 1 to 5:

Jane _____

Toni _____

Chris _____

Jeff _____

Miss Smith _____

Cooperative Problem-Solving Through Brainstorming

Objective Students will learn to work cooperatively to generate as many ideas as they can think of to solve a given problem situation.

Materials Chalkboard, chart paper or tag board
Colored markers
Transparency #6/Handout #15 - "Rules of Brainstorming" and/or
Transparency #7/Handout #16 - "Brainstorming Solutions to a Problem"
Transparency #8/Handout #17 - "Narrowing Down Solutions to a Problem"
Transparency #9/Handout #18 - "Looking At Consequences"
Handout #19 - "Group Climate Questionnaire"

To the Teacher Brainstorming is a well-known, widely used problem-solving tool. It is especially useful when there is an identified problem that could use a creative solution, i.e., how the early settlers could have lived peacefully with the native Americans; how to redecorate the classroom; how to make the class a happier, more enjoyable place to learn; ways to make new friends; how to have an innovative fund-raiser; the best way to memorize times tables; etc. It is designed to produce a large body of data which can later be worked on and refined.

Brainstorming can be used in conjunction with other exercises whenever an interesting question or problem arises, and it often succeeds in generating a high level of group energy as a number of different minds and perspectives focus on the same topic. It can be used in an exercise on categorizing ideas on a given topic. An example could be cars. Items in that category are engine, body, uses, colors, makes, fuels, etc. Subheads of fuel are octane, additives, brands, etc. Students could go on categorizing until the sub-headings (or the students) are exhausted.

Because of the nature of the ground rules for brainstorming, this strategy is particularly useful in assuring participation of all group members. Brainstorming separates idea production from evaluation by calling for rapid, noncritical listing of any and all ideas, no matter how wild, on a given topic. By encouraging the freedom to express even silly thoughts, brainstorming often brings out some truly creative ideas. Imagination becomes a group skill. For these reasons, it is a fine strategy for students to use when they are working cooperatively to find a solution for a given problem.

Lesson Presentation

Review with students the value of working together to solve problems and of listening, encouraging, and responding. Say or paraphrase the following:

Now that you have practiced some of the important cooperation skills and have worked cooperatively with each other to solve some problems, I would like to teach you to use the technique of brainstorming. Brainstorming will be helpful in many of the group cooperation activities we will be doing in our classroom, and will also give you a tool that you can use in groups all your life. Brainstorming is a good first step in solving a problem, a way of getting out the greatest number of ideas for consideration. The most important thing is to spill out ideas as quickly as possible without criticism of your own thoughts or anybody elses.

Transp. #6/ Handout #15

Use Transparency #6, "Rules Of Brainstorming," as you go over the following guidelines to brainstorming with students: (You may wish to give students a copy of the rules.)

1. **Try to come up with as many ideas as possible; no idea is too wild or crazy.**

2. **Write down all suggestions. If you judge and evaluate ideas as they are thought up, students tend to become more concerned with defending their ideas than with thinking up new and better ones.**

3. **No criticism of anyone's ideas. It doesn't matter how wild they might be. It's easier to tame down a wild idea than to pep up a bland idea. If wild ideas are not forthcoming in a brainstorming session, it usually means that students are censoring their own ideas. They are thinking twice before they shout out an idea because they're afraid others might think it's a silly or stupid idea and put them down or laugh at them.**

4. **Don't try to decide if the ideas are good or bad. The goal is quantity, not quality. Quantity eventually breeds quality. When a great number of ideas come pouring out in rapid succession, evaluation is generally ruled out. People are free to give their imaginations wide range, and good ideas result.**

Cooperative Problem-Solving... Lesson 6
Page 93

5. Use others' ideas to think of new ideas of your own. Everyone is encouraged to build upon or modify the ideas of others. Combining or modifying previously suggested ideas often leads to new ideas that are superior and more creative than the ones that sparked them.

After discussing the rules for brainstorming, engage the class as a whole in a brainstorming session so that you can coach them through the brainstorming steps. Choose an actual class problem situation for which you would like to see a creative solution, or use one of the following topics:

- *How to weigh an elephant*
- *How to keep from getting off the subject in our class or small group discussion*
- *Ways to set up a science fair*
- *Ways to divide a group assignment*
- *How to learn spelling words rapidly*
- *How to make learning long division more fun*
- *What students can do to make the school look better*
- *Ways to have an innovative fund-raiser*
- *Ways to stop environmental pollution*
- *Ways to use a Coke bottle on a desert island*
- *Ways to express caring to someone far away*
- *Ways to work for peace*

Give the class the following instructions:

During the next 5 to 10 minutes, let's try to come up with as many ideas as we can that might solve the problem we are working on.

First we'll work on quantity. We'll try to generate as many ideas as possible as quickly as we can. Don't hold back an idea just because it seems worthless, impractical, or dumb. Don't discuss or judge others' contributions. We will discuss the ideas later. Don't even say you think someone's idea is really good. Just listen to every idea without commenting. If someone's idea reminds you of an idea kind of like it, say it, even if it isn't completely original.

Remember: No praise and no criticism! We're all just thinking up as many ideas as we can!

You may want to have a bell near you, which you ring whenever a student forgets and starts to evaluate or discuss an idea during the brainstorming session.

Transp. #7

Write all suggestions students offer on the chalkboard or on overhead Transparency #7, "Brainstorming Solutions to a Problem." Begin the next step, sorting and refining the ideas. Review with students the suggestions they made and help them discard all proposals that are too difficult or unrealistic. In general, any idea requiring a major decision or major effort by people outside those involved in the problem ought to be eliminated. For example, an idea that would require convincing a school board to remodel a school cafeteria, or a principal to put in a pop or candy machine would probably be unworkable.

Determine which of the solutions seems most workable by asking questions like:

- *Who would have to do what to make this idea work?*
- *How much time would it take?*
- *What kind of help would be needed?*

Transp. #8
Transp. #9

Decide by a show of hands which are the three most feasible ideas or solutions. For each of these three solutions, have students list as many possible consequences as they can. Write student responses on overhead Transparency #8, "Narrowing down Solutions to a Problem," and Transparency #9, "Looking at Consequences." If you prefer, outline a grid on the chalkboard similar to one of these and write responses there. After using one of these procedures, have students make their final choice of a solution by voting or using a show of hands.

Handout #16

Now that you have modeled leading a brainstorming session, divide the class into groups of four or five students and explain that you would like them to try brainstorming in their small groups. If the room has enough chalkboard space, each group can gather around a section of the chalkboard. If a chalkboard is not available, each group can gather around a desk or table equipped with a large sheet of paper or you can give each group a copy of Student Handout #16, "Brainstorming Solutions to a Problem." Designate or have each group decide who will act as the recorder of all ideas generated by the group.

Choose a brainstorming topic from the list on the previous page, or focus on a problem relevant to your particular students.

Instruct the groups to list as many solutions to the problem as they can think of. After 5 minutes, stop the listing. Have the groups quickly count and share the number of items they have recorded. Take a few minutes to discuss questions like these:

- *Are you expressing all the ideas that come to you?*
- *Is everyone getting a chance to put in ideas?*
- *Are you able to avoid being critical of each other's contributions?*

Tell students to take a few more minutes to continue brainstorming. Then ask the groups to review their lists and choose the three solutions that their group feels would be most useful.

Handout #17
Handout #18

After the three top solutions have been determined, have students follow the procedures for evaluating these alternatives suggested earlier. You may wish to give each group a copy of one of the forms for evaluating solutions: Handout #17, "Narrowing down solutions to a Problem," and Handout #18, "Looking at Consequences," or they may continue to use the chalkboard for these steps.

Reconvene the total group and have each small group report its top three suggestions and final solutions. You may wish to have the class as a whole discuss and evaluate the solution. Post in the classroom each group's entire list of possible solutions so all can see how many ideas emerge in a short time through brainstorming.

Summarize the brainstorming sessions by discussing the following questions:

- *Was this a good way to get your ideas listened to?*
- *Did many good ideas come out?*
- *Can you think of other times we might use this method of sharing ideas to solve problems in our class?*

Handout #19 *Give students Handout #19, "Group Climate Questionnaire," to fill out individually and return to you.*

Use "Sentence Starters for Promoting Thinking" in the Appendix to elicit verbal comments about their thoughts and feelings during the lesson and to help them think of ways to apply and transfer lesson concepts.

Sup. Act. *The supplementary activities, "A Tough Decision," and "Millions of Marshmallows," that follow this lesson can provide more practice in brainstorming and are enjoyable activities for students.*

Rules of Brainstorming

1. Try to come up with as many ideas as possible.

2. Write down all suggestions.

3. No criticism of anyone's ideas.

4. Don't try to decide if the ideas are good or bad. The longer the list of ideas, the better.

5. Use others' ideas to think of new ideas of your own.

Brainstorming Solutions to a Problem

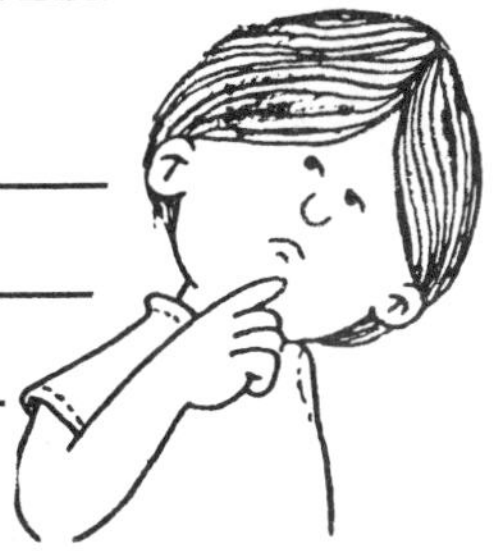

The problem is ____

____

____

Possible solutions are

____

____

____

____

____

____

____

____

____

____

____

____

____

____

____

____

____

____

____

____

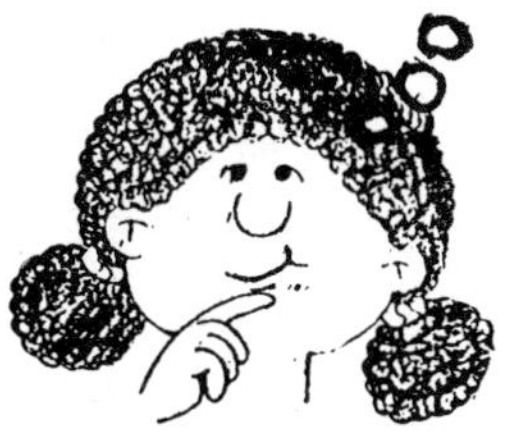

Lesson 6 Transparency #8/Handout #17

Narrowing Down Solutions To A Problem

Our best solution.	What's good about the solution?	What's bad about the solution?
1.		
2.		
3.		

Lesson 6   Transparency #9/Handout #18

Looking at Consequences

Solution #1	Solution #2	Solution #3

Group Climate Questionnaire

Below is a series of statements, each beginning "With this group I . . . " Use the five-point scale provided below to indicate how you feel about each statement. Circle the word that most closely represents your response. There are no right or wrong answers. What is important is that you indicate honestly how you feel. Do not sign your name to this form.

With this group I . . .

1.	like letting others know my ideas.	Never	Seldom	Frequently	Always
2.	worry about my goofs or mistakes.	Never	Seldom	Frequently	Always
3.	feel comfortable.	Never	Seldom	Frequently	Always
4.	can let others know my feelings.	Never	Seldom	Frequently	Always
5.	talk to only a few members of the group.	Never	Seldom	Frequently	Always
6.	feel that others ignore me.	Never	Seldom	Frequently	Always
7.	feel that others care about me.	Never	Seldom	Frequently	Always
8.	feel that others do not listen to me.	Never	Seldom	Frequently	Always
9.	feel that others put down my ideas.	Never	Seldom	Frequently	Always
10.	feel that others make fun of me when I make mistakes.	Never	Seldom	Frequently	Always
11.	feel that others like me.	Never	Seldom	Frequently	Always
12.	usually have a chance to say all I want to in our group activities.	Never	Seldom	Frequently	Always
13.	help others express their ideas.	Never	Seldom	Frequently	Always
14.	am overly stubborn about my opinions.	Never	Seldom	Frequently	Always
15.	give in too quickly when I'm opposed.	Never	Seldom	Frequently	Always
16.	am too quiet.	Never	Seldom	Frequently	Always
17.	participate enough.	Never	Seldom	Frequently	Always
18.	am tolerant of opposition viewpoints.	Never	Seldom	Frequently	Always
19.	dominate the conversation.	Never	Seldom	Frequently	Always

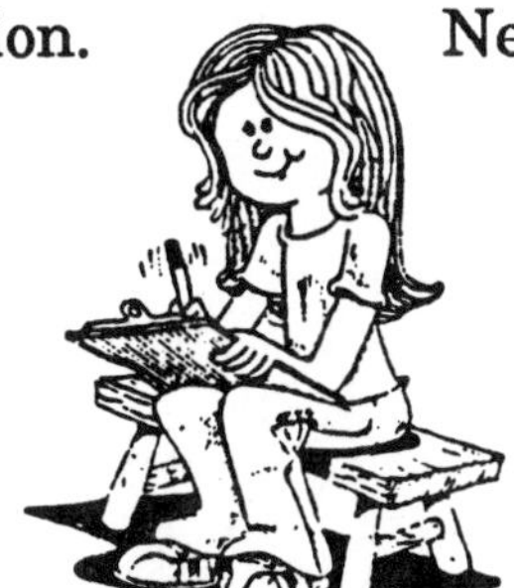

Lesson 6 — Supplementary Activity

A Tough Decision

Objective Students will cooperate as a large group to problem-solve a given situation by brainstorming solutions and evaluating consequences.

Materials Transparency #8, "Narrowing Down Solutions to a Problem"

Procedure Tell the students to imagine that they are the main character in the following story, "A Tough Decision." Read the story and have them brainstorming possible solutions. Record all brainstorming on a transparency. Help students narrow their solutions to three possibilities. Use transparency #8, to lead students through an evaluation of their three solutions.

Lesson 6　　　　　　　　　　　　　　　　　　　　Supplementary Activity

A Problem for Brainstorming
A Tough Decision*

The year is 1800. You are the captain of an American ship with a crew of 35 men, carrying a cargo of wheat. Your destination is Egypt. Along the way pirates are a constant threat to ships like yours. You and your crew are ready to fight. Lookouts are watching the horizon for the approach of other ships. Suddenly, the lookout in the crow's nest cries out, "Ship off the port bow. She's flying no flag."

Using your spyglass, you locate the ship. It seems to be in trouble. Most of its sails are gone and you can see other signs of damage. It looks as though the ship has been severely damaged in a storm.

You notice that a number of men, a few women, and a couple of children are waving shirts and other objects in order to attract your attention. As far as you can tell, these people are in trouble and may die unless you choose to rescue them.

As captain, though, it is your responsibility to protect your crew, cargo, and ship. Quickly, you meet with the other ship's officers who help you command the ship and crew. One officer says, "It's a trick. The pirates are using those people to lure us in. Let's sail away quickly." Another officer disagrees. "I see no sign that this is a trick. There are women and children on that ship who need our help. We must rescue them."

A third officer suggest a compromise. "Let's take no chances. Let's send some men over in a longboat. If it's a trick they'll find out. We can't afford to risk all our men. We must find out whether or not it is a trick. It's better to lose a few men and the longboat than it is to lose our whole crew, cargo, and ship."

The first officer does not like this suggestion. "That's not right. If it's a trick, the men we send over are dead men. We should not ask any of our men to take such a chance. Besides, we need our full crew to run the ship."

You as the captain make the final decision. You may choose to support one of your officers, or you may decide to do something they have not recommended.

What are some possible solutions to this problem?

* J.D. Casteel, *Learning to Think and Choose*, 1978, p. 88.

Millions Of Marshmallows

Objective Students will practice the techniques for brainstorming and problem solving by writing an advertisement.

Materials Handout - "Millions of Marshmallows"

Procedure Review the rules of brainstorming with the students: Tell them that brainstorming is a technique in which 1) you list as many ideas as possible (all suggestions are written down); 2) no discussion or judgment of others' ideas is allowed; 3) the longer the list of ideas, the better; and 3) all ideas are worthwhile even though they may sound wild, as they may help someone think of another idea.

Divide the class into groups of four or five and then ask them to apply these rules to the following situation:

"You own a small grocery store in a small town and have placed an order for 10 boxes of miniature marshmallows. When the shipment arrives, you discover that you made a big mistake: You ordered 1000 boxes instead of 10! The marshmallows cannot be returned and will soon become hard. The shipment has been paid for and you don't want to lose your money. You must convince your customers that there are many uses for hard miniature marshmallows."

Brainstorm all uses imaginable for these marshmallows. Record responses on the board when all groups are done (i.e., paint and thread them for necklaces, melt and use them as glue, flatten them and use them as Bingo markers, etc.). Distribute copies of "Millions of Marshmallows" and ask them to create an advertisement that will entice customers to buy the marshmallows. The advertisement may show just one or many uses, and students may create more than one advertisement. Display the ads in the classroom.

Lesson 6

Supplementary Activity
Handout for "Millions of Marshmallows"

Millions Of Marshmallows

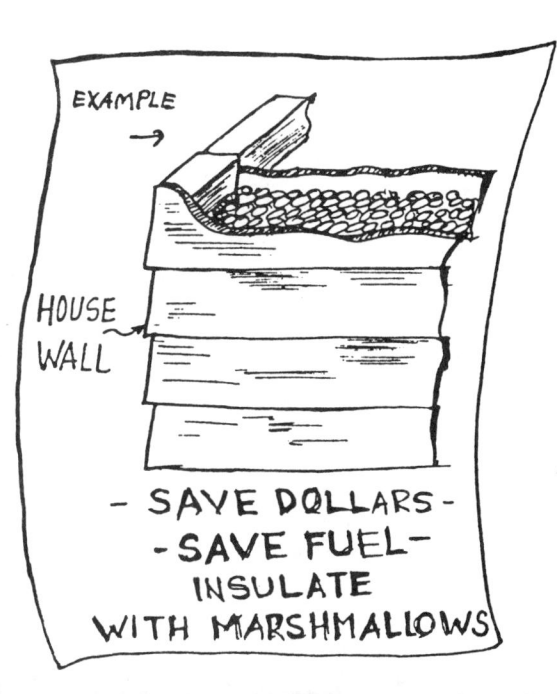

Advertisement created by: _____

Cooperative Decision-Making Through Consensus

Objective   Students will learn to cooperate by striving toward consensus regarding a given problem situation.

Materials   Handout #20 - "Questions for Observer"
Handout #21 - "Group Behavior Tally Sheet"

To the Teacher

"Well, we out-voted you! That settles it!"

"No, it doesn't. Just because there are more of you doesn't make you right. It's still not a good plan."

"Oh, don't be such a sore loser!"

"It's not being a loser that bothers me. I just don't think you guys know what you're doing."

"What do you mean?"

"You haven't listened to why we don't agree. Some of us have some very good reasons for not wanting to go along with you."

Conversations like this are quite likely to occur after a conflict has been handled by voting on the issue. In some classrooms group decision-making can result in one or two powerful individuals railroading decisions through intimidation.

Although decision-making by a few individuals or by voting has advantages in that decisions can be made quickly and efficiently, there are many disadvantages. Among these is the fact that a few individuals or even the majority may not always have all the information needed to come to a wise decision. Also, if all members of a group haven't been consulted on a particular decision, they will not be as committed to it as they might have been if they had been involved in making it.

Teaching students to reach consensus gives students a mechanism to facilitate group decision-making and helps make group decisions fairer and more representative of the views of all group members. Consensus is based on the concept of shared power.

While it may be difficult to simulate problem-solving issues in the classroom that all students will become deeply invested in, there will be issues in their adult life that they'll feel strongly about. There will be times when they'll disagree with others' opinions on these issues. Students should have access to a procedure other than voting at these times. Voting can sometimes be a useful tool in reaching decisions where there is disagreement, but voting has its disadvantages. When an issue is decided simply by polling the members and letting the majority win, groups tend to become "polarized." In a voting situation there are not necessarily winners and losers. Losers don't readily support decisions forced on them by the majority. Many times they look for opportunities to sabotage decisions with which they disagree.

The most effective method of group decision-making is through consensus, but it also takes the most time. In consensus an attempt is made to arrive at a solution that all can agree with, or support, or at least live with. The ideas and opinions of all members are taken into serious consideration by the entire group.

Unanimity is often impossible to achieve. There are degrees of consensus, all of which bring about a higher quality resolution than does majority vote or other methods of decision-making. Consensus is more commonly defined as a collective opinion reached by a group of people working together under conditions that permit communication to be sufficiently open, and the group climate to be sufficiently supportive, so that all members of the group feel they have had their fair chance to influence the decision. When a decision is made by consensus, all members understand the decision and are prepared to support it. Operationally, consensus means

- that all members can rephrase the decision to show that they understand it;
- that all members have had a chance to tell how they feel about the decision; and
- that those members who continue to disagree or have doubts will, nevertheless, say publicly that they are willing to give the decision an experimental try for a period of time.

Consensus demands patience and skills in group interaction. The cooperation skills of listening, encouraging others to contribute, and summarizing are important prerequisites for the use of consensus.

Despite its advantages, consensus-seeking should not be attempted in every problem-solving situation. Arriving at consensus is difficult and can be time-consuming. Too frequent attempts to reach consensus can be frustrating to students, who prefer quick decisions so they can get on with the task.

Nevertheless, it is important for students to know the different ways that consensus can be reached. The following lesson teaches students the

Cooperative Decision-Making Through Consensus

Lesson 7
Page 99

guidelines for reaching consensus and encourages them to consider thoughtfully the points of view of all group members, not just the noisy few or the majority.

Lesson Presentation

Remember when we learned about brainstorming and how we can come up with some really creative solutions to problems? We solved the problem of which solution to pick by voting on what we thought was the best choice. In voting, some people get what they want or "win," and others don't get what they want or "lose."

Today we are going to try another approach to solving problems or reaching decisions when working in a group. It is called reaching "consensus." *(Write this word on the board.)* **When a group reaches consensus, we mean that everybody in the group either agrees with the idea, or at least can live with it. It means that everybody's opinion in the group was listened to and thought about and that the group tried to come up with decisions or solutions that made everybody at least a little happy. Consensus means everybody feels that they had a part in deciding what would be done.**

Sometimes this is really easy to do because everybody picks one idea that seems to be the best one. But sometimes there are two or three ideas that seem to be good ones, and it's hard to pick one that everyone can agree on.

Sometimes a group reaches consensus by working it so that each side gives in a little. Let's say that a teacher told the class they could decide when to have their science test. Part of the class wanted to have their test right away because they had studied for it and didn't want to forget anything that they knew. The rest of the class hadn't studied yet and wanted to have the test in a week, so that they would have plenty of time to get ready for it. Let's say that the class decided to have the test in three days. This way, everybody gave up a little of what they wanted rather than one side getting all they wanted. They reached consensus!

When a group is trying to reach consensus, it can happen that a lot of people in the group might even change their minds for the sake of a few people. Let's say that a class is trying to decide what day to have a class picnic and almost everybody wanted to have the picnic on the following Sunday. Suppose that two students didn't agree because they couldn't come and they gave good reasons why they couldn't attend. The whole class may decide that it is important for them to give up the day they want rather than exclude two members of the class. Can anyone think of a time when this has happened in a group you've been in? *Allow for student response.*

Sometimes the way people reach consensus is to find a new solution. A group may have a hard time reaching consensus or agreement because part of the group wants one thing and the rest of the group wants another thing. One way out of this dilemma is to find a new solution that will satisfy everyone. For instance, let's say a class is trying to decide on a reward for the kids who bring in the most papers in a paper drive. Some kids want candy bars, several other kids in the class want sugarless gum because they say their parents won't let them eat candy. Finally, someone in the group suggests popcorn because there is no sugar in it and most kids like it. Finding a new alternative like this is a way to satisfy everybody. Neither group feels it has won or lost. Can anyone think of a time a group they were in solved a problem this way? *Allow for student response.*

In consensus, people don't "give in" just to avoid an argument or because they are outnumbered. If they really believe they're right, they stick with their solution. But then they continue to listen to see if anyone else comes up with a solution better than theirs. In consensus, the important thing to learn is when to give in and when to continue to fight for your ideas. You should feel free to change your mind if you learn something new that you hadn't thought about. You shouldn't look on this as "giving in," but as simply admitting that someone else had a good point or that their argument made more sense.

It is really hard for a group to reach consensus if they don't know how to use the cooperation skills you've been learning. A group whose members haven't learned how to be observers, participants, and helpers, and who haven't learned to encourage each other to speak, to respond to each other, or to brainstorm, would probably never reach consensus on anything. Because you know these skills now, you're ready to work on the hardest cooperation skill of all, consensus. You're ready to work as a group to solve problems or make decisions that everyone in the group supports.

You may wish to put the following list on the chalkboard or on a chart for students to refer to.

Here are some things to remember when you are trying to reach consensus or agreement:

1. **All group members have equal time to give their opinions.**
2. **Don't put down or ridicule anybody else's ideas.**
3. **Don't get involved in arguing for your ideas just so you can win.**
4. **Listen carefully to the reasons others give for their opinions.**
5. **Don't be afraid to change your mind when you hear new information.**
6. **Don't change your mind if you think you are right just to avoid a hassle. Instead, be willing to explain carefully your reasons for your opinion.**
7. **Don't take the easy way out by suggesting that people take a vote or flip a coin.**
8. **Keep thinking of alternative solutions.**
9. **Arrive at a decision that everyone in the group can support.**

In consensus it's really important for group members to help during the cooperative activity. There needs to be someone who will write down everybody's ideas. Then, when all have finished giving their ideas, a group helper needs to summarize all the different opinions.

- A helper needs to see if anyone in the group can come up with a solution that would be accepted by everybody.
- Helpers need to ask group members who talk too long to sum up what they have to say.
- Helpers need to ask students who haven't spoken to give their opinions.
- Helpers encourage other members who won't listen or who stubbornly stick to only their own ideas to think about what others have to say.
- Helpers may say things like, "Would you tell us your reasons?"

In consensus there is a need for helpers in the group who say things like the following: *List these comments on the chalkboard or overhead.*

- John, what's your opinion?
- Becky, what are your reasons for refusing to change your mind?
- Does everybody agree with Becky?
- How many would feel O.K. if we did it this way?
- Alice has a good point, though. What are we going to do about what she said?
- Would Bob's solution work?
- What if we took part of Sally's idea and part of Bill's idea and did this?
- What if the kids that want to do it this way give in a little on one idea and the kids that want to do it that way give in a little, too?

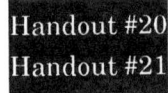

After you divide students into small groups you may wish to let each group decide who will take the helper roles, or you may wish to pick two or three students to be helpers in each group. You should also select one student from each group to fill the observer role. Explain to the group that this student will be observing to see how well each group member is using the cooperation skills taught in previous lessons and will report back to you regarding this. Give the observer either student Handout #20, "Questions for Observers," or Handout #21, "Group Behavior Tally Sheet."

Have groups work in a corner of the room, away from each other as much as possible, so that if one group finishes early they can be given another task and they won't disturb other groups (see supplementary activities following this lesson). After students have been divided into groups of four or five and some have been designated to take the role of helper, give each group a bag of small, individually wrapped, sugarless candies. There should be one and a half times as many pieces of candy as there are students.

Outline the problem to the class by saying or paraphrasing the following:

Each group has a bag containing ____ pieces of candy and there are ____ students in each group. You can have the candy as soon as you can reach consensus or all agree on how the candy should be divided. You can't cut the candy. You have ____ minutes *(give a time limit that would be reasonable for your students)* **to find a method of distributing the candy that everyone agrees with. If you haven't reached agreement when the time is up, return the candy to my desk.**

A good way for you to start might be to brainstorm all the possible ways the candy might be divided and then select the ideas in the list that everyone likes best. Next, try to narrow these ideas down to one solution that all feel is a good one. Remember to use all the cooperation skills you have learned so far.

Be particularly careful to use these skills:

- listening carefully to others' ideas,
- encouraging all to share their thoughts,
- responding to what others have said before you speak, and
- summarizing others' ideas.

Don't forget to have fun as you work toward a solution you feel is a good one.

Circulate among the groups, prompting students now and then to use the cooperation skills you have taught them previously. After an appropriate amount of time for your students, assemble the class as a whole. Collect the observers' forms, scan them, and then discuss how each group went about their task. After groups describe their procedure for dividing the candy, discuss these questions: (Refer to information on the observer forms when appropriate.)

- **Did everyone who wanted to talk get a chance?**
- **Did you feel others were listening to you?**
- **Did you really think about others' ideas?**
- **Did the group move smoothly from brainstorming alternatives to discussing and agreeing on a few, narrowing down possible solutions?**
- **Who did most of the talking in your group? Did that help or hinder the group?**
- **Who suggested that enough ideas were given?**
- **Would the group have reached a decision without this person's help?**
- **Which of these words best describe the way your group made you feel: lonely or part of the group, bossed around or not bossed around, frustrated or pleased, satisfied with the group decision or not satisfied with the group decision?**

If students express dissatisfaction with the way things went in their group or report unresolved controversies, explain that this is common when people are trying to reach consensus. Remind them also that reaching consensus can be very difficult and there are bound to be times when opinions clash, especially if the problem the group is trying to solve is a hard one. Explain that you will be teaching them some things they can do to reduce this kind of controversy in the next lesson.

Sup. Act. *On the following pages are supplementary problem situations that would be useful in helping students practice the skill of reaching consensus. Following that are five high-interest supplementary activities that challenge students to reach consensus. Use one or more of these activities before proceeding to the next lesson. Always appoint an observer for each group and have them use one of the observation forms in the introduction.*

Lesson 7

Handout #20

Questions for Observers

1. Who is talking the most? _____
   _____

2. Who is talking the least? _____
   _____

3. What attempts do members make to encourage others to contribute? _____
   _____
   _____

4. What attempts do members make to link their contributions to previous contributions? _____
   _____

5. Do group members listen to one another? If not, jot down examples of when they don't. _____
   _____

6. What could members do to improve the way they are working together? _____
   _____
   _____
   _____

Things would go better next time if....

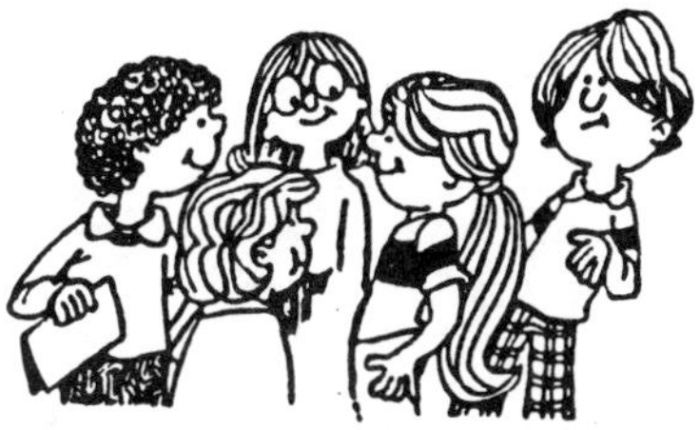

Group Behavior Tally Sheet

____
Observer

List the names of group members down the left-hand side of this form. Put a check in the appropriate box in Column A every time you observe a group member helping the group get the job done. Put a check in the appropriate box in Column B every time you observe group members not helping get the job done.

Things That Help a Group get a Job Done

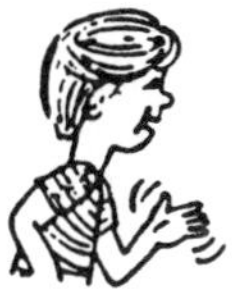

1. Listening to others
2. Giving ideas
3. Asking questions
4. Replying to ideas
5. Working well with others
6. Getting others involved
7. Keeping things under control
8. Keeping everyone on the subject
9. Summarizing what has been said
10. Encouraging and complimenting others

Things That Don't Help a Group Get a Job Done

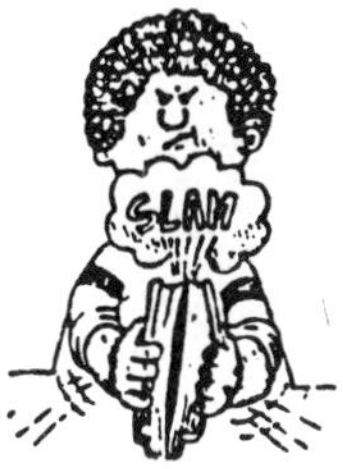
SLAM

1. Not listening
2. Interrupting
3. Acting silly
4. Fooling around
5. Putting others down
6. Letting others do all the work
7. Saying things that get the group off the topic
8. Refusing to consider other ideas
9. Acting bored

	A	B
Names of Group Members	Helped the Group Get the Job Done	Didn't Help the Group Get the Job Done
1.		
2.		
3.		
4.		
5.		
6.		
7.		
8.		

Problem Situations for Reaching Consensus

Objective   Students will cooperate in small groups to reach consensus regarding a specific problem situation.

Materials   One copy of an observation form for each group: Handout #20, #21, or one of the forms in the Introduction.

One copy of the problem situation, "The Tree House" or "What Should Gloria Do?" for each group.

Procedure   Divide the class into small groups. Appoint or instruct groups to select an observer for each group. Tell students that they are going to be asked to use their best cooperation skills to solve a problem situation; review those skills with the class:

- listen carefully to one another's ideas
- encourage all to share their thoughts
- respond to what others have said before speaking
- summarize others' ideas

Read aloud one of the problem situations, "The Tree House" or "What Should Gloria Do?" Give a copy of the situation to each group and an observation form to each observer. Tell groups that they will be given a certain amount of time to come to consensus in their groups as to the solution to the dilemma. Remind observers as to their role as silent members of the group. After the specified amount of time, reconvene as a large group and debrief the content of the groups' discussions. After appropriate closure, allow observers to share their observations, omitting personal references. Compliment the groups for their willingness to receive feedback from their observers and discuss ways group process could be improved.

Lesson 7

Supplementary Activity
Handout for "Problem Situations..."

The Tree House Dilemma*

For the last four weeks something strange has been going on in the town of Rainwood Forest. The television sets have been turned off, kids seem busy, and the familiar words, "I'm bored; There is nothing to do," haven't been heard. Across the street from where these kids live is a lot where many trees grow. However, the trees had been cut down and houses had been built. There was a big pile of leftover lumber by one of the houses. A boy, Tom, asked a worker who was standing nearby what he was going to use the lumber for.

"We're going to burn it," he answered.

"May I have it?" asked Tom.

"Sure. But what are you going to do with it?"

"Build a tree house. My friends and I have been wanting one for a long time. We could use it as a club house."

"You can have the lumber if you can have it moved by this afternoon. Tomorrow morning some men are coming to plant grass and shrubs, so we have to burn any wood that is left."

Tom raced home and asked his mother if he could store the lumber in their backyard. She agreed, so he ran from house to house and asked his friends to help. They were as excited as he was. They all wanted a club house, and for it to be a tree house on top of that was really great! After a short time, the lumber was all stacked in Tom's backyard.

The next morning everybody met at Tom's. They chose a big oak tree in which to build their house. Then they made a list of the tools they would need. The boys' and girls' parents let them use their hammers, handsaws, and a large ladder. But they needed more than that! Nails, rope, paint, roofing, a window, a door... Luckily, some of the parents had the needed items in their garages and workshops. Every family contributed something. For almost 3 weeks the boys and girls worked hard, and the parents lent a hand here and there. When the tree house was finished, everybody was very proud! The roof didn't leak, the door worked well, and after some practice everybody could pull themselves up the rope to get into the tree house.

* J.D. Casteel, *Learning to Think and Choose*, 1978, p. 105-106.

Lesson 7

Supplementary Activity
Handout for "Problem Situations..."

On Saturday morning Tom met at the tree house with all the boys. They pulled themselves into the club house, pulling the rope in after them so nobody could bother them. Then they sat down and decided on a name for their club, and Tom was elected the first club president of "The Rainwood Boys." They talked about entrance fees, dues and who could join the club. After a while, the girls who had helped build the club house arrived. They wanted to try out the tree house, too, but weren't able to get in because the rope was pulled in.

Marie yelled, "Hey somebody let the rope down!"

Tom replied, "Sorry, but this is just a boys' club. You can't come up!"

One girl after the other protested. "That's not fair! You used my ladder!"

"Give me back my nails!"

"I want my door back!"

"We helped build it. We've got just as much right to use it as you have!"

The girls complained to their parents. The parents said the kids had to work out a plan that would be fair to everybody. What do you think would be the best solution?

Lesson 7

Supplementary Activity
Handout for "Problem Situations..."

What Should Gloria Do?*

Gloria's cheeks burned, but the rest of the class was laughing. Even Charlene, sprawled on the floor with the tray of paint jars, was laughing. Gloria had been reading her science book and hadn't even noticed Charlene going by till she felt something hit her foot and heard the crash of the paint jars.

"You and your big feet!" Charlene yelled as she hit the floor and everybody laughed.

But this was the last straw for the teacher. Everything had gone wrong all day long. She decided that Gloria had tripped Charlene on purpose, and so she announced that Gloria was to stay in at recess for 1 week.

Gloria wanted to explain, but she just sat there and couldn't get the words out. It wasn't so much the punishment. It was the humiliation of being ridiculed by the teacher in front of the class.

All afternoon Gloria burned inside. She could hardly speak when the teacher asked her a question in math. Never before had she felt so angry and helpless.

"It's so unfair," she thought. "I'll get even. I won't do another thing for her as long as I live."

At the end of the day, Gloria purposely banged her chair against her desk so the teacher would know she was mad at her. At dinner that night she hardly ate a thing. She finally told her family what had happened.

"Refuse to stay in at recess," her little sister said.

"Report your teacher to the principal," said her brother.

"Well, do something," her mom said. "Don't just stew about it." It was hard for Gloria to get rid of a grudge. Maybe she was taking it all too seriously. The rest of the class had thought it was funny. But it was no joke to her. She was really angry and had to get it off her chest. What should she do?

* *Unfinished Stories*, NEA Publication.

Lesson 7   Supplementary Activity

 # Guess Who's Coming to Dinner?

Objective   Students will reach consensus on a given problem situation.

Materials   None

Procedure   Have each student write down, privately, five people (real, fiction, living, or dead) they would like to invite to dinner. Form students into small groups. Each student shares his list, giving reasons for each choice. The group members then combine their lists and reach consensus on 10 guests whom they, as a group, would like to invite.

Have each group read its choice to the class. After students have agreed on whom to invite, have them discuss and agree upon any or all of the following:

- What kind of menu would you plan?
- What would the seating arrangement be?
- What would you have each guest bring for a potluck?
- If the guests were to bring gifts, what would you have each one bring?

Just for fun, have students discuss the following:

- Do any of the guests have anything in common with each other?
- Which of the guests might become friends after meeting each other at your dinner? Why?

Lesson 7 — Supplementary Activity

Baker's Dozen

Objective Students will reach consensus on a given problem.

Materials None

Procedure Ask students to list 13 items which they frequently use at home and that are powered by electricity (anything with plugs). When they are done, ask them to get into small groups of four or five. As a group, they are to reach consensus as to what three items they could live without the easiest if electricity were suddenly cut off. In addition, have them reach consensus on three items that would be the last ones they would want to give up.

After groups have finished, have volunteers read from their group's list and tell why they chose those items.

This exercise can also be done with other situations. Students can list three things they liked best and least about an event. They could also list three things they would never want to have to learn again and three they would be glad to study again.

Lesson 7 Supplementary Activity

Which Substitute Do You Want?

Objective Students will reach consensus on selection of a substitute teacher from six fictional candidates.

Materials Handout for each student describing the six fictional candidates

Procedure Divide class into groups of four to six. Introduce the task by reading the following to students:

This is not a real situation. Pretend that I will be attending a meeting away from school for three days next week. You will be able to help choose the substitute. There are six people on the substitute list. You will get a brief description of the six pretend people. In your groups, discuss each person and decide on your recommendation.

Give each student a copy of the descriptions of the six candidates. You may wish to read the descriptions to the class. Ask the groups to discuss the six candidates and decide whom they want; then have them share their decision and the reason for their choice.

Lesson 7

Supplementary Activity
Handout for "Which Substitute Do You Want?"

*
Name   Mr. Jim Lewis
Age   24 years old
Status   Married, one child
Experience   Has substituted in all grades.

Finished college one year ago, but has not been able to find a full-time job. A P.E. major in college. Gives the teacher's instructions for the whole day first thing in the morning; students are on their own the rest of the day.

Name   Mrs. Elizabeth Anderson
Age   62 years old
Status   Married, no children
Experience   30 years' experience as a kindergarten and first grade teacher.

Follows teacher's lesson plans, but tries to add extra art and music activities. Lets students talk as much as they want. Sends students who won't work to the principal's office.

Name   Mrs. Susan Davis
Age   36 years old
Status   Widowed, two children
Experience   Taught 4th and 5th grades for 6 years in another state.

Follows teacher's lesson plans and instructions exactly. Has a firm set of rules. Keeps the room quiet so students can work. Gives extra recess time to students who finish assignments.

Name   Mr. Bill Brown
Age   58 years old
Status   Married, four children
Experience   18 years' teaching experience in intermediate grades (4,5,6)

Mr. Brown believes in an orderly classroom and is strict at times. He desperately needs a job because his wife requires a lot of expensive medical care. He is always willing to help students if they have a problem.

Name   Mr. Tom Smith
Age   35 years old
Status   Married, no children
Experience   6 years' experience in public schools. Taught at various levels, from kindergarten through 6th grade.

This teacher is considered not very hard and easy to get along with, but students have said they didn't feel they learned as much as they did from other teachers. His classes do a lot of fun activities, such as special art projects, having parties, and going on field trips.

Name   Mrs. Nancy King
Age   38 years old
Status   Married, two children
Experience   5 years' experience as probation officer.

This teacher is considered very strict and demands a lot from her students. However, former students have said that they learned a lot in her class.

---

*   *Project S.E.L.F.*

Lesson 7 — Supplementary Activity

Learning From the Experts*

Objective Students will learn to identify their values and gain experience in consensus decision-making through making choices as a group from a list of alternatives.

Materials Handout of "Experts"

Procedure Have students look at the list of "Experts" while you read it aloud. Tell students to decide on two "Experts" they would like to invite to their classes to tell about their expertise; then divide the class into groups of four or five. Each group must select, by consensus, two "Experts." The choices may differ from those made individually. Remind the class of the consensus technique: no voting, no bullying, each group member has a chance to speak, one person is chosen to report the group decision.

Give groups 15-20 minutes to make their decisions.

After writing their choices on the blackboard, discuss the group choices and the process with the class. You may want to use the following questions in your discussion with students:

- Do the choices have a common characteristic?
- How did the group's choices differ from your own?
- Did everyone have a chance to speak?
- Were your views listened to?
- Was it easy to achieve consensus or difficult?
- Did one person in the group dominate the discussion?
- How did it feel to argue your individual choices publicly?
- How did it feel when you had to compromise a value you hold?
- Would you stand by the final two choices?

* K. Martin, M. Black, and C. Wolter, *It's Up to Me*, 1980.

Lesson 7

Supplementary Activity
Handout for "Learning From the Experts"

Learning From the Experts

1. J. Paul Gettrick:   Will teach you how to handle money successfully, and how to become a multimillionaire in weeks.

2. Dr. I. Q. Brainey: Guarantees to make you a genius. You will be able to instantly master any mental task you attempt.

2. Ma Thusela:  Is a sorceress whose herbs and potions will increase your life expectancy to as much as 500 years of vital, productive life.

4. Atlas Armstrong: Teaches a course on diet and exercise guaranteed to make you ten times stronger, with no loss of agility or distortion of body image.

5. Lotta Chuckles:  Helps you develop your sense of humor. You will be able to laugh at your own mistakes and see the funny side of many things that used to get you down.

6. Dr. Will B. Charming: Instructs you in the art of winning and keeping friends. People will find you charming and lovable; you will never again be lonely.

7. I. M. Jock:  Trains you to achieve superstar status in the professional sport of your choice: baseball, football, soccer, tennis, golf, etc.

8. Ms. Mary Selfworth: Will help you increase your self-esteem, and self confidence. Will enable you to become your own best friend.

Lesson 7 Supplementary Activity

What We Value

Objective Students will reach consensus on selection of three aspirations from a list.

Materials Handout for each student with a list of aspirations.

Procedure Divide the class into groups of four or five. Hand out to each student a copy of the list of aspirations. Ask groups to discuss the list and decide which three they would consider most important. After they have reached consensus on this, ask them to write down their rationale for their choices. They have 10 minutes to complete the activity.

Lesson 7

Supplementary Activity
Handout for "What We Value"

What We Value

Select three of the following and give your rationale for your choices.

1. To rid the world of prejudice.
2. To serve the sick and needy.
3. To become a famous person (movie star, baseball hero, and so on).
4. To be the richest person in the world.
5. To be the President of the United States.
6. To be the most attractive person in the world.
7. To have a house overlooking the most beautiful view in the world, in which you may keep for 1 year 40 of your favorite works of art.
8. To live to be 100 years old, with no illness.
9. To master the profession of your choice.
10. To have a vaccine to make all persons incapable of lying or stealing.
11. To control the destinies of 500,000 people.
12. To have the love and admiration of the whole world.
13. To have your own all-knowing computer, for any and all facts you might need.
14. To be the best musician in the world on an instrument of your choice.
15. To have the power to make everybody happy.

_____
_____
_____
_____
_____
_____
_____
_____
_____

Dealing With Conflict in Cooperation Groups

Objective Students will learn the skill for giving negative feedback. Students will learn to adapt to the give and take of working with others.

Materials Transparency #10/Handout #22 - "How I Feel and Act When Someone is Doing Something That Bothers Me"

Transparency #11 - "Steps for Giving Negative Feedback"

Handout #23 - "Dear Abby Letters"

To the Teacher

"Not everything that is faced can be changed but nothing can be changed until it is faced."

- James Baldwin

When students are working together and sharing ideas, information, resources, and materials, they are bound to encounter problems. These can be problems like the unwillingness of some members to contribute, the tendency of some members to stray off the topic, the attempt of some to dominate the group, or conflict between two group members. When group members ignore a problem, it seldom disappears, but rather continues to plague the group. By taking the time to confront these problems directly, the group is relieved of a problem that can be distracting to members and can sap emotional energy. They can then keep their attention on their work.

Confronting interpersonal problems openly is essential if a group is to develop maximum effectiveness. Openness has an additional benefit. Students develop skills that will be useful in countless interpersonal situations in the future. Instead of feeling helpless when things are not going well when working with others in a group, students will have the skills to examine the problems and work out satisfactory solutions. They will not be dependent on a teacher or group leader to take responsibility for making things right.

Many students never say anything about issues that are bothering them because they want to avoid conflict and being seen as complainers. This can lead to holding in anger until the feelings surface in a fight or indirect expression of anger such as sulkiness or uncooperativeness. Alternatively, there are students who frequently talk about what's bothering them but do so in a nonproductive manner, becoming hostile or putting down the other person. This style of giving negative feedback turns others "off." The result may be that such students are not listened to and don't have their needs considered.

This lesson will emphasize learning how to give negative feedback in a non-hostile and appropriate manner. Students will practice this in role play situations. They will also have an opportunity to compare their reactions and experiences to others' in the group and explore common problems which may have arisen when attempting to work cooperatively.

When students are urged to talk openly about things others do that bother them, they need to understand the difference between constructive feedback and confronting one another in a hurtful way or with brutal honesty.

While it may not be possible to preclude completely the possibility of students hurting the feelings of others when talking openly about problems in the group, chances of students confronting one another in a harmful way can be minimized by teaching the skills in this lesson.

Many students become uncomfortable when asked to talk about the way they are working together, because they equate it with "telling on" one another. Help students understand that the purpose of describing the behavior of others is not to identify and punish offenders. The purpose of bringing up problem behavior is to help the group improve its work and ultimately make everyone feel more comfortable.

In this lesson students are taught the difference between "I" messages and "You" messages. An "I" message is a statement of how something someone is doing makes you feel, e.g., "I feel annoyed when I see you throw paper on the floor." A "You" message is the way most of us habitually communicate with people, especially with those over whom we have authority. "You" messages tell a person what's wrong with them. "You're messy;" "You are inconsiderate of other people;" "You shouldn't be so bossy;" "Why can't you be more careful?" An "I" message gives accurate information about the effect a person has on you, whereas a "You" message is an attempt to label or blame the person.

During conflict, to a certain extent, it is helpful simply to avoid statements that begin with "you" ("You never get done on time.") and attempt to begin statements with "I feel . . . ("I feel worried when I realize how little work is done.")."

Students will find the "I-message" approach valuable in dealing with all conflicts. Explain the difference between describing the other person ("you" message) and reporting one's own feelings ("I" message), and

Dealing With Conflict in Cooperation Groups

encourage them to practice replacing "You" messages with "I" messages whenever conflicts erupt in the classroom.

You may also want to use some of the components of two lessons in the ASSIST manual *Helping Kids Handle Anger:* Lesson 11, "How to Tell a Friend You're Mad" and Lesson 12, "What to do When a Friend is Mad at You."

Lesson Presentation

Say or paraphrase: **In this lesson you're going to learn how to tell someone that something he or she is doing bothers you when you're working with them in a group.**

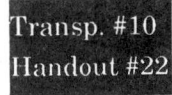

Show students Transparency #10, "How I Feel and Act When Someone is Doing Something That Bothers Me," or give them each a copy. Say or paraphrase:

These are some of the ways most people feel and act when someone is doing something that bugs them. As I read through them, think which ones are most true about you.

Read through and discuss items on the list.

Even though you may not feel like doing it when someone you're trying to work with is bothering you, it's usually best to say something to the person about it. This lets others know directly how you feel and saves you from being sarcastic or uncooperative. If you do it right, you can often tell others how you feel without hurting them or making them angry. You can also get other people to listen to your side of a problem. This way you'll be more likely to get the other person to stop doing what's annoying you.

For example, there might be someone in your group who always interrupts you when you're talking so that you never get a chance to get your ideas out. You don't want to be enemies with the person, but you're tired of being interrupted.

Ask students to recall situations where they wanted to tell someone they were bothered by something the person was doing. Explain that it doesn't have to have occurred in the classroom.

You might want to record situations on the chalkboard or overhead with student initials by them to use later for role playing. Go around the group until several students have contributed.

There are two things you should keep in mind about giving negative comments: First, what the other person is doing should directly affect you. Suppose you heard that another kid in your group is always borrowing people's things. He's never borrowed anything from you. If you go up to him and say, "Hey, stop making off with other people's stuff all the time!" you're butting into something that's really not your business.

Second, if they are doing something that annoys you, it should be something they can change. For example, saying something about somebody's looks such as "I don't like the way your eyes bug out when you laugh" isn't fair. It can't be changed and it can hurt the person's feelings. Or, if a student is taking what seems to you to be a long time to do something, but is working as fast as he/she can, it really isn't fair to ask him/her to go faster.

Transp. #12 *Go through the following steps for giving negative feedback. Write the steps on a chart or on the chalkboard, or use the Transparency #12, "Steps for Giving Negative Feedback."*

Now let's talk about some specific things to do when it is appropriate to tell someone that he or she is bothering you. There are four steps:

First **of all, stay cool. Relax and don't lose your temper. Think about what you are going to say ahead of time. That way you'll be less likely to get mad when you are talking. Taking a deep breath first can help, too.**

Second, **look right at the person. Don't look down or fidget.**

Model for students the varying effectiveness a statement has with or without eye contact.

Third, **tell the person just what it is that's bothering you. Don't attack, call him or her a name, or get nasty. A good rule of thumb is to start with the word "I" instead of a "You." When you start with "You," it's easy to end up blaming or calling someone a name. When you start with "I," you're reporting how you feel. For instance, it's better to say "I don't like it when you don't do your share," rather than "You're lazy."**

Brainstorm with students other examples of "I" statements as well as some examples of inappropriate "You" statements and list them on the board. Below are some ideas:

- *"I don't like it when you take the best materials for yourself and don't share them with anybody else;"*
- *"It makes me mad when you tell everybody else what to do and don't give anybody a chance to say what they think;" or*
- *"I don't like it when you borrow my things and don't bring them back."*

Fourth, **say what you want the person to do instead. This means you tell the other person what you'd like them to do instead of annoying you. For example, after you said, "I don't like it when you borrow my things and don't bring them back," say "I'd appreciate it if you would return my stuff when you're through with it."**

Review these four steps and post them in the class in abbreviated form as suggested below:

Steps for Giving Negative Feedback

Step 1. Relax. Don't lose your temper.

Step 2. Look at the person.

Step 3. Say what's bothering you. Start with the word "I . . . ," and say how you feel about it.

Step 4. Say what you want the person to do instead.

Let's see how it looks when we tell someone we're mad using these steps.

[Model]

Select a student. Have him/her role play a behavior and pretend that it's bothering you. Then model for the class, giving that student negative feedback, making sure to include each of the four guidelines. Ask students to look for the steps as you model them. You may wish to model the steps several times. Set up a role play with students where they give you negative comments using the four steps. Coach them through the steps when necessary and ask the rest of the class to be looking for each step.

Say or paraphrase:

Let' say that I'm a student working in the group and I just want to play around. I keep making dumb remarks to try to get you to laugh and I'm not doing anything to help. You want to get the job done so you won't have homework. I'm going to call on some of you now and all I want you to do is to say what it is you're annoyed about without attacking me personally. Try to use the four steps as you do this.

[Handout #23 Role Play]

Next, ask two student volunteers to role play in front of the class, giving negative feedback and using the four steps. You may wish to give students Handout #23, "Dear Abby Letters," and have them role play, giving negative feedback using one of those scenarios. Call on several students to role play. Praise them for the steps they included, pointing out any steps they may leave out as they do this. Finally, set up role play student-to-student, until all students have had a chance to practice the steps for giving negative feedback to others.

Say or paraphrase:

We haven't dealt yet with the feelings of the person receiving the negative feedback or how to handle their response. Usually, when a person is asked in a polite and reasonable way to stop doing something, they will cooperate. There will be times, however, when they will respond negatively. In the next lesson we'll look at negotiation and compromise as ways to give them a chance to share their feelings and how to handle it if they get mad, try to pick a fight, or refuse to do what you want them to.

For now, let's just focus on giving negative feedback. A time when it's especially valuable to do this is when we're discussing a cooperation activity that we've done in the classroom. This is a time when we should all feel free to be honest, should express and expect both positive and negative feedback, and should be willing to listen graciously to how others are feeling about what we do.

Encourage thinking and discussion of the main concepts of the lesson by using the "Sentence Starters for Promoting Thinking" in the Appendix. For example,

- *"The main ideas seem to be . . . ,"*
- *"This is similar to what I know about . . . ,"*
- *"Another point of view is . . . ,"*
- *"If this is true, then . . . ," and*
- *"What I wonder is . . ."*

Lesson 8   Transparency #10/Handout #22

How I Feel and Act When Someone Is Doing Something That Bothers Me

How I feel: *I usually . . .*

a. _____ am afraid to say anything directly, because I don't want to hurt their feelings.

b. _____ am afraid that if I do say something, they won't like me.

c. _____ am afraid to say anything for fear they'll get mad and retaliate.

d. _____ feel confused about how to bring up the subject.

e. _____ feel a nice person would just forget it and not say anything.

What I do: *I usually . . .*

a. _____ make matters worse by getting angry and "blowing up."

b. _____ talk about the person behind his/her back.

c. _____ avoid the person or act rude to the person but not bother to tell them why.

d. _____ act friendly, as if nothing is bothering me.

e. _____ drop hints about how I feel, hoping they will get the message.

Steps for Giving Negative Feedback

Step 1: Relax. Don't lose your temper.

Step 2: Look at the person.

Step 3: Say what's bothering you. Start with the word "I . . . ," and say how you feel about it.

Step 4: Say what you want the person to do instead.

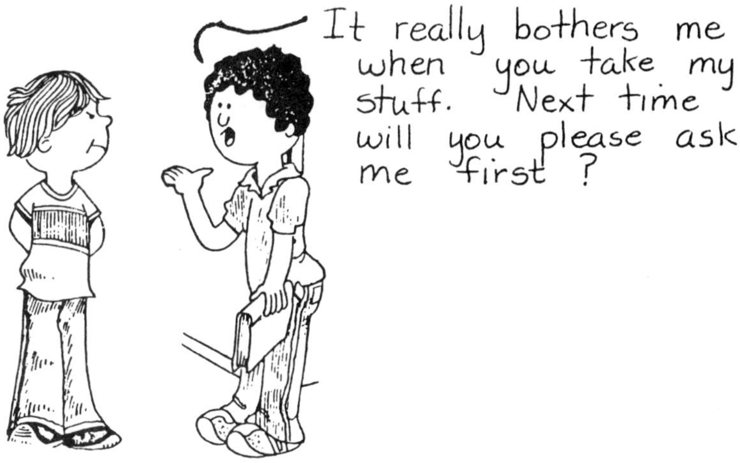
It really bothers me when you take my stuff. Next time will you please ask me first?

Lesson 8   Handout #23

Dear Abby Letters

Dear Abby,
One kid in my group is always doing her homework for another subject when we're supposed to be working on a group project. It really bugs me.

>Signed,
>"Disgusted"

Dear Abby,
Because I always contribute, the rest of my group often says or does hardly anything. I'm tired of always having to get the group started on the work and keep it going. How can I get other people in the group to do their share?

>Signed,
>"Tired"

Dear Abby,
There is a person in my group who always interrupts or takes over. We hardly ever get a chance to hear everybody's ideas. How can I get this person to give others a chance to talk without hurting this person's feelings?

>Signed,
>"Tired of Being Quiet"

Dear Abby,
There is a person in my group who is always making smart aleck comments or wisecracks, or putting kids down. People don't feel like being in our group anymore. They are afraid to talk because they think this kid will put them down. What can I do to get our group back together?

>Signed,
>"Worried"

Dear Abby,
There is a person in our group who always criticizes everybody's ideas. When we're trying to agree on something, he says he doesn't like the way we're doing it and that our ideas won't work. He never has any better ideas.

>Signed,
>"Tired of Being Criticized"

Learning to Negotiate and Compromise

Learning to Negotiate and Compromise

Objective Students will learn the skills of negotiation and compromise so that they may more effectively resolve conflict situations that arise in cooperative learning.

Materials Transparency #12/Handout #24 - "Steps for Negotiation"

To the Teacher When students work on tasks together, there are bound to be problems or personality conflicts. Every decision contains potential controversy, as a decision is a choice among alternative courses of action. When communication is effective, students will find themselves in disagreement and will engage in a discussion or debate to determine which assumptions, ideas, information, or course of action to adopt and follow. In order to function effectively with a cooperative group, students will have to have skills in managing controversies.

In this lesson an attempt is made to help students get past seeing conflicts as "win-lose" situations where one person has to dominate. Instead, students are introduced to the concept of negotiation and compromise. These tools provide a "no-lose" approach, where a solution is sought to meet the needs of both parties so that neither party will have to "give in."

In this lesson students are taught six steps of negotiating, and they practice these steps using role play situations. Students are encouraged to use these steps to solve conflict situations themselves.

There may be times when students need your assistance in resolving a conflict. When this occurs you may wish to use the following conflict resolution steps to help students arrive at a mutually satisfactory solution:

<u>Step One:</u> Assure both students that you are not willing to take sides, but will help them work towards a solution that they both can live with. Also, make clear that, in order for this to happen, both of them have to be flexible and willing to compromise.

<u>Step Two:</u> Have both parties (one at a time) describe the conflict. If they interrupt or are not listening carefully, have each summarize the other's position before responding.

<u>Step Three:</u> Have both students explain how the conflict makes them feel. (This helps make students more vulnerable and amenable to compromise.)

Step Four: Have both students tell what, from their points of view, would be the ideal outcome of the conflict. Encourage them to suggest an outcome that they can accept.

Step Five: Feel free to suggest any possible alternative students may have overlooked.

Step Six: Ask students what changes they would each be willing to make in order to have the solution they both agree they want. Remind them they may each have to give in a little bit in order to get an outcome that is mutually acceptable.

Step Seven: Write down what both parties agree to do and include provision for checking back with you so all can evaluate how the solution is working.

Lesson Presentation

Say or paraphrase:

In our last lesson we discussed the importance of being honest and to the point with someone who is doing something that bothers us or that we don't think is fair. We practiced telling someone in a nice way what it is he or she doing that bugs us and asking them to do something else instead. Usually, when people are asked in a polite and reasonable way to stop doing something or to consider our point of view, they will do so.

However, there will always be times when you tell someone how you feel or make a request and they will disagree with you or ignore you, get mad, put you down, or try to pick a fight about it. You can always say something like, "Look, I really don't want to fight with you about this." But there is more that you can do. You can learn how to negotiate and compromise. That's what we will focus on today. Learning these skills will help you deal more effectively with situations when you tell someone how you feel and what you want, yet that's not enough to solve the problem.

Write the word "negotiate" on the board or overhead. Ask students what they think negotiation means. Try to bring out that negotiation involves people having a difference of opinion.

Learning to Negotiate and Compromise

Say or paraphrase: **Negotiation is a way of reaching an agreement with someone even though you start out seeing things differently. So negotiation involves**

- **a difference of opinion,**
- **talking,**
- **using your head, and**
- **compromising.**

Write the word "compromise" on the board or overhead. Ask students for their definition of the word "compromise." Try to bring out that a compromise calls for a "deal" or a "meeting in the middle" where each gives up something to reach an agreement so that neither person loses.

Think for a minute about the choices you have when someone says "no" to what you want. You can get angry, upset, nag, try to con him or her, or lie. You can go ahead and do it anyway. Can you think of any more?

Negotiation is a much better way to deal with "no's" in life. It can give you what you want or a part of it and let you get it without a big hassle. Negotiation gives you power and makes you stronger.

You get this power by learning to understand what other people want, and how to give them what they want, too. In negotiation your job is not only to say how you feel and ask for what you want, but to find out why the person won't give it to you and what it may take for them to give you what you want.

If you learn how to negotiate skillfully, you will be more likely to get your own way, avoid fighting with people in difficult situations, and make the other person feel that he or she has won something, too. Negotiation can be broken down into some simple steps. Let's go through them.

Transp. #12/ Handout #24

At this point, put on Transparency #12, "Steps of Negotiation," write the steps on a chart, or give students a copy of them. Go through these steps with students, discussing each step:

1. **State your problem or ask for what you want in a clear, simple way:**

   "I don't like it when ..."
   "Things would be better if ..."

2. **Listen carefully to the person's response:**

   "I do this because ..."
   "You're wrong about ..."
   "I don't want to ..."

3. **If you are ignored or told "no," ask "why."**

4. **Think about why the other person might feel this way.**

5. **Suggest a compromise.**

When you follow these steps, there is something else you have to keep in mind — the way you talk to a person. You have to remember to keep your cool, look at the person, and talk in a calm voice. If you lose your temper, you'll also lose your chance to negotiate because the other person will get angry too and will probably ignore what you want.

Model

Suggest some typical problems that might come up when students work together in cooperation groups. Model the negotiation steps by taking the role of the person who is trying to negotiate and ask another student to participate with you in the role play. For instance, you might suggest the following situation: you both are working cooperatively in a group to write a group report. There are two jobs left in the group to do. One is to be the person who reads the final report to the class and the other job is to prepare a short quiz for the class to take after they hear the report. You want to be the one who gets to read the report to the rest of the group because you feel you could read it in a really interesting way. Another person in the group refuses to write the quiz because he says he doesn't know how to write test questions. He keeps insisting he wants to be the presenter. Model for students the steps for negotiating one by one. The compromise you make might be offering to help the other student write the test questions if he'll agree to let you be the speaker. If you use this situation, say or paraphrase the following:

What I've done is ask the other person to tell me why he felt the way he did. I thought about his feelings. Then I suggested something that would take care of the other person's problem. That's the key to negotiation — taking care of the other person's problem and still getting what you want. In this situation, by asking the other person "why," I found out that he/she didn't care much about being the presenter. He/she just didn't want to have to write the quiz. Notice also that I talked to him/her in a calm and friendly manner.

Suggest some other situations and again model for students one by one the steps of negotiation, pointing the steps out on the chart or on Transparency #12, "Steps for Negotiation."

Role Play

Next have students brainstorm conflict situations that could arise when they are working together and could be resolved through the use of negotiation. Select students to role play before the class some of the situations, coaching them through the steps. Using one of the conflict examples that students have given, have students break up in pairs and work towards negotiating a solution for a given conflict. Urge students to listen carefully to one another and to try to understand how the other person is feeling. Have them work towards a solution that will, at least in part, take care of what the other person needs or wants.

Urge students to use the skills of negotiation and compromise when conflict arises during cooperation activities. Explain to them that with these skills they will be able to resolve most conflicts themselves. On the occasions that they can't, they can each ask another student for an opinion regarding what would be a good compromise. If both these measures fail, assure students you will be available as a mediator.

If the problem is a serious one that students feel requires a consequence, some teachers have students come up with three consequences and then it's the teachers option to pick one or decide on an alternate solution.

Sup. Act. *The supplementary activity, "Negotiating for What You Need," provides a good opportunity for further practice of the skills presented in this lesson.*

Use "Sentence Starters for Promoting Thinking" in the Appendix to help students summarize and process what they have learned in this lesson and to deal with any remaining questions or confusion.

Steps for Negotiation

Step 1: Ask for what you want in a clear, simple way.

Step 2: If you are ignored, or told "no," ask "why."

Step 3: Listen carefully to the reply.

Step 4: Think about why the other person might feel this way.

Step 5: Suggest a compromise.

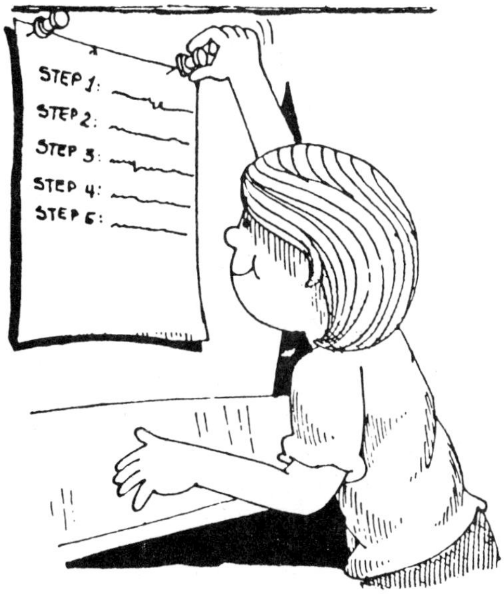
STEP 1:
STEP 2:
STEP 3:
STEP 4:
STEP 5:

Lesson 9　　　　　　　　　　　　　　　　　　　　　　　Supplementary Activity

Negotiating for What You Need

Objective　Students will practice negotiation skills.

Materials　Group 1 - Scissors, ruler, paper clips, pencils, and two 4" squares of red paper and two of white

Group 2 - Scissors, glue and two sheets of gold, white, and blue paper, each 8-1/2" x 11"

Group 3 - Felt-tipped markers and two sheets of green, white, and gold paper, each 8-1/2" x 11"

Group 4 - 5 Sheets of paper, 8-1/2" x 11" - one each of green, gold, blue, red, and purple

Tasks sheets for each group

Procedure　This activity provides students with a chance to practice using resources which have been unequally distributed and lets them negotiate to obtain the resources they need. You may divide the class into groups of two to four. This activity should take less than an hour.

Distribute an envelope of materials and a Tasks Sheet to each group. Explain that each group has a different set of materials, but they all have to complete the same tasks. Tell them that they are to negotiate for the materials so they can complete the tasks. The first group to finish is considered the winner. Give the signal to begin.

Stop the competition when all groups have completed their tasks. Discuss how resources were shared, how negotiation was done, what the competition was like, and how power was used.

Lesson 9   Supplementary Activity
Handout for "Negotiating for What You Need"

Tasks Sheet

Each group is to complete the following tasks:

1. Make a 3" x 3" inch square of white paper.
2. Make a 4" x 2" inch rectangle of gold paper.
3. Make a T-shaped piece 3" x 5" inches in green and white paper.
4. Make a four-link paper chain, each link in a different color.
5. Make a 4" x 4" inch flag, in any three colors.

The first group to complete all tasks is the winner. Groups may negotiate on using resources in order to complete the tasks.

Working Cooperatively on a Long-Term Simulation Project

Objective   Students will learn to negotiate, to reach consensus, and to work cooperatively while implementing a simulated farming adventure.

Students will gain skills in the academic areas of math, social studies, language arts, ecology, economics, and career education.

Simulation game

Materials   Cardboard or wooden boxes lined with larger plastic bags. There should be one box for every four students. Boxes should be approximately 1 yard long, 1/2 yard wide, and 4"-5" deep. Each box should be filled with a layer of gravel and then a layer of rich soil. Earthworms should be added if possible.

Miniature farm animals: These can be purchased at most toy stores. They come in packages which include cows, horses, goats, chickens, pigs, ducks, turkeys, etc.

Optional miniature equipment: Available at most toy stores. Wheelbarrows, speed spreader, trucks, tractors, boats, sea planes, windmills, etc.

Handout #25 - "Letter from U.S. Dept. of Agriculture"
Handout #26 - "Starting Your Farm"
Handout #27 - "Government Price List"
Handout #28 - "Ye Old Savings and Loan" check deposit and withdrawal slips
Handout #29 - Bartering tokens
Handout #30 - Play money

To the Teacher   This activity is a wonderful way to teach a host of academic and social skills. Because of the nature of the simulation, the students become very emotionally involved in this experience and, as a result, learning is heightened.

Students participate in a simulation activity whereby they form small cooperatives and each homestead an "uninhabited island." They actually plant, harvest, and sell crops and go through the steps of building a life in a small community. As they acquire income, they advance in small steps toward approximating a technological society. They are faced with decisions regarding everything from land use and equipment expenditures to family size. They must plan for meeting the entire hierarchy of human needs: shelter, food, safety from vandalism, medical care, recreation, leisure time, and education. They are confronted with numerous value decisions. The greatest challenge is that these decisions must not be made individually, but cooperatively with the other members of their small homesteading cooperative. Students will have continual opportunity to use the cooperation skills they have been exposed to in each of the preceding lessons. Use these opportunities to remind students to encourage one another, to listen, to summarize, to brainstorm, to work for consensus, and to negotiate. Review and model these and the other cooperative skills whenever you can.

The entire process of this activity can take several months. Students generally engage formally in farming co-op activities and lessons once a week, but they often like to "tend to their farms" during free moments in the school day. The entire activity as outlined below contains many suggested procedures. Each class and teacher, however, will develop their own procedures and spinoffs, as this activity is a great stimulus for creativity and imagination.

If you have difficulty acquiring the items listed in this section, ask students if they have some items at home that would work well for the government store to sell, and if they would lend them for the duration of the simulation activity. Many students have the little farm animals that are mentioned in this section as well as many other items that can be incorporated into the project. Students should not be permitted to bring things from home for their own farms. This wouldn't be fair to the other co-op members.

Lesson Presentation

Say or paraphrase: **We are going to assume that the country you were born in is facing many big problems. There is a shortage of land, housing, food, water, and power. Pollution is causing problems everywhere. The President has asked for volunteers to homestead some small uninhabited islands. Of those who responded, you have been chosen to plan and farm the usable land on the island. You will each be given an island with three or four other people. Your group is a cooperative and will work**

Working Cooperatively on a Long-Term...

together on the land assigned to you. Each cooperative will have a large box of soil which will represent the island you are going to farm.

At this point, decide on a method of forming groups of four or five students. You can let students decide on the formation of their own groups (the most recommended procedure), or simply number students or the boxes off and have students draw a number that corresponds.

Handout #25 *Give each cooperative a copy of the letter from B.A. Wiseacre of the U.S. Department of Agriculture (Handout #25). Once the cooperatives have been formed, students must reach consensus on a name and the names of the members of their cooperative on their box. Students must then elect a group leader for their cooperative.*

The group leader is responsible for coordinating affairs and relaying information to and from the "outside world."

Each farming cooperative receives essential supplies from a government representative (the teacher) who manages a government store. The following initial supplies are issued to each cooperative:

Enough toothpicks or wood splints to build a simple dwelling	=	*3,200 board ft. lumber*
Glue	=	*10 bags cement*
A paper cup	=	*1 watering system*
20 seeds - radish, corn, beans, onion bulbs	=	*5 per co-op member*
scissors, ruler, etc.	=	*tools*

Handout #26 *The first two essential tasks co-op members have is to build dwellings and plant their crops (Handout #26). These two tasks involve a lot of group* *planning and decision-making. Co-ops must come to agreement as to how the four or five of them are going to use the land allotted to them. How many homes will they build? Where will they plant their crops? (Students typically start by each constructing their own home and planting their own crops and then, as the simulation proceeds, they build cooperative housing and rearrange land use so as to have more space to plant crops and raise animals.) Give students graph paper and have them draw to scale their plan for land usage. State that, as the U.S. Government Representative, you must approve their land use plan before they can start any construction or planting. You may need to remind students of their negotiation techniques as they try to come up with one land use scale drawing that represents the ideas of all co-op members.*

As houses are completed and the first crop is planted, explain to students that the government store will buy any excess crops produced after co-op members have harvested and stored their own necessary food reserves. Depending on how your students' crops grow, you can reach a mutual decision regarding how much of their harvest they must retain for their own use. (Two inches per student is a good round figure.) It will probably take about 2 or 3 weeks for plants to grow to the point of being able to be harvested. Students should then cut only an inch or so off the top of each plant so that the plants will continue to grow.

Students take their harvested plants to the "receiving" section of the government store. You will probably wish to "hire" store employees so you will be free to oversee the entire project. Often students whose crops are growing rather slowly are quite eager to make some money working for the store. Together you can determine a fair wage.

Payment for the harvest brought to the store is determined by laying each plant harvested along a yardstick. Students receive payment on a "per inch" basis ($2.00 per inch works out well).

Handout #27

Students are free to purchase whatever merchandise they wish from the government store with their profits. Post a list of current prices for merchandise, or provide Handout #27, "Government Store Price List." The prices can be determined by you and your students or you can use the "suggested price list" provided at the end of this lesson. Students can also practice bartering with one another by using the bartering tokens to symbolize farm products that are surplus.

Once students start making a profit on their farms, it is time to start talking with them about long-range planning. Each co-op should discuss together which is the wisest use of their funds. Help students to ruminate on the repercussions of their purchases by saying things like the following:

- *If you buy a milk cow, you will have fresh milk.*
- *If you buy a horse, you will have some help as you labor in your fields.*
- *If you save your money until you have enough to buy a male and a female goat, you could start a goat herd.*
- *If you go in with another co-op on a bull, you might be able to build up a herd of cows.*
- *If you save a lot of money, you may be able to buy a tractor and then you wouldn't have to work in the fields all day, etc.*

Handout #28
Handout #29
Handout #30

When students get to the point of willingly wanting to save money, open up the co-op bank, "Ye Old Savings and Loan Association." Hire employees to work in the bank and teach students to use the forms provided at the end of the lesson for their banking procedures.

As the project develops over the weeks, draw from it as many learning experiences as you can. The following are a few suggestions but you and your students will probably come up with many other ideas. Point out the importance of the right environmental conditions for crops to grow. If all boxes do not receive an equal amount of sunlight, have students rotate them on a regular basis. Discuss the benefits and disadvantages of using pesticides. Discuss using fertilizer.

Have students assume that as time passes they will marry and have families. Don't let them get involved in whom they will marry or when; just explain that, as things go, we will assume some islanders will marry and have families and that membership in the co-op will increase. Discuss the "carrying capacity" of each island and the whole issue of population dynamics, and the effect of population growth on resources and environment.

Allow co-op members to be as enterprising as they wish and to open up small business and service industries.

Present co-op members with hypothetical plans that the government might have to build a freeway or some similar venture and discuss the repercussions.

Present co-op members with hypothetical plans of private developers to begin ventures on the islands such as shopping centers, amusement parks, wildlife preserves, marinas, etc., and discuss the advantages and disadvantages.

Present the whole issue of local vs. central government. Address the issue of the need for schools and medical facilities, as well as selection of personnel. One way to do this is to have a representative from each island for a council and then interview those who would like to be hired as teachers, medical personnel, architect/contractor, etc.

Simulate the inevitable natural disasters encountered in farming by listing possible disasters on slips of paper, cutting them up and putting them in a sack from which each co-op must draw on occasion. For instance: a blizzard, a tornado, rats and mice, rabbits, crows or locusts destroying crops, hoof and mouth disease striking cattle, drought, floods, etc. Students should brainstorm ways to cope with these occurrences. They may decide, for example, to open up a Red Cross to help disaster victims.

Letter from U.S. Department of Agriculture

UNITED STATES DEPARTMENT OF AGRICULTURE
B.A. Wiseacre, Secretary
Grow M. Bigg, Under-secretary
3902 Green Avenue NW
Washington, D.C. 20001

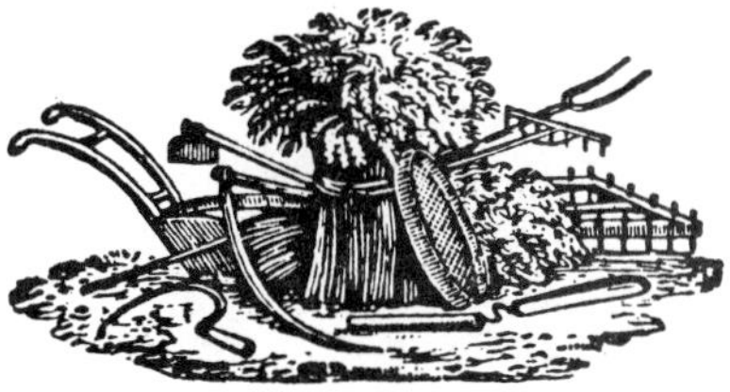

Dear Friend,

Welcome to your island. We encourage and congratulate you for the adventure you are about to undertake. The government feels that this project will do much to solve the problems our nation is facing.

The following services and regulations are provided to help you as you begin to build your co-operatives. Please contact us if you need further information or advice.

Each co-operative has been assigned a tract of land and will be given seeds and tools in the listed quantities:

- 3,200 board ft. lumber
- 24 4 x 8 st. sheet metal
- 10 bags cement
- 10 gal. paint
- 20 seeds per homesteader
- 1 watering system per co-operative
- use of project tool pool.

Supplies for the first year have been shipped in and you may secure them as needed from the government warehouse. Survival the second year will depend upon the success of your crops.

Each homesteader must raise enough plants per year for his/her own consumption.

Each colonist must erect one building on his land for his/her personal use or may join with others in the co-operative and erect a communal building.

Additional construction of ditches, ponds, buildings, bridges, roadways, etc., is subject to approval of all members of the co-operative.

Each co-operative may legislate its own laws and regulations and may name and divide property by consent of all members.

We wish you well in your efforts to create a peaceful, productive, pollution-free, population-balanced place to live.

Sincerely,

B.A. Wiseacre

B.A. Wiseacre, Secretary

Lesson 10   Handout #26

Starting Your Farm

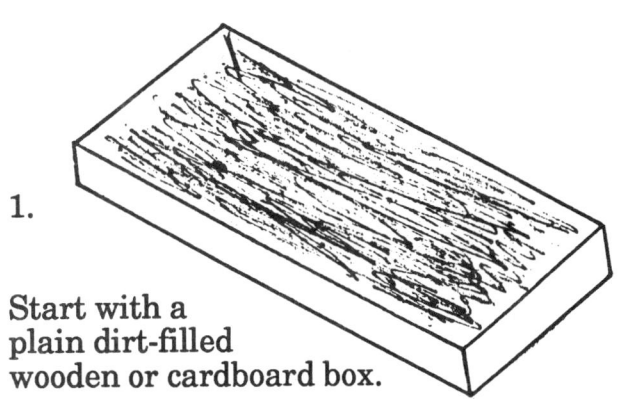

1. Start with a plain dirt-filled wooden or cardboard box.

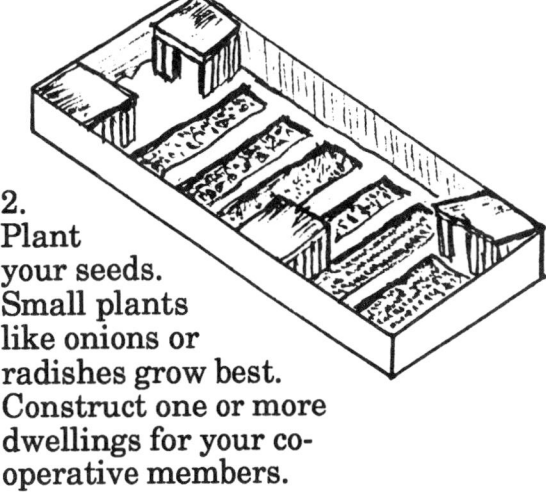

2. Plant your seeds. Small plants like onions or radishes grow best. Construct one or more dwellings for your co-operative members.

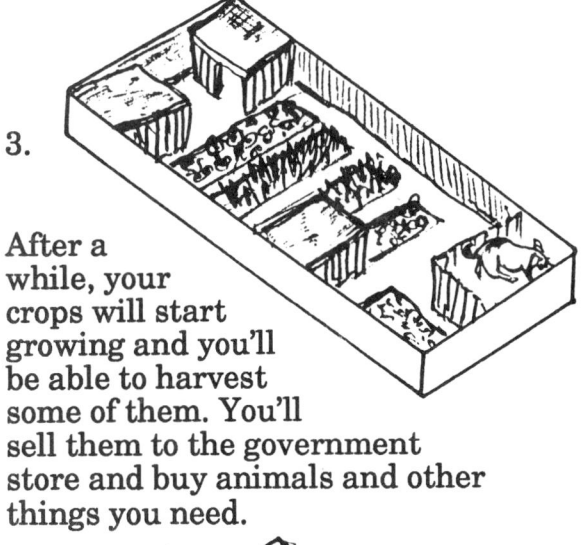

3. After a while, your crops will start growing and you'll be able to harvest some of them. You'll sell them to the government store and buy animals and other things you need.

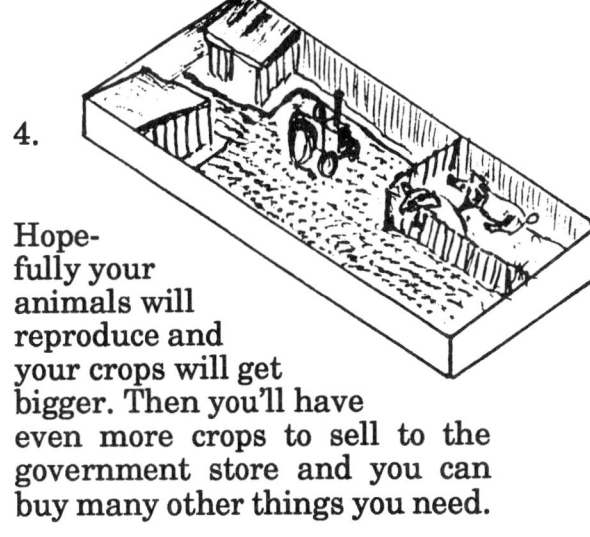

4. Hopefully your animals will reproduce and your crops will get bigger. Then you'll have even more crops to sell to the government store and you can buy many other things you need.

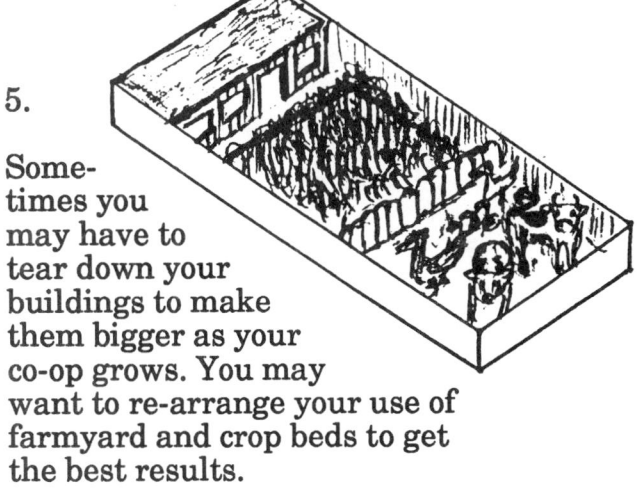

5. Sometimes you may have to tear down your buildings to make them bigger as your co-op grows. You may want to re-arrange your use of farmyard and crop beds to get the best results.

6. Still more planning and construction will go on. You may even start a small business.

Government Store Price List

Livestock

Bull	$200
Cow	$100
Horse	$100
Pig	$75
Pig with babies	$100
Sheep	$60
Goat	$60
Chicken	$25
Pony	$40
Turkey	$25
Duck	$40
Rabbit	$20

Equipment

Tractor	$500
Seed spreader (rent)	$100/wk
Windmill	$800
Truck	$200
Animal shelter	$75
Fishing boat	$300
Car	$100 (gas - $1.25/gal)
Wheelbarrow	$20

Miscellaneous

Apple trees	$20
Onion seeds	$1.00/four
Fertilizer	$2
Rice	$5 (5 rice crackers)
Flour	$5 (5 wheat crackers)
Salt	$1/bag

Lesson 10 Handout #28

Ye Old Savings and Loan Association

Date _____

Previous Balance _____

Deposit _____

Check Drawn _____

Balance _____

Check Number _____
Date _____

Pay to the Order of _____ _____ Dollars

_____

_____
Signature

2511: 3426: 47036: 336

Ye Old Savings and Loan Association

Name _____

Date _____ 19 ____

_____
Signature - (Refund Received)

SAVINGS DEPOSIT

Account Number:

CASH		
Checks - List		
Transfer From		
Refund Received in Cash		
TOTAL DEPOSIT	$	

Ye Old Savings and Loan Association

Check Payable To _____

Special Instructions _____

Signature _____

Signature _____

Date _____ 19 ____

WSFV-9

SAVINGS WITHDRAWL

Account Number:

AMOUNT OF WITHDRAWL		
#	Cash	$
#	Check	$
#	P.M.O.	$
#	T.C.	$
#	Transfer To	
	TOTAL	$

Bartering Tokens

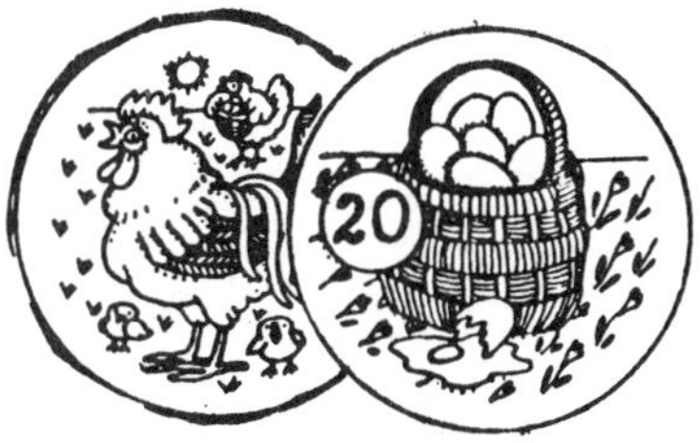
20

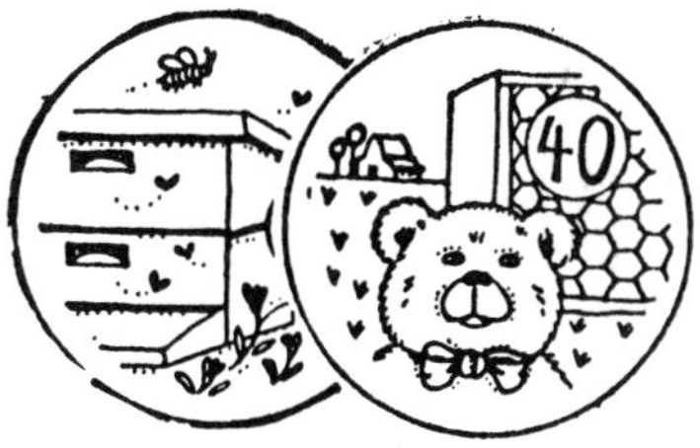
40

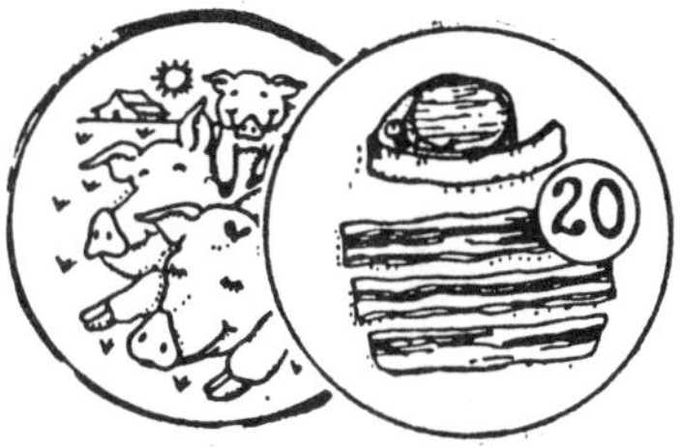
20

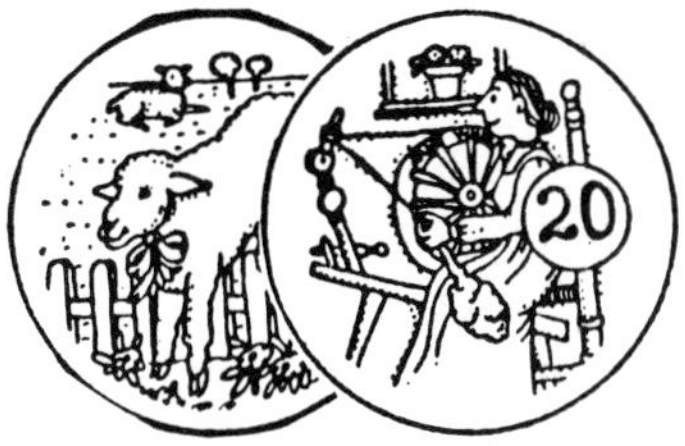
20

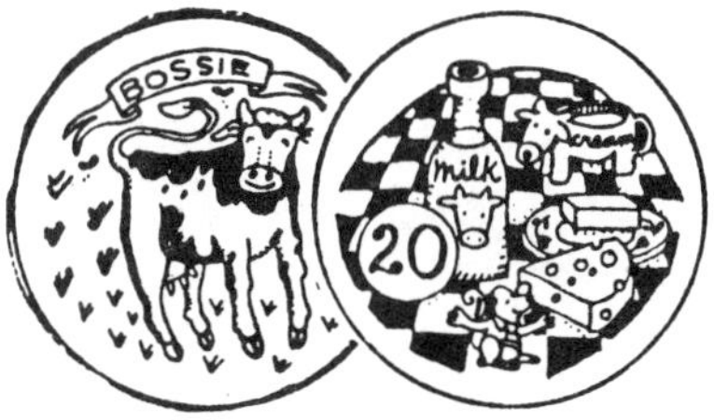
BOSSIE
milk
20

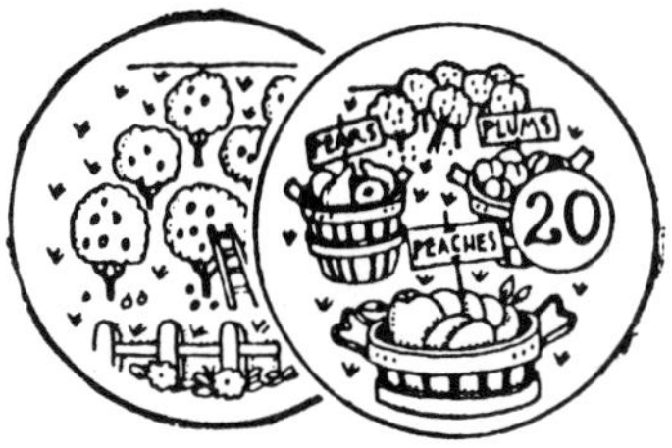
PLUMS
PEACHES
20

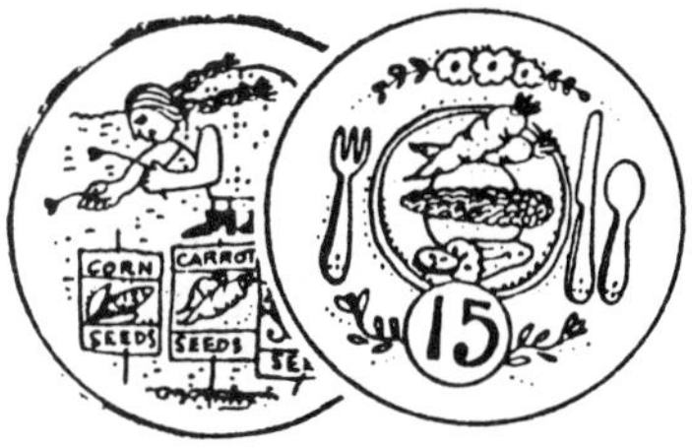
CORN SEEDS
CARROT SEEDS
15

Play Money

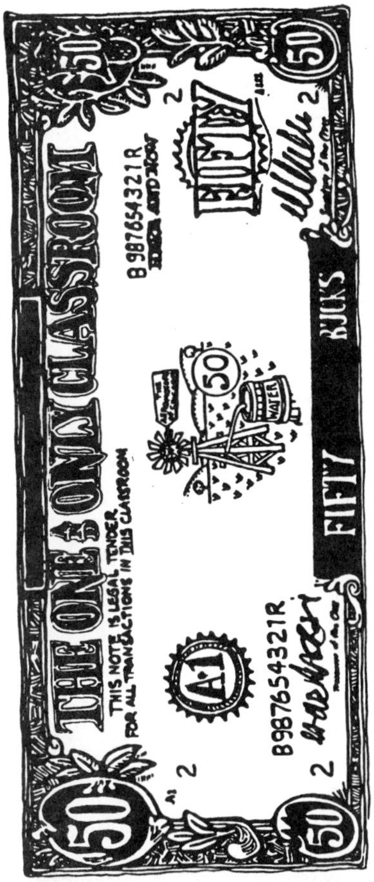
THE ONE AND ONLY CLASSROOM
THIS NOTE IS LEGAL TENDER FOR ALL TRANSACTIONS IN THIS CLASSROOM
B987654321R
HERE AND NOW
FIFTY
FIFTY BUCKS
50

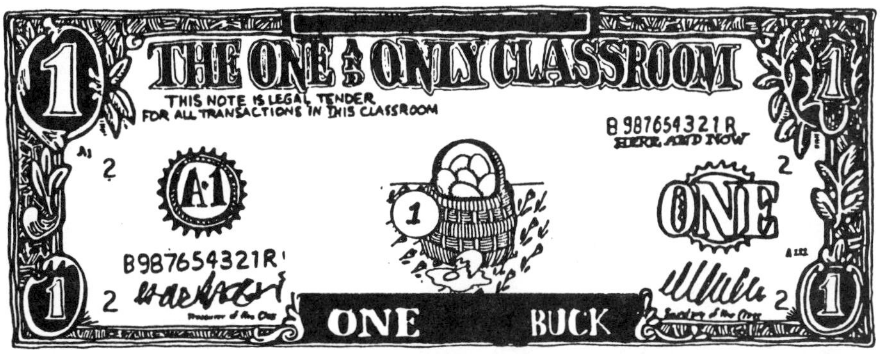
THE ONE AND ONLY CLASSROOM
THIS NOTE IS LEGAL TENDER FOR ALL TRANSACTIONS IN THIS CLASSROOM
B987654321R
HERE AND NOW
ONE
ONE BUCK
1

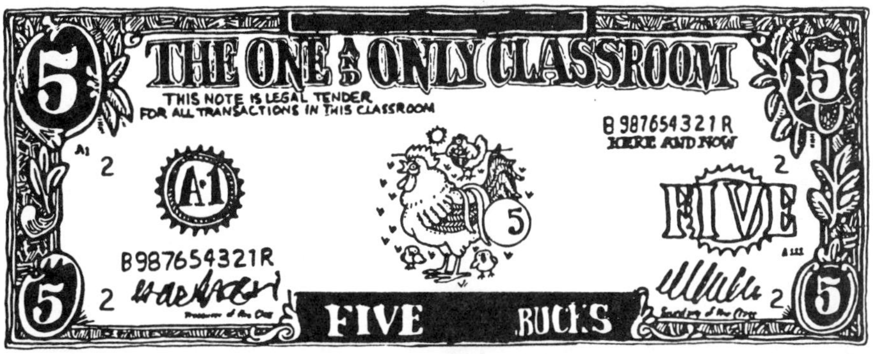
THE ONE AND ONLY CLASSROOM
THIS NOTE IS LEGAL TENDER FOR ALL TRANSACTIONS IN THIS CLASSROOM
B987654321R
HERE AND NOW
FIVE
FIVE BUCKS
5

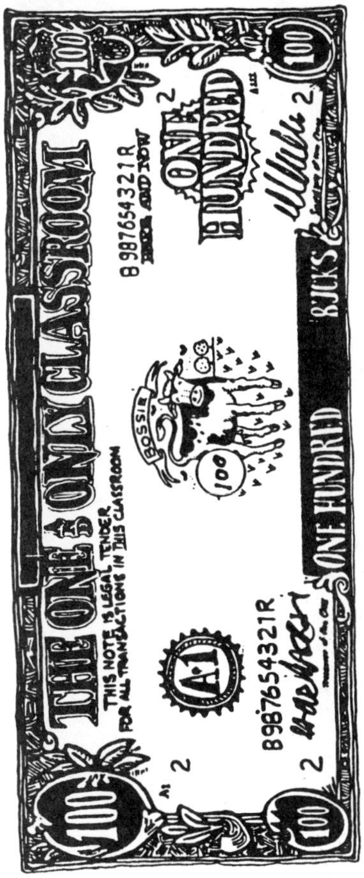
THE ONE AND ONLY CLASSROOM
THIS NOTE IS LEGAL TENDER FOR ALL TRANSACTIONS IN THIS CLASSROOM
B987654321R
HERE AND NOW
ONE HUNDRED
BOSSIE
ONE HUNDRED BUCKS
100

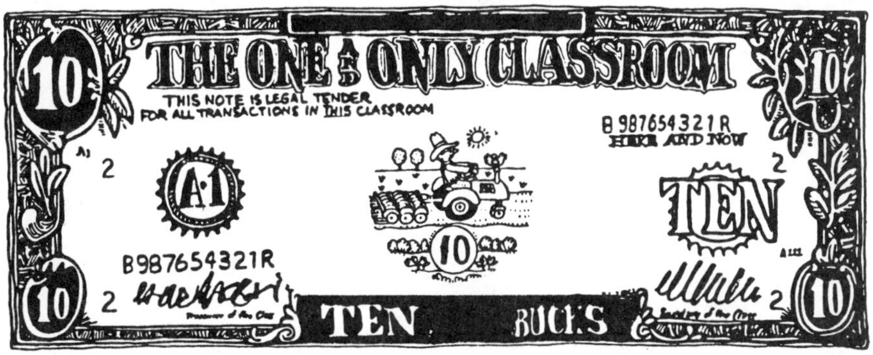
THE ONE AND ONLY CLASSROOM
THIS NOTE IS LEGAL TENDER FOR ALL TRANSACTIONS IN THIS CLASSROOM
B987654321R
HERE AND NOW
TEN
TEN BUCKS
10

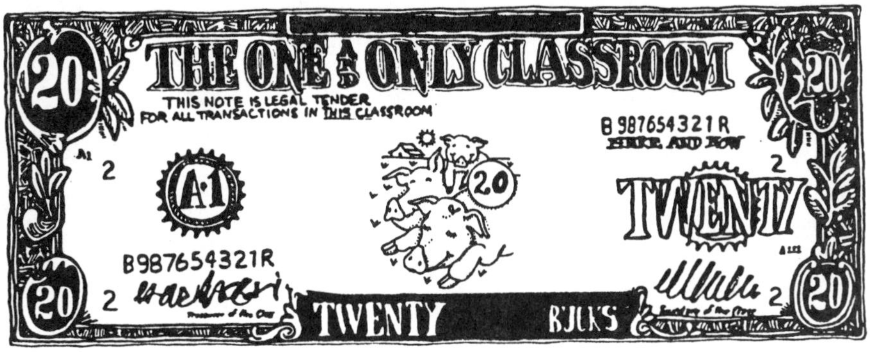
THE ONE AND ONLY CLASSROOM
THIS NOTE IS LEGAL TENDER FOR ALL TRANSACTIONS IN THIS CLASSROOM
B987654321R
HERE AND NOW
TWENTY
TWENTY BUCKS
20

Using Cooperation Skills in Large-Group Class Discussions

Objective   Students will participate effectively in classroom meetings and discussions.

Students will gain skill and confidence in expressing themselves.

Materials   Debriefing "Sentence Starter" signs (in Appendix)

To the Teacher   Establishing the practice of classroom meetings and discussions provides a vehicle for students to share their thoughts and feelings about classroom life. A positive classroom climate is more likely to come about when all students in the class are involved in discussion, problem-solving, and decision-making.

The terms "class meetings" and "class discussions" are often used interchangeably in educational literature. The main difference between the two appears to be that class meetings tend to focus on school issues that involve current problems in students' lives and are often used to solve conflict situations. Class discussions are also used for these purposes, but the term at times is given a broader meaning and also encompasses discussions related to academic subject matter. Because the procedures themselves and the guidelines for implementing them are so similar, we will use the terms interchangeably.

Both class meetings and discussions can be a very important part of classroom life. However, students must be taught how to behave during these activities. Class meetings and discussions are not open-ended forums without restrictions. Their purpose is always to teach something. They are only worthwhile if a clear educational objective has been established. In problem-solving meetings and discussions, students may suggest solutions to classroom problems or make recommendations, but the final decision of any action to be taken always rests with the teacher.

Productive meetings and discussions require the same fundamental skills and attitudes necessary for cooperative learning. A review of the basic principles taught in the preceding lessons might be helpful for students. The following are some further general guidelines for assuring the success of either classroom meetings or discussions:

- Whenever possible, it is best to sit in a circle or semicircle. It is much harder to have a class discussion if the students have to talk to the backs of heads. The circle format allows the students to participate as equals with the teacher, to make eye contact with one another, and to note others' non-verbal behavior. Students have the opportunity to speak to one another instead of only to the teacher. It's worth the time it takes to move the furniture, if this is necessary. It is often productive to instruct students in methods of forming a circle or semicircle quietly and efficiently, and to give them time to practice this. The supplementary activity following this lesson entitled "Organizing a Group Circle" teaches this skill during the actual class meeting or discussion. Try not to place yourself at any focal point in the circle.

- Before having class meetings or discussions, review ground rules, and emphasize that everyone will follow them. You may wish to make a chart of rules and display it for all to see.

<u>Ground Rules</u>

a. Everyone gets a turn to talk.
b. You can skip your turn to talk if you wish.
c. Listen to the person who is talking.
d. The time is shared equally.
e. There will be no interruptions, put-downs, or gossip.

- Assure students that when they take their turns, they will be listened to and they will not be interrupted, probed, advised, preached to, criticized, ridiculed, or put down.

- Make sure students know what they are supposed to accomplish. Many class meetings or discussions fall flat because students are not aware of the teacher's purpose in holding the meeting or discussion. The discussion's purpose cannot always indicate a specific outcome and may not lead to a plan of action, but it should at least be clear in its goals. For example, you might say "The purpose of this meeting is to explore why some students are mean to each other," or "The purpose of this discussion is to talk about changing some classroom rules."

- The teacher's main function in a class meeting or discussion is to preside over an exchange of ideas and opinions. Whatever questions you ask should be for the purpose of keeping the group on the subject and thinking with greater clarity. The art is in asking questions, or getting students to ask questions, that require clarification of ideas and that move the class toward resolving the issue being discussed.

- Always ask a question before naming a person to answer it. In this way everyone thinks about the question, not just the student called on to answer it.

- Don't always call on the first student whose hand goes up. Allow time for several hands to go up, and from time to time call on the last one up; it may be that of a shy contributor who needs encouragement.

- Keep track of who has spoken and who has not. Involve shy students, inviting them to review what someone just said. If they can say even a few words, you can give them recognition for listening.

- Never force participation. Students must always be allowed the option of refraining from speaking. Don't assume that those who remain quiet are not getting anything from the session -- they can be learning by listening to the comments of others. If you are respectful of all students' comments, quiet or shy students eventually gain the motivation and courage to speak.

- When students get off the topic being discussed, use a review to bring digression back to the topic. Don't "put down" someone who digresses, but say something like, "Thanks, Ed. Now let's see what we've talked about so far."

- Work toward looking at students' statements from their viewpoints without judging rightness or wrongness of any response. It is important that you develop the ability to accept unconditionally what is being said. This means not showing a shocked reaction, nor an exceptionally pleased one.

- Above all, model good listening! Your demonstration of listening skills will do far more to encourage student growth and learning than will your own comments even if you know how to say something better than students can. Model external signs of listening by eye contact, nodding when appropriate, smiling, gestures, posture, etc. Before you begin to have class meetings or discussions, it would be helpful to teach Lesson 3, "Learning How to Listen to Others," and the activities that follow it in this section. This will give students an opportunity to learn key listening skills.

- Teach students to focus on the person who is speaking by imagining that the speaker is on stage with a spotlight on him or her. Explain that it is the speaker's show and everyone else's job is to look at the speaker and listen. No one needs to "steal" the spotlight when another is speaking because they will have their chance to speak later. Sometimes it's helpful to use a prop, like a microphone or a ball, which is handed to the person who has been called upon to speak.

- Do not allow non-listeners to make new contributions. If during a classroom discussion, it is apparent that certain students have not been listening carefully to previous speakers, do not allow them to share their own ideas until they have established that they know specifically what the preceding contributors were saying. Often a new contribution is an interruption. The student has not been listening at all but has just been waiting for a chance to shoot up a personal skyrocket.

- Don't repeat a student's comment. It is all too common for teachers to repeat or paraphrase, in a loud, clear voice, what a student has said so that everyone will be sure to hear and understand it clearly. This says to students they needn't speak up because the teacher will help them out. It also reinforces in students the habit of not listening. "Why bother, when the teacher is going to repeat everything anyway?" It communicates to the students that they don't need to listen to one another, only to the teacher. When the teacher refrains from repeating and, if students haven't heard, redirects them to ask the speaker to repeat, students begin to listen to each other more attentively.

- At times, summarize what you've heard. Although repeating students' answers can have the harmful result of encouraging students not to listen to one another, there are occasions when summarizing what a speaker has said can be valuable. For example, when a student shares some personal views on a controversial topic, summarizing what the student has said shows that you've understood and encourages the student to continue speaking. You might use the following words in restating or paraphrasing students' comments: "In other words . . . ," "You felt . . . ," "Sounds like . . . ," "Are you saying that . . . ," "I hear you saying . . . ," "It's important to you that . . . ."

- Use praise to encourage the kinds of behavior that are helpful in a discussion. For example, when students show the connection between their own new ideas and previous contributions, or point out how two or more ideas are related, comment on the helpfulness of what they have done.

- Emphasize that in most situations there is no single right answer. Use the brainstorming technique when a number of creative ideas would be useful (see Lesson 6 on brainstorming).

- Do not permit personal matters to be the focus of a classroom discussion. In general, students have an excellent notion of what is appropriate to share in a class discussion and what should not be shared. If a student does begin to share personal and potentially embarrassing information regarding himself or family members, say something like, "Most parents prefer that we don't talk about family matters when they are not present." If a student expresses a strong feeling regarding something not related to school, the teacher should make a clear distinction between the right a student has to his or her feelings and his or her responsibility to keep family matters private. It is important not to imply that what the student alluded to was bad or weird, but simply that this kind of information should not be shared in class discussions. If you sense that a student who begins to discuss such information really needs to talk about it, say something like "Jim, why don't you talk to me later about that?" and then direct attention to another student.

- Never probe or pressure a student to respond to a particular topic or to divulge his or her feelings. An explicit norm should be established for the "right to privacy" and the right to be silent should be respected at all times.

- Keep from reinforcing disruptive behavior by giving it as little attention as is possible. Place students who tend to be disruptive near you. If a student is disruptive while another speaks, it is sometimes helpful to touch that student on the knee while keeping your eyes on the student who is speaking. If a student ridicules, interrupts, or puts another student down, remind the student immediately of the ground rules. Any time that disruptive behavior persists, deal directly and firmly with it in the way most appropriate to your setting.

- If many students are misbehaving, end the meeting or discussion. Explain to students that having class discussions or meetings is a privilege, not a right, and if the privilege is abused, they lose it for the time being. This must be said calmly. If you appear angry, some students may feel they have gained control of the situation. If you end the discussion calmly, they will see that the discussion has ended because of the inappropriate behavior, not because they managed to get the teacher angry.

- Establish a definite time limit to curb rambling (from 10 to 25 minutes is a good rule of thumb for elementary-age students). Reduce resistance to quitting when you call "time" by giving a 2 - 3 minute warning.

- Always review, or sum up, what happened during the meeting or discussion. This is important because it helps students identify the main thoughts and feelings that were expressed, as well as how they felt about the experience.

Lesson Presentation

Identify the topic for the classroom meeting or discussion. This may be a "real life" issue that has come up in the classroom and needs to be dealt with. It may be a hypothetical situation which, as a result of class discussion, can provide some important learning or insights for students.

Topics and situations that can be used for such a discussion have been provided at the end of this lesson.

After selecting the topic for the classroom meeting or discussion, encourage students to suggest a list of "Do's" and "Don'ts" to be used as guidelines for a successful meeting/discussion.

Example:

Do	Don't
— One person talks at a time.	— Don't interrupt.
— Try to contribute to the discussion.	— Don't force others to speak.
— Try to be sensitive to the feelings of others.	— Don't make "put-down" remarks.
— Try to make group members feel comfortable and safe.	— Don't use more than your share of time.
— Give full attention to the speaker by eye contact.	— Don't get off the topic.
— Allow each group member equal time to contribute.	
— Stay on the topic.	
— Listen to the speaker.	

After the guidelines have been established, explain the purpose of the meeting/discussion. If the purpose is to identify reasonable solutions to social problems in the classroom, the following questions will facilitate the process:

- *What is the problem?*
- *Are there some parts of the problem we are ignoring or running away from?*
- *Is there something about our class that has changed and resulted in the problem?*
- *What are the alternatives open to us?*
- *What are the consequences of each alternative?*
- *Are there any risks involved in deciding a certain way?*
- *Are we being honest about the problem?*

- *What are some other ways of thinking about what happened?*
- *Does anyone see the situation differently?*
- *How can we make sure our solution works?*
- *Who is responsible for solving this problem?*
- *Are we being concerned about the feelings of the people involved?*

At times during the discussion, summarize points of view. At the end of the discussion, ask students questions like the following:

- *Are there any specific actions we should take as a result of our meeting?*
- *What did you like or dislike about this meeting?*
- *How did the guidelines help our discussion?*

You may wish to continue to debrief the meeting/discussion by having students respond to "Sentence Starters for Promoting Thinking" in the Appendix.

Sup. Act. *On the following pages are some topics and problem situations you might wish to use to practice class discussion skills.*

Lesson 11   Supplementary Activity

Organizing a Group Circle

Objective Students will participate in planning the logistics of organizing the class into a circle for discussion.

Materials Chalk, chalkboard, tagboard (optional)

Procedure *Say:* **TODAY we are going to learn how to form a circle for discussion.** *Draw a circle on the board.* **LOOK at this circle. What do we need to do to move from our desks to a circle on the floor?** *(Option is that children may bring chairs to form circle.) Answers need to include quiet movement, selecting a place, being able to see all students, posture, and other behavior that will promote forming a circle quickly and efficiently. Try forming the circle.* **RETURN to your desks. Let's form our circle again.** *Have students evaluate with you about the formation of this circle if satisfactory. The optional tagboard noted above can be used to prepare name tags if students aren't yet familiar with each other.*

Lesson 11   Supplementary Activity

Inner-Outer Circle Discussion

Objective Students will act as both participants and observers in a class discussion.

Materials None

Procedure The procedure is useful when having a discussion with a large class of students. Have students sit in two concentric circles, one within the other. After the circles are formed, tell the class that the inner group will discuss a topic while the outer group observes how the discussion is going. When the discussion is finished, the outer group will share and discuss its observations with the inner. Then the two groups will change places and repeat the procedure.

This way everyone has a chance to be both participant and observer to discuss the topic, and to become more aware of what happens during a discussion.

Do these before the discussion:

1. Either choose the topic of discussion for students or suggest several and let a student committee choose one of them.
2. Choose a timekeeper.
3. Choose some simple method of dividing the class into two groups. It is best to mix boys and girls, talkers and shy ones. Any random method should work, such as dividing by halves of the alphabet or putting half the girls and half the boys into each group.
4. Decide how to form the inner and outer circles. If the desks are immovable, have the students take seats so as to roughly form two circles.
5. Divide up tasks for students in the outer circle. Have some students count how many in the inner circle talk. Have other students note which people look as if they want to say something, but don't. Finally, choose some students to keep track of who gets interrupted and who does the interrupting. Remind all students in the outer circle that they are to watch the discussion in silence.

Do these things during the discussion:

1. Have students in the inner circle begin the discussion, let them talk together for 8 or 9 minutes, then call time.
2. Have the observers report on what they saw and heard while the inner group listens in silence. Then let the inner group comment on the observers' reports and the discussion itself.
3. Have the groups reverse roles and repeat the above.
4. Evaluate the discussion by asking students what helped or hurt it.

Variation You can leave one chair empty in the inner circle so a member of the outer circle may enter, contribute, and then leave.

Some Open-Ended Topics for Class Discussion

Objectives Students will cooperate as a large group, using ground rules and skills for discussion presented in Lesson 11.

Materials None

Procedure Review skills and ground rules for large-group discussion before introducing one of the open-ended discussion topics listed below.

- What one thing do you wish did not exist?
- If you were suddenly sent to an unknown destination, what three things would you want to have with you?
- What's the hardest thing about being a friend?
- Which would be a more valuable possession -- perfect health or great wealth? Why?
- If we all looked and acted exactly the same, what problems would it cause?
- Why is it important to have people of all ages living in a community, or is it?
- If we could never change our minds, how would this affect our lives?
- If the world were about to blow up and only you and five other people could escape in a spaceship, whom would you take with you?
- If you could pick any time in history to live, what period would you choose?
- If you did not have to go to school, how would you spend your time?
- What do you like about October? Or May? Or . . .
- What would be a good Christmas present for the whole world?
- What is the most important thing in life?
- What would make the world a better place to live in?
- What can teachers and students do to get along better with one another?
- What is the greatest problem facing this school?

Lesson 11   Supplementary Activity

Problem Situations for Class Discussion

Objective Students will cooperate as a large group, using ground rules and skills for discussion presented in Lesson 11.

Materials Story, "What Should Guy Do?"
Story, "What Should Pete Do?"

Procedure Review skills and ground rules for large-group discussion before reading one of the following problem situations for class discussion.

Lesson 11

Supplementary Activity
"Problem Situations for Discussion"

What Should Guy Do?*

Guy hated his new school so much that he didn't have time to like anything any more. Just one month ago, he was spending the summer in the same house where he'd lived all his life and was planning to start sixth grade in the same school he'd gone to since kindergarten. His friends would all be in his room and he was a cinch to make the baseball team. And then, just before school opened, the family had moved to a little town Guy hadn't even been able to find on the map. As far as Guy was concerned, the world had come to an end.

Guy didn't like their new house or the town or the people. He started school and the school was so different from the one back home that Guy could hardly stand it.

"Don't be such a poor sport, Guy," his mother said to him one night after he had spent the dinner hour complaining. "We'll only be here a year and then we'll be going back. Make the best of it."

In a year, all the gang at home would have forgotten him, Guy thought. That night he went to sleep trying to pretend that he was back in his old bedroom.

The next day, things seemed worse than ever. "What a school!" Guy thought. "So small that there isn't even a cafeteria, so all morning long you keep smelling what people have in their lunch bags."

Today, the room was unusually stuffy and somebody had brought some kind of cheese that smelled terrible. Even though a light drizzle was falling when the noon bell rang, Guy went outside and hunched up against the schoolhouse wall while he ate his sandwiches.

Looking glumly at the mud puddles on the dreary school yard, he munched away without knowing whether he was eating peanut butter or bologna. He was thinking about what his father had said at breakfast that morning.

* *Unfinished Stories,* NEA publication.

Lesson 11   Supplementary Activity
                       "Problem Situations for Discussion"

"Guy, you're too smart to spend a whole year griping about things that can't be changed. Surely, you can find something else to do besides wasting your time on hating."

Guy wanted to figure out a way to have a good year, but he didn't know how to start. How could he have a good year in this miserable school away from all his friends? What should Guy do?

Lesson 11

Supplementary Activity
"Problem Situations for Discussion"

What Should Pete Do?*

Miss Cary's new pen was missing. The children had admired it when she used it to take the roll that morning and she had told them that her brother had sent it to her from Japan. She had let the class pass it from one person to another so that everyone could look at the ship floating mysteriously in liquid inside the cap. Now the pen was gone. Miss Cary asked everybody to look in his desk to see if it might be there by mistake.

"I'll bet somebody took it," Pete said to his friends at recess. And all during the game of softball, he kept wondering who might have done it.

When the recess bell rang, Pete took the ball and bat to the P.E. equipment room. On his way, he passed by the principal's office and he saw the principal talking quietly, but very seriously, to Keith Bronson. Keith, with his face a deep red, was standing by the door looking almost ready to cry. Pete quickly ran back to class.

"Hey," he called to his friends. "I'll bet that Keith took Miss Cary's pen. The principal was bawling him out about something, and boy, did he look scared."

When the boys took their seats, they gave Keith a dirty look to let him know that they knew. Keith looked puzzled for a minute and then his face turned red again. He's the one, all right, Pete thought.

The next day, Pete saw the pen back on the teacher's desk. "Oh, you have your pen again!" he said to the teacher. "Yes, I found it between the pages of the grade book," Miss Cary laughed. Pete stood still. "You . . . you found it in the grade book?" he said. "Yes, wasn't that crazy! I must have closed the book on it."

Pete didn't answer. By now, almost everyone in the class thought Keith was a thief, and it wasn't true. Whatever Keith had been upset about in the principal's office, it wasn't about the pen. Well, what of it? Pete tried to tell himself. I didn't say for sure that he took it. I said I bet he had because I thought the principal was bawling him out, and that much was true. But Pete didn't feel any better. He was the one who had started the rumor. Now what should he do?

* *Unfinished Stories,* NEA publication.

Activities Designed to Promote Cooperation Skills

Cooperative Decision-Making Activities . . . . 139 - 165
Cooperative Art Activities . . . . 167 - 174
Cooperative Structure-Building Activities . . . . 175 - 184
Cooperative Survival Simulation Activities . . . . 185 - 219
Cooperative Puzzle-Solving Activities . . . . 221 - 257
Cooperative Free-Time and Recess Activities . . . . 259 - 266

Section B

Involving Students in Cooperation Activities

Your students have now been introduced to the skills needed to work cooperatively. The following activities provide students with varied opportunities to practice cooperation skills. These activities involve small-group discussions and peer projects. They promote communication, sharing, and mutual respect. Look through the activities and select those that would be appropriate for your class. Prepare students for involvement in the activities by reminding them of the cooperation skills that were introduced and practiced when you taught the cooperation lessons in this manual.

Student participation in these activities will be enhanced if you appoint one or more students as observers and have them use one of the group observation sheets in the introduction to this manual. While involving students in the cooperation activities suggested here, as well as in small cooperative working groups in academic subject areas, you may wish to occasionally repeat the procedure of having students draw a cooperation role behavior card and practice that particular behavior at least part of the time as they engage in the cooperation activity. Be sure to debrief with students after they have completed an activity, using the guidelines for debriefing presented in the introduction. Also use the "Sentence Starters for Promoting Thinking" in the Appendix. These should be hanging in your classroom. These practices will foster the internalization of the cooperation skills you have presented in lessons.

Debriefing the Activities

The following questions can be used to debrief most cooperation activities. The debriefing can be formatted a number of ways:

- discuss questions as a class

- form discussion groups consisting of one member from each cooperation group to discuss questions

- discuss questions in dyads or triads

- answer individually on paper for submission to teacher or for sharing with cooperation group

- remain in cooperation groups to share opinions as the questions are asked

Questions

1. Was any time lost in getting organized? How could that be improved?
2. How did your group decide who would do what? How did you resolve differences?
3. Did everyone in your group participate? How did members of your group try to get others involved?
4. What was the climate like in your group? Encouraging? Competitive? Enthusiastic? Sluggish?
5. What did you like least about your group product or decision?
6. What did you like best?
7. What are some ways you group could improve their group work?
8. What did you like best about working with your group?

The sentence-starters in the Appendix are also effective debriefers.

Cooperative Decision-Making Activities

Who Gets the Ice Cream? 141
Ideal Island 142
Planning a Party 143
Designing a Game 144
Group Drama 145
Starting a Factory 146
Making Team Decisions 147
Play Ball . . . . 148 - 149
A Petition . . . . 151 - 153
A Trip to Hawaii . . . . 155 - 157
Cooperation Auction . . . . 159 - 161
Space Ambassadors . . . . 163 - 165

Conclude each of these activities with debriefing exercises found in the Introduction and/or on page 138.

Who Gets the Ice Cream?

Objective Students will cooperate as a small group to reach a group decision within a short time span.

Materials Ice cream bar for each student

Procedure Divide the class into groups of four or five. Give each group an ice cream bar and tell them that they have 5 minutes to decide who gets the ice cream bar. They have to set up their own criteria for the recipient of the ice cream bar, and they must decide on the person within the given time span. If they can't decide, they lose the bar.

If at the end of 5 minutes the groups have decided on who gets the ice cream bar, each member of the group gets a bar. Do not let the groups know this ahead of time.

Ideal Island

Objective Students will cooperate in small groups to create a life style on a fictitious island.

Group cooperation activity

Materials Large pieces of paper and marking pens

Procedure Divide class into groups of five or six. Give each group a large piece of paper and a marking pen. Tell them that they are going to make their own special island. The piece of paper represents a map of the island. There is nothing on it yet. Each group is to put 15 things on the island which would make it an ideal place to live. If someone wants to put something on the island that the other members of the group do not want, they will have to negotiate.

Allow 20-25 minutes for the exercise. Display islands around the room and discuss what was put on each island and how decisions were made. You may wish to have groups order 15 items according to importance.

Planning a Party

Objective Students will cooperate in small group to plan a social gathering.

Materials None

Procedure At special times of the year, such as Valentine's Day, St. Patrick's Day, Thanksgiving, etc., it is fun for the students to plan their own party. It might be beneficial to hand out a brief questionnaire asking the students what kind of food they want, entertainment, games, prizes, etc. In this way everybody has the opportunity to express what they would like for a party.

Divide the class into groups of three or four. Ask them to choose what committee they would like to be, i.e., clean-up, decoration, food, games, etc. Then have them cooperate on planning the party within their various committees. When everyone is done, ask a group member from each committee to report to the class on what his or her committee has decided to do.

Designing a Game

Objective Students will cooperate in small groups to design a game.

Materials Set of common objects, such as paper cups, a rope, a bucket, a piece of cloth, etc.

Procedure Divide class into groups of four or five. Show each group the same set of objects. Each group is to design a game that can be played which uses all of the objects. At the end of a specified time period, one representative from each group is asked to share its game with the class. Ask groups to share their success or problems with the activity.

Group Drama

Objective Students will cooperate in small groups to create a play.

Materials Several paper bags, filled with about six different objects (Example: a book, play money, broken toy, a photograph)

Procedure Divide students into groups of four or five. Give each group a paper bag and ask them not to look inside until it is time to begin. Tell them that the bag holds props for a play. The plays are group projects in which each student takes part. They will be silent plays with plots built around the objects in the groups' bags. Time allowed for preparation is 30 minutes a day for 3 days, after which they will present the plays to the class as a whole.

After the plays have been presented, discuss the following questions:

- Did everyone agree on the play?
- Was there a leader?
- How did the leader become a leader?
- Was it fun?
- How did you decide on the story and actors?

Starting a Factory

Objective Students will cooperate as small groups in planning an imaginary factory.

Materials None

Procedure Have students divide into small groups. They are to plan the start of a small factory. This factory should make a product that students think people need and would want. It could be something already being manufactured or something that nobody has thought of yet.

Students need to decide on

- what the product will be
- price of the product
- salaries of the employees
- how the product would be made
- advertising, and
- how to come up with money for starting the company.

When everyone is finished, have a representative from each group report to the class about their factory.

Making Team Decisions

Objective   Students will cooperate as members of a team to make decisions in a game.

Materials   None

Procedure   In this activity, students divide into teams and participate in group decision-making as they compete for points with another team in a game.

The group decision is simply to pick one of two colors, blue or green, but the group needs to develop a strategy to make the decision.

The game works like this: divide the class into two teams and space them so that they cannot hear each other's discussions. The game will last for nine "innings." During each inning, the teams have to choose either the color blue or the color green. After the teams state their choices, you will tell them how many points they have earned. Points are determined in this manner (students are not told how points are determined):

1. If both teams select blue, both teams get five points.
2. If both teams select green, both teams lose five points.
3. If one team chooses blue and the other green, the team that chose blue loses 10 points and the team that chose green receives 10 points.

Begin the game by having each team select a color. If the group does not entirely agree, suggest that the choice of the majority should rule. Allow them two to four minutes per inning. A member from each team announces the team color selection.

Add up the points at the end of nine innings to determine the winner. After the game, have a class discussion regarding strategies the team used to decide on a color and whether it is hard to get a group decision in the time allowed.

Play Ball

Objective Students will cooperate in small groups to invent a game.

Materials Rubber play balls about 8" in diameter - one ball for each group, "Play Ball Process Sheets"

Procedure Divide the class into groups of 6 to 10 members. Place a ball in the center of each group and tell the student that they are to invent a game to be played with the ball they have been given. They will be allowed 10 minutes to plan the game. At the end of that time they should be prepared to demonstrate the game to the other members of the class. They may use any other material available to them. The game should be designed so that it can be played in an approved place, such as a gym, playground, sidewalk, or whatever is available.

At the end of 10 minutes, the "Play Ball Process Sheets" are handed out, and students are asked to take 2 or 3 minutes to fill them out while the planning session is still fresh in their minds.

Each group demonstrates its game for a 5-minute period. Have the following discussion focusing on the process each group used to design its game. Students should be discouraged from thinking of the activity as a competition for the best game.

Cooperative Decision-Making Activities   Handout for "Play Ball"

Play Ball Process Sheet

Answer the following questions about the activity you just did:

1. What part of the final plan do you feel was your contribution?

2. Did you feel free to contribute your ideas?

3. On a scale of one to seven, how satisfied are you with the final plan?

4. Could you have made up a better game alone?

5. Does the game take into account the variety of abilities present in your group?

6. Does your game have provisions for rule enforcement? Why or why not?

A Petition*

Objective   Students will cooperate in small groups to identify issues and express their opinions publicly.

Materials   Copy of "Petition" worksheet

Procedure   Divide the class into groups of four or five. Hand out the petition form and explain its use. Each group chooses an issue about which they feel strongly, such as whether some classes should be graded only pass/fail, or whether there should be no homework in certain classes. Give groups about 5 minutes to think of their petitions. Then have a member of each group briefly get up in front of the class and state his petition and why the group feels strongly about it.

Students then carry their petitions around the room, trying to get others to support their positions. Students sign in the "Agree" or "Disagree" columns or are free not to sign at all. It should be stressed that no one should sign unless he or she is convinced of the validity of the petition. You might give them a day or two to gather as many signatures from classmates as they can. Students may sign as many petitions as they want.

After the petitions have been signed, display them where the class can read them.

Discuss the exercise with the class. Ask them what beliefs they found their classmates to have, whether there were issues on which they themselves had no opinion, how it felt to sign in the "Disagree" column, whether it was harder to sign "Disagree" for a friend, etc.

---

*   K. Martin, M. Black, and C. Wolter, *It's Up to Me,* 1980.

PETITION

We, the undersigned, believe that _____
_____
_____
_____
_____

AGREE   DISAGREE

A Trip to Hawaii*

Objective Students will cooperate in small groups to consider qualities and make choices of traveling companions.

Materials List of roommates

Procedure Tell the students that they are to imagine they have won a trip to Hawaii. They each need to pick four other students with whom they will room, eat, and be a group for all activities during the 2-week trip. Give them each a copy of the list of potential roommates and have them make a mental note of four roommates they would like. Then divide the class into groups of four or five.

Each group is to select four students from the list to be their roommates. All the students in the group must agree on the final choices.

Finally, have the groups explain to the class why they have chosen their particular traveling companions.

---

* J. Wilt, and B. Watson, *Relationship Builders*, 1978.

Possible Traveling Companions

Matt Richie — Matt is very rich and knows it. He is spoiled because he always gets everything he wants. His parents will give him a lot of money to bring on the trip and he will buy things like ice cream, candy, and other snacks for his group. He will also bring some of his expensive and fancy toys.

Betty Beautiful — Betty is the most beautiful girl going on the trip. She is very shy and always does what everybody else wants to do. Betty's group never gets into trouble because the grownups assume any group with Betty in it couldn't be doing anything bad.

Alan Athlete — Alan is the best athlete of the group. He is so talented that his group always wins the athletic competitions. He is always telling the other members of the group what to do and when to do it. If one member is not very good at a certain sport, Alan is quick to tell him, but the team manages to win because of Alan.

Tammy Truth — Tammy will always tell the truth. She will never sneak anything or cheat at any of the games. If someone in the group does something wrong, she will let one of the adults know about it.

Freddy Friendly — Freddy is small and not very athletic. He has a bad heart and therefore cannot participate in many activities. But he is very friendly and always nice to everybody.

Tommy Talent — Tommy is very talented. He can play the guitar and sing. He entertains the group with jokes and they enjoy his music. He is loud and sometimes gets the group into trouble because he keeps them up singing and laughing late at night.

Heather Helper — Everyone likes Heather. She always likes to help the group and would do anything for the other members. Sometimes, in order to help the group, she is sneaky and tells small lies.

Mitzi Moody — Sometimes Mitzi is very happy and lots of fun. But sometimes she is unhappy and complains a lot and is terrible to have around.

Cooperation Auction

Objective Students will cooperate in small groups to make effective decisions for a fictitious auction.

Materials Auction List, Play Money (Lesson 10, Handout 30)

Procedure Divide students into groups of three or four. Give each group a copy of the auction list and $150 in play money or a certificate for that amount. Explain to students that the items on the auction list will be auctioned off, in order, to the highest bidding group. There will be no individual bids. (Each member of the group gets one of everything that the group purchases.) If a group runs out of money, it may no longer bid on items. Students must reach a decision together regarding how they want to spend their $150. When the auction is over, have students discuss what their group purchased, what they wanted and didn't get, and what they received. Discuss how each group worked together or didn't work together.

You may wish to have the class make up their own auction list.

Auction List

1. $1,000 for each member of the group to spend in any way they wish.

2. A perfect report card for an entire year

3. A free, all-expense paid trip to Disneyland, the World Series, or a rock concert with anyone of your choice

4. A chance to spend the day with your favorite TV character

5. Ten minutes in a store of your choice, collecting whatever you can cart out in a wheelbarrow

6. A perfect backyard, filled with every toy, game, or amusement that you can imagine

7. A guarantee that you will become President of the United States when you are older

8. A week in which no one can tell you what to do

9. A chance to run your school for a week

10. Perfect health for an entire year

11. A chance to become the most beautiful or most handsome person in your entire community

12. The opportunity to eat whatever you want for a year

13. The chance to personally solve the world's pollution and environmental problems

14. The promise to have a perfect friendship for life -- your friend will be exactly what you want him/her to be

Cooperative Decision-Making Activities

Space Ambassadors

Objective Students will cooperate as small groups to make decisions based on values.

Materials Student handout "Space Ambassadors"

Procedure Divide the class into groups of four or five. Tell each group that they have been given the responsibility to select five people to represent the Earth as ambassadors to a distant planet. These persons will be that planet's first contact with our civilization and should therefore be the best representatives of Earthly life. The groups are to choose five persons from the list of volunteers given to them on the student handout. The information provided on this list is the only data available on these people.

Give the groups 15 to 20 minutes to make their choices. Write the choices on the blackboard and have a spokesperson from each group briefly explain the rationale for the choices.

You may want to ask the following questions:

- What values do you think were reflected in the choices you made?
- Did the choices you made reflect anything about the composition of your group?
- How successful were you, individually, in getting the choices you wanted? How did the group process work for or against your wishes?
- What kind of civilization do your choices represent?

Space Ambassadors

1. Assistant Manager, large downtown bank, resident of the suburbs, age 39

2. His wife, age 37

3. Welfare recipient, mother of six, age 32

4. Head of local construction firm, son of Mexican immigrant, age 48

5. Minister, white, age 28

6. Editor of a daily newspaper, age 30

7. Army major, Vietnam veteran, age 46

8. Model for television commercials, male, age 49

9. High school dropout, working in neighborhood youth center, age 18

10. Artist whose work appears in leading national magazines, age 41

11. His younger wife, writer of unpublished children's stories, age 19

12. Doctor, just published major research on cancer, female, age 47

13. Chief of an American Indian tribe, age 87

14. Principal, elementary school, black, age 43

15. Insurance salesman, age 25

Cooperative Art Activities

A Cut Paper Mural 169
Group Mural 170
Group Collage Project 171
A Group Drawing 172
Patchwork Project 173
Building Bee 174

Conclude each of these activities with debriefing exercises found in the Introduction and/or on page 138.

A Cut Paper Mural*

Objective Students will cooperate as a large group to complete a cut-paper mural.

Materials Construction paper

Procedure In this activity students each contribute to a mural by creating a visual image out of cut paper. Cut paper murals can add a new dimension to learning parts of speech or grammatical construction by combining a visual image with the printed word. For example, each student can choose an idea that illustrates a subject-verb-object language pattern such as "Paula rides horses," and illustrate it. "A Day at the Beach" mural which focuses on adverbs and verbs might combine printed phrases and colorful images that say "runs swiftly, swims fast, sails gracefully, fishes happily, shines warmly, dives deeply," etc.

Cut paper can also be used to illustrate literature such as folk tales, fairy tales, myths, limericks, haiku, proverbs, etc. Each student contributes at least one cut paper form to the assembled product and adds the appropriate word, phrase, or sentences. Students see their contribution combined with those of their classmates to form a finished product. Assembling the mural should involve group decisions related to aesthetic arrangement, balance, and unity.

To ensure that students' images are in scale, they should be told to make all their figures about the size of their hands, with really large animals somewhat larger and smaller creatures smaller than their hands. Their written words, phrases, or sentences that go with their image should be part of their design. This is best accomplished by letting it curve around to be close to their cut paper object.

---

* B. Herberholz, "Double Value: Visual Images/Verbal Reinforcement," *Arts & Activities*, November, 1980.

Group Mural

Objective Students will cooperate in groups to create a theme mural.

Strategy Butcher paper, scrap pieces of colored paper, crayons, or felt-tip pens or paints, magazines

Procedure Divide the class into groups of 5 to 10 students. Give each group a theme for its mural. They could all use the same theme or each group could use a different one. Some possible themes are things that make me happy, things that make me feel sad, fun in the spring, favorite summer activities, how I feel today. Each student can express his or her feelings and contribute to the mural by painting, coloring, drawing and/or cutting and pasting.

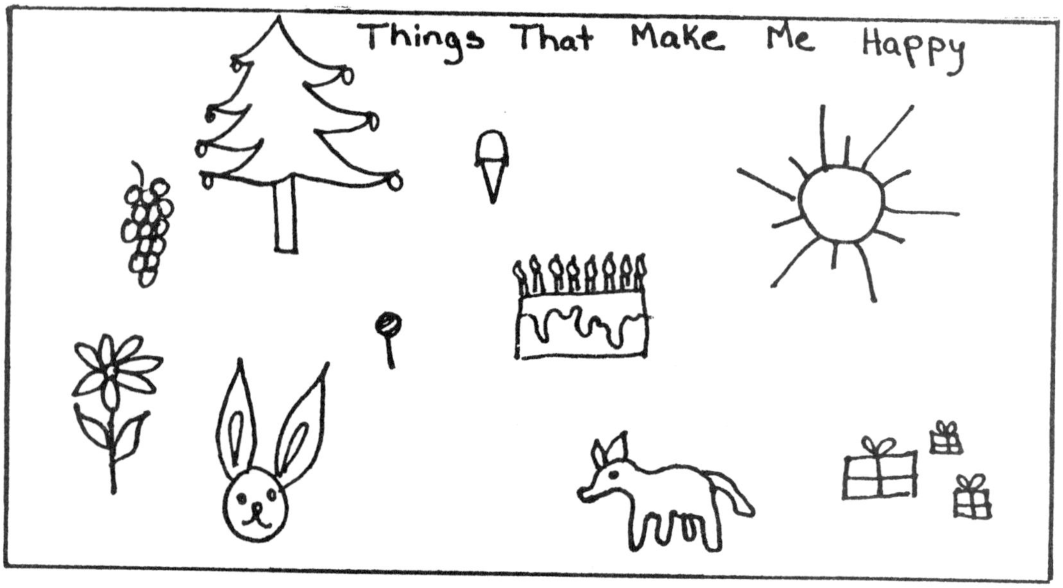
Things That Make Me Happy

Group Collage Project

Objective   Students will cooperate in small groups in planning to complete an art project of their choice.

Materials   Shoe boxes filled with art materials, e.g., clay, blocks, macaroni, paper clips, construction paper, glue, paint, brushes, crayons

Procedure   Divide the class into small groups, and give each group a shoe box filled with art materials. Their task is to develop a group art project, which results in some type of artistic product. Each group needs to agree upon a theme and a title for its project. Also, each member of the group must participate in the project.

Allow 15 to 30 minutes for completion of the projects. Have each group select a spokesperson to explain the project and each member's contribution. Following that, group discussion could focus on the following questions:

- How did it feel to be working with others on an art project?
- Was it hard to decide what each person should do in the project?
- What things did you learn from this activity?
- Are there any benefits to working this way rather than alone?
- Would you like to do this type of group art project again? Why or why not?

A Group Drawing

Objective Students will cooperate in small groups on a group drawing.

Materials Large sheets of butcher paper for each group, crayons, pencils, paints

Procedure Divide students into groups of three or four. Give students a list of topics for doing a group drawing. Each group must decide upon a specific topic from the list and make a single drawing according to the topic. Every member of the group must contribute to the drawing. After everyone has finished, have members of each group explain their drawing and encourage others in the class to ask questions. Here are some suggested topics:

- The perfect toy
- A perfect classroom
- A person from outer space
- An ideal vehicle
- An ideal bedroom or kitchen
- An invention - household, form of transportation
- A new kind of animal
- A robot

Patchwork Project*

Objective Students will cooperate in small groups on a class collage.

Materials Fabric remnants, rubber cement, pinking shears, 1 square of fabric approximately 12" square for each group, 1 large piece of fabric approximately 24" x 48"

Procedure Divide students into groups of four. Have each student use pinking shears to cut two squares approximately 2" x 2". Give each group a 12" x 12" square and have each person glue his/her small squares into a design. Have the groups get together and glue their 12" squares to the largest piece of fabric. This finished mural can be used as the background for a bulletin board, as a piece of art for the wall, as a tablecloth for special occasions, or as an attractive way to display special projects.

---

* J. Wilt and B. Watson, *Relationships Builders* (WORD Educational Products Division, Waco, Texas, 1978).

Building Bee

Objective Students will cooperate in small groups on a planning map.

Materials Large sheets or roll of paper, crayons, rulers, etc.

Procedure Review with the class the need for cooperation when working with a group. Talk about good listening skills, taking turns when speaking, and sharing materials.

Ask students to imagine a certain type of building. This might be a restaurant, an apartment building, a factory, a house, etc. Have them think in detail about this building -- the purpose, size, color, details, etc. Then have them work in groups of four or five. Give each group a large sheet of paper, pencils, rulers, and crayons. Explain that you would like each of them to draw the building they imagined then as a group to arrange their individual buildings as if they were all on one or adjoining streets.

When buildings have been drawn and colored, the group may add trees, sidewalks, people, and vehicles to their street. Each group member is to put his/her name on his/her building (George's Grocery, Samantha's Beauty Parlor, etc.).

When the class has finished the activity, have each group select a spokesperson to describe to the rest of the class the picture his/her group has completed.

Cooperative Structure-Building Activities

Paper Clip Structures 177
The Straw Man 178
Peas and Toothpicks Sculpture 179
Designing and Constructing a Building 180
Shelter 181
Bridge Building . . . . 182 - 183
Tinker Toys 184

Conclude each of these activities with debriefing exercises found in the Introduction and/or on page 138.

Paper Clip Structures*

Objectives Students will cooperate in pairs to build a paper clip structure.

Materials Paper clips, pliers (optional)

Procedure Have students work on a structure by joining paper clips together. They may do so by pulling one end out, twisting two ends together, making an eye or circle, opening the paper clip all the way and forming a "W" with a loop in the center.

Have students describe their structure to the class then display the finished product somewhere in the classroom.

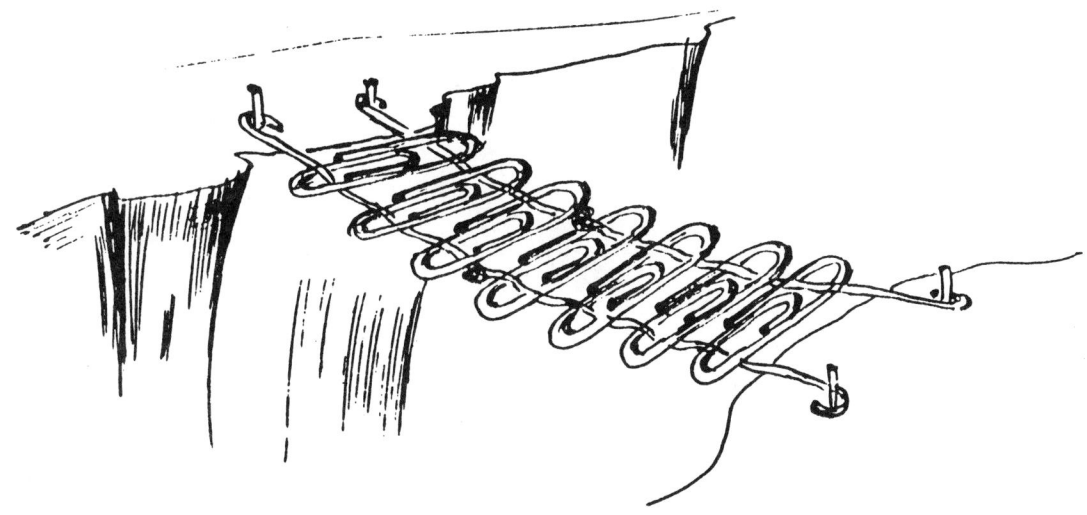

* J. Wilt, and B. Watson, *Relationship Builders*, 1978.

The Straw Man

Objective Students will cooperate in small groups to build a figure out of drinking straws.

Materials Plastic straws, a package of straight pins per group, scissors

Procedure Explain that today the class will be working on an exercise that will help them learn to cooperate with others in a group. Divide the class into groups of four. Group them at individual tables and give each group a bunch of straws, a package of straight pins, and scissors. Give them 10 to 15 minutes to work on the straw man. They are to try to build the most aesthetically appealing, free-standing straw man they can.

At the end of the work period, have the groups place their straw men on a table for display. Ask the various groups how they organized themselves, how the members worked together to help the group, and what they might have done better.

Cooperative Structure-Building Activities Primary/Intermediate Level

Peas and Toothpicks Sculpture*

Objective Students will cooperate in pairs to build a toothpick sculpture.

Materials Dried peas or beans (soaked overnight) or marshmallows, toothpicks

Procedure Have students work on a sculpture together by sticking toothpicks into peas or marshmallows, connecting them to create something either recognizable (a chair, a table, a car, etc.) or abstract.

Display the sculptures when they are finished. Students can also add a small sign explaining anything about the structure they wish.

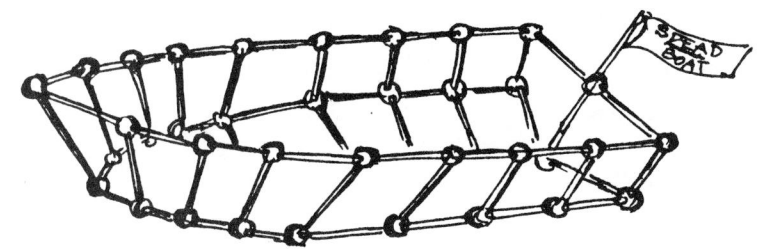

* J. Wilt, and B. Watson, *Relationship Builders*, 1978.

Designing and Constructing a Building

Objective Students will cooperate in small groups to construct a building.

Materials Boxes of common materials, such as scissors, tape, glue, two boxes, egg carton, three styrofoam trays, four paper cups, newspaper, and ice cream sticks

Procedure Divide class into small groups. Give each group a set of materials. They are to build something using all their materials. They will have 30 minutes to plan and construct their design. Before building, they must write or sketch their plans and show them to the teacher.

Each group's construction will be judged according to the following criteria which are announced to the whole class before building begins: height (exact measurement of height), sturdiness, beauty or attractiveness, and how closely the design follows the original plans.

When all groups have completed their projects or the allotted time has run out, students are to vote for the best one, using the above criteria. Students may not vote for their own group.

EXAMPLE
PUBLIC OBSERVATION PLATFORM
TRAY
DECORATED EDGE (PAPER)
SUPPORT (CUP)
BASE SUPPORT (ICE CREAM STICK)

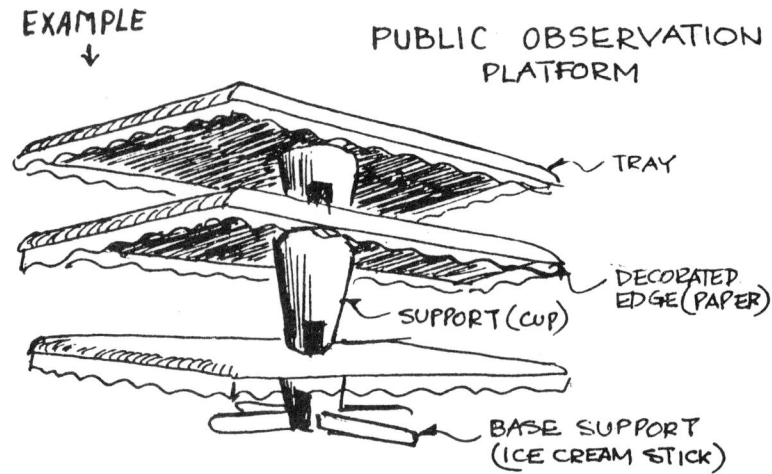

Shelter

Objective Students will cooperate in small groups to plan and build a group-sized shelter.

Materials 5" stack of newspapers and roll of masking tape per group

Procedure Divide the class into groups of four or five. Each group is given a stack of newspapers and a roll of tape.

Instruct students that they are to plan and build a shelter into which they can all fit, using newspapers and tape along with other props that they might need. The total planning and building time for this activity is 30 minutes. You might suggest that they spend no more than 10 minutes planning their shelter and use the remaining 20 minutes for the building of it. Give the students a warning signal to inform them when they have only 5 minutes left.

After you have called time, discuss with students what went right and what went wrong, and why.

Bridge Building

Objective Students will cooperate in small groups to build a bridge.

Materials A 6" to 8" stack of newspapers and a roll of masking tape for each group, a weight such as three bricks bound together, and a cardboard box one foot square.

Procedure Divide the class into groups of five to eight students. Place a stack of newspapers and a roll of masking tape in the center of each group. The bricks and cardboard box should be placed in the center of the room, equidistant from each group.

The groups are to use the newspapers and tape to design and build a bridge which will be strong enough to carry the weight of the three bricks placed on the middle of the span, and high and wide enough for the box to pass under. They have 10 minutes for planning and ten minutes for construction. During the planning period, they may touch the materials, but may not prefabricate any parts or arrange the newspaper into different piles. They may go to the bricks and box at any time to test their weight and size, but the bricks and the box must remain in the center of the room until the end of the building period.

Call out a 2-minute warning before the end of each period. If no bridge has been completed, you may extend the building period for a fixed amount of time, such as five minutes.

At the end of the building period, one member of each group tests that group's bridge by passing the box under the bridge and then resting the bricks on the center of the span.

The activity should be followed by a class discussion focusing on issues such as how much collaboration and how much competition there was among group members, what pleased students most, what procedures could be changed so that students might feel more satisfied, and whether the groups felt that they were competing against each other.

Ask students to think back over their behavior during the planning and construction and to write down two or three changes in their own behavior that they might make if they were to do the activity again. They need not put their names on their papers.

Students will want to discuss the bridge-building and various solutions during the post-building discussion period. This is natural, and there is validity in this kind of discussion. But try gently to redirect the discussion to the group process of planning and building.

Tinker Toys

Objective Students will cooperate in small groups to build a Tinker Toy structure in silence.

Materials Tinker Toys, Leggos or other similar building materials

Procedure Divide the class into groups of six to eight students. Place a box of Tinker Toys in the middle of each group. Instruct the students that they are to plan and build a structure of Tinker Toys which will be judged for height, stability, beauty, and use of materials.

The time limit for the entire activity is 16 minutes. During the planning period the students may talk, but may not touch the materials. During the building period they may touch the materials but not talk with each other or write notes. The planning period must last at least five minutes, but may not be more than 10 minutes. After five minutes the students may begin building at any time, but once they start building, they may no longer talk and may not go back to the planning stage.

Notify the students at the end of 5, 10, and 14 minutes. At the end of the building period, groups may examine each other's work, and then the activity should be discussed, first in the small groups, then with the entire class. Questions for discussion may be similar to those in the "Bridge Building" activity. Additional questions can be, "How should beauty be judged? How well were the group members able to communicate non-verbally during the building period? How was the time to begin building negotiated? How did the finished structure differ from each individual's conception of the structure at the end of the planning period?"

Cooperative Survival Simulation Activities

What Should We Bring? . . . . 187 - 189
Going Camping . . . . 191 - 193
Surviving at Sea . . . . 195 - 197
Stranded in the Desert . . . . 199 - 202
Stranded on an Island 203
Adventure on Rugged Rock Pass . . . . 204 - 207
Surviving in the Mountains . . . . 209 - 213
Rescue Plans . . . . 215 - 219

Conclude each of these activities with debriefing exercises found in the Introduction and/or on page 138.

What Should We Bring?

Objective Students will cooperate in small groups to compile a survival list.

Materials Student handout

Procedure *Divide the class into groups of four or five and say or paraphrase the following:*

> As a field trip, your group has taken a boat ride to see some islands which lie off the Washington coastline. The boat is now by a large island. We know that this island is deserted: there are no people on it. We do not know if there are animals on the island or if there is water on the island. From your boat you can see that there are some trees and greenery on the island. Suddenly the boat scrapes along a large rock which tears a hole in the boat's bottom. The boat will sink in 30 minutes. Fortunately, there is a small lifeboat that you can use to get to the island, but it is not big enough to sail on the open ocean back to the mainland. There is room for all the people in your group and for five things that you can take with you from the larger boat.
>
> I will give you a list of things on the boat. Which five things will your group take? This must be a group decision. You have 10 minutes to decide.

Map and List of Items on the Boat

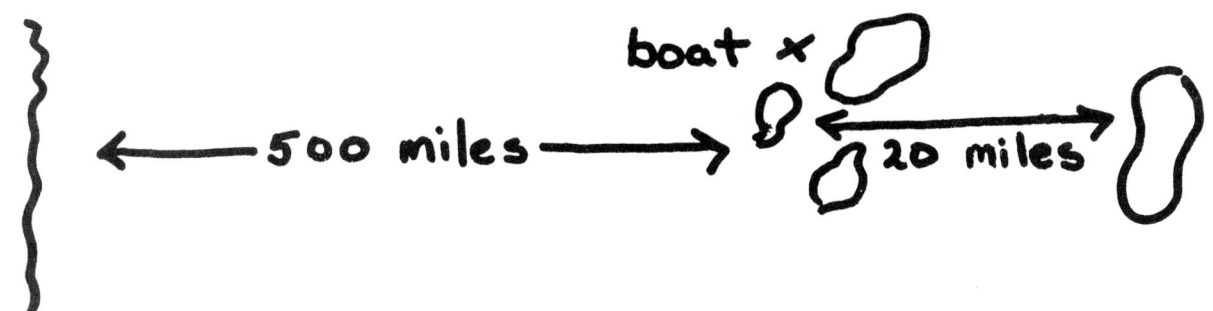

Choose five things that your group wants to take along:

1. Five jugs of water
2. Rifle and 10 boxes of bullets
3. Canvas sail from the boat
4. Fishing rod and tackle
5. One box of kitchen matches
6. 50 feet of old heavy-duty rope
7. 6-volt battery lanterns
8. Ten flare kits
9. Axe
10. Knife
11. First-aid kit
12. Pair of rabbits
13. Sleeping bags
14. One 6-person nylon wall tent

Which five things did your group decide to take?

1. _____

2. _____

3. _____

4. _____

5. _____

Going Camping

Objective Students will cooperate in small groups to solve a problem on a camping trip.

Materials List of items to be taken on the camping trip

Procedure Tell the students to imagine that they are going on a camping trip. The road is blocked and they must walk 10 miles in order to get from the car to the campsite. They are unable to carry all the things they brought along and must leave some in the car. In what order would they leave things in the car? Now divide class into groups, and give them the Student Handout.

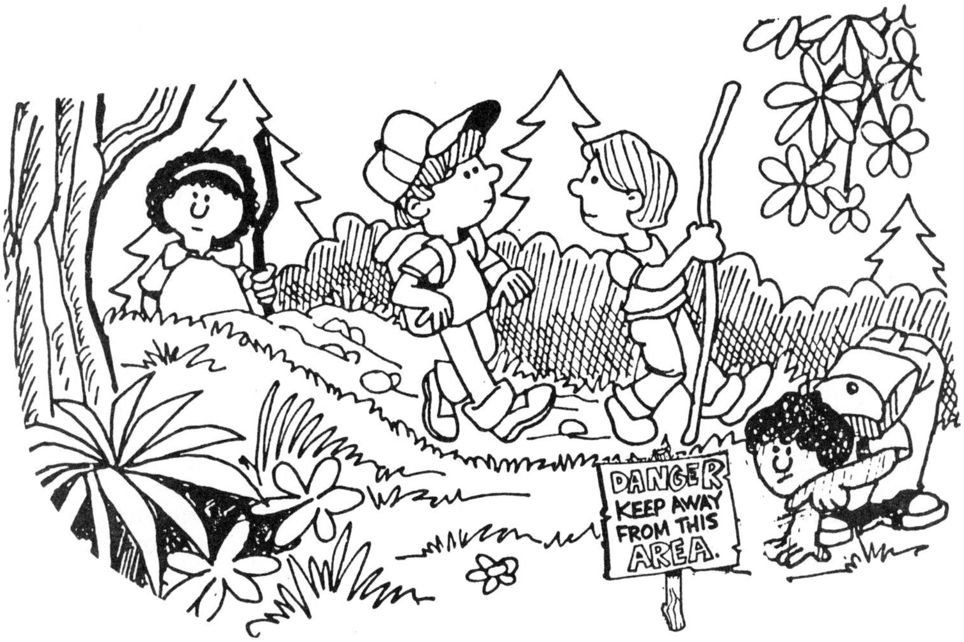
DANGER
KEEP AWAY
FROM THIS
AREA.

Cooperative Survival Simulation Activities   Handout for "Going Camping"
                                                              Page 193

Put #1 by the most important item, #2 by the next most important item, etc.

_____ Water

_____ Tent

_____ Flashlight

_____ Food

_____ Sleeping Bag

_____ Matches

_____ Cooking Pan

_____ Compass

Surviving at Sea

Objective Students will cooperate in small groups to prioritize a list of survival items.

Materials Student handout

Procedure Divide students into small groups and provide them with the handout. Ask each group to come up with a rank ordering of the objects listed. Have them put a #1 by the most nonessential item on a sinking boat, a #2 by the next most nonessential item, and so on.

Surviving at Sea

You are members of a fishing party on a 50-foot fishing boat. You have run into both bad weather and engine trouble more than 150 miles from the nearest shore. The captain of the ship has stated that because of rough seas, the boat weight must be lightened or the boat might sink. Decide, as a group, in what order you would throw things overboard.

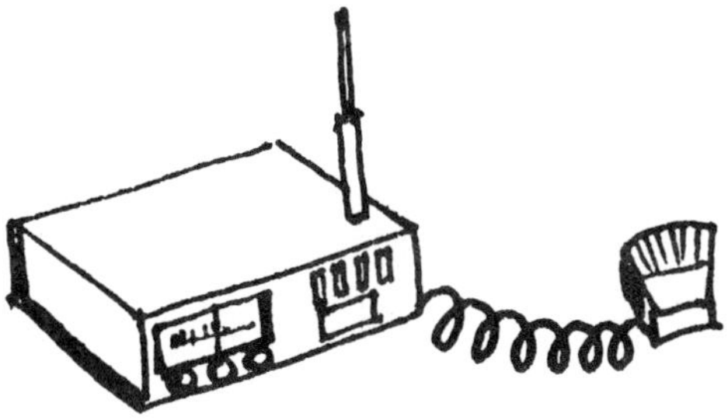

_____ Box of matches

_____ Ship-to-shore radio

_____ Compass

_____ Navigational map

_____ 10 gallon container of water

_____ Signal flares

_____ Life rafts

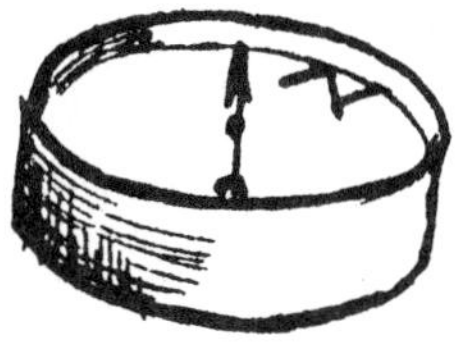

_____ 100 ft. of rope

_____ Flashlight

_____ Life jackets

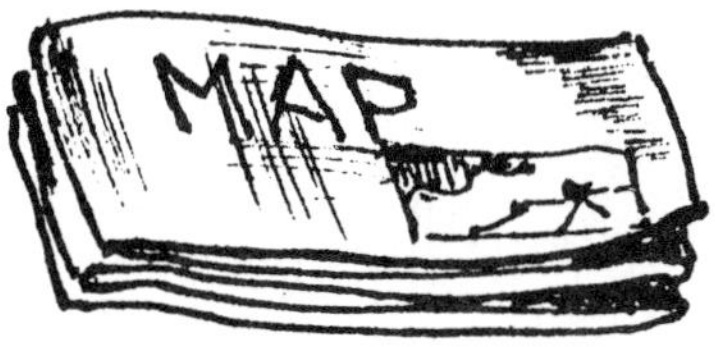
MAP

Stranded in the Desert

Objective Students will cooperate in small groups to solve a problem while role playing different characters in a crisis simulation.

Materials Role playing sheets and item list

Procedure Divide the class into groups of eight or less. Tell them that they are to imagine that they are members of science club that is on a school field trip to study rock formations in the desert. They are driving over old trails, far away from any road, when suddenly the van in which they are riding starts skidding, plunges down a ravine and overturns. The driver and the teacher are killed, but the rest of the club is relatively unhurt. The bus burns.

The nearest ranch is around forty-five miles away and there are no other human beings around that anyone knows about. The school knows generally the destination of the field trip, but it would be difficult to pinpoint the exact destination of the group. The school would surely alert someone to the fact that the expedition did not return when it should have.

The surrounding area is dry and rugged. The weather report early that morning predicted temperatures to reach 110 degrees, making surface temperatures 130 degrees. Everyone is dressed in lightweight clothing, including hats and sunglasses. Before the van caught fire and burned, members of the club were able to salvage the following items: (write these on the board)

Flashlight
A magnetic compass
Animals of the Desert, a book
Rearview mirror
Four canteens, each containing two quarts of water
Large, light-blue canvas
One jacket per person
A Beebee gun
Bottle of 1,000 salt tablets
Map of the area

The group needs to make some decisions -- either to stay where it is or to try to walk out and to hunt for food or not to hunt. The group members will have to rank the salvaged items in the order of their importance. Whatever decisions are made, the group must stay together.

Hand out the role playing sheets to the group members, instructing them not to show or discuss their roles with other group members. Give students a few minutes to read their role sheets, then give the signal for the session to begin. Groups will have up to 30 minutes to make their decisions. Tell students that, while at the beginning of the discussion they should assume their assigned role, they are free to change their minds if someone else has convincing evidence. In the end, everybody in the group must come to the same decision.

Give a warning when there are 5 minutes left in the session. After 30 minutes have elapsed, have the groups share their decisions with each other.

Role 1

You believe that the group should stay at the scene and not hunt for food. You think that nobody should get excited and move around much, since everybody should try to conserve energy. You believe that the mirror is the most important part of the salvaged equipment, since with it you can signal any search planes that will come looking for you. It can also reflect enough light to be shown beyond the horizon. The water you have, while easing the effects of dehydration, will not significantly prolong your lives. There are cacti around, from which you could suck some moisture, but the work of cutting them open and sucking at them will probably take more energy than you would regain from the moisture.

Role 2

Your position is that the expedition should try to hike to the nearest ranch and hunt for food along the way. Forty-five miles doesn't seem to be such a terrible distance to you and the water and salt tablets should be enough to get you through the hike. Additional moisture can be gotten from cacti along the way and with the gun you can hunt animals for food. The water, salt tablets, and gun all seem equally important to you. The only real danger is if you all wait too long to set out on the hike.

Role 3

You feel that the group should set out for the nearest ranch, but not stop along the way for anything like hunting. The water is sufficient for every person and, with a compass and a map, you can't get lost. The canvas can serve as a sun shade during the day and the group should walk at night.

Role 4

Your position is that the group should stay where it is and wait to be rescued. You think the salt tablets are very dangerous, as they require a lot of water to dilute them; otherwise it would be like drinking sea water. You don't think there is enough water to last for a 45-mile hike. You think hunting would be a good idea, both as a source of food and as a diversion, since it may take several days to be rescued. The most important items to you are the mirror and the flashlight, since they can signal search planes. The water is also very important.

Role 5

You believe that the group should stay where it is, not using energy to hunt. The canvas and the jackets are the most important items to you, since the canvass can keep the sun away and the jackets keep the air from getting at your body and dehydrating it. The mirror is important to signal any search party. Because you believe that you will be found eventually, you think your best bet is to stay by the wreckage, since the school manager knows your approximate location.

Role 6

You think the group should walk out but not do any hunting. The meat of any animal you would be lucky enough to kill would require extra water to digest, and there is no water to spare. Hunting would be an unnecessary waste of energy, since a body can go without food for a long time. The compass and map are most important, as they will keep you from getting lost. The water is important too, but the most important thing is to start walking immediately.

Role 7

You believe that the group should stay where it is and wait to be rescued. You think hunting while waiting is a good idea, but that walking to the nearest ranch would be crazy. Nobody in the group has ever walked that far and the shock of the accident decreases the strength you have for such a hike. With the gun and the book you can get food and conserve energy to signal the search parties.

Role 8

The most important thing to do, in your opinion, is to walk out immediately. You have heard of people being stranded in the desert and never found. The map and compass aren't that important, because you can follow the tire marks of the van. The group should not sit around and bake, but set out and hunt along the way for food, chewing cactus for moisture. The jackets are also important, because nights get cold in the desert. The book can help you with hunting.

Items Saved From Van

Flashlight
A magnetic compass
Animals of the Desert, a book
Rearview mirror
Large, light-blue canvas
Four canteens, each containing 2 quarts of water
One jacket per person
A Beebee gun
Bottle of 1,000 salt tablets
Map of the area

Stranded on an Island

Objective Students will cooperate in small groups to decide what items are essential if they become stranded on an island.

Materials None

Procedure Divide students into small groups and have them imagine that they are to be left on a tropical island for a year. They are permitted to take along with them seven items to sustain their lives. What would they take? Have them try and agree on a list and explain their choices to the larger classroom group.

?
TV

?
PAN

?
ENCYCLOPEDIA
A
B
C
D
E
F
G
H
I

?
AXE

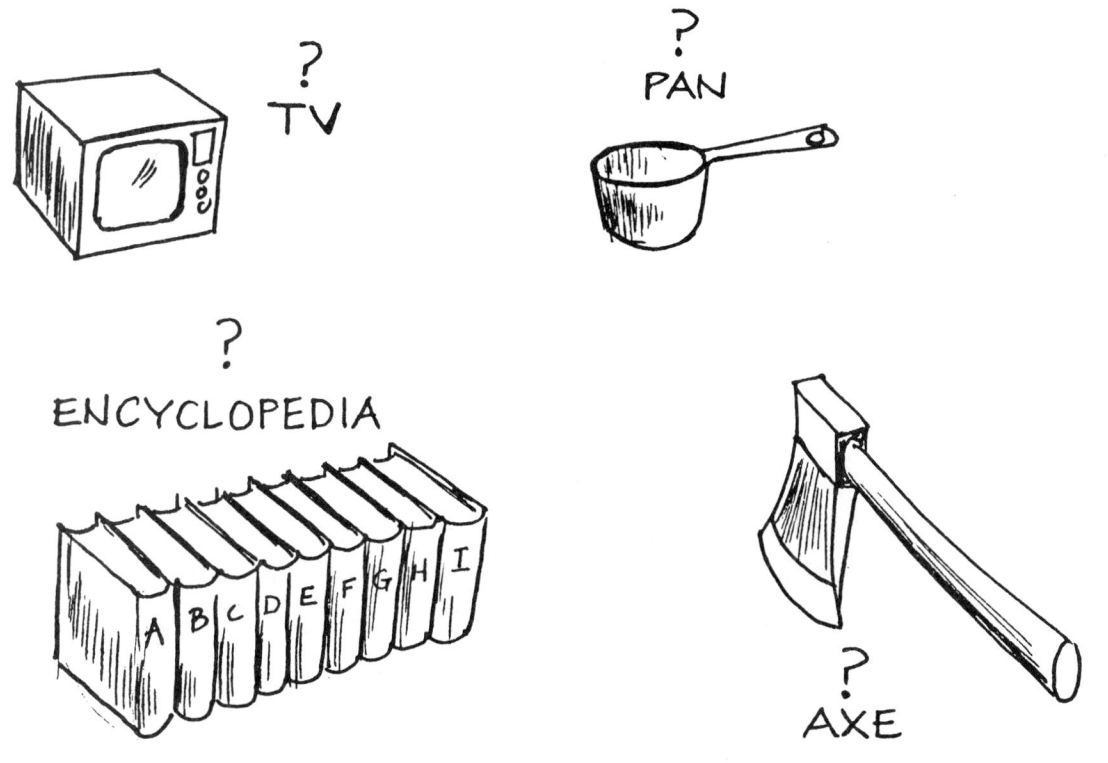

Adventure on Rugged Rock Pass

Objective Students will practice brainstorming as a large group and then reach consensus.

Materials Activity sheet "The Adventure on Rugged Rock Pass"

Procedure *Introduce the lesson by stating that the class is going on an imaginary hiking trip. Instruct students to rest their heads on their desks and close their eyes. Ask them to visualize a hiking trip.*

Read the following story to the students, dramatizing it as much as possible:

We're going on an overnight hike. We will be hiking up an old Indian trail through Rugged Rock Pass. The climb is steep and the path is narrow. This will be a difficult hike and we must plan very carefully what to take in our backpacks.

Raise your heads. We all need to contribute our ideas about what to take. Each person make a suggestion and I will write it on the board. Let's see how many ideas we can come up with.

After recording all responses on the board, continue with the story.

We all have to carry our own supplies. All of the items which have been suggested will not fit into our backpacks. Let's decide which things are most important.

Let's remove all duplicate ideas from the board. Now let's decide which items we will take.

Ask students to place their heads on their desks.

Our backpacks are ready to go. We hop on a bus to take us to the beginning of the trail. We can hardly wait to get started! Now we are on the trail, singing, and happy to be on our adventure. The path gets steeper and winds around a high cliff. Just as we get around the cliff, we hear a loud rumbling noise. We look back and see that a huge boulder has completely blocked the narrow path behind us! There is no turning back. Slowly we move along the path and find, to our horror, a deep gorge that can be crossed only by a narrow, rickety, old swinging bridge. What should we do now?

The bridge will not hold our weight plus the full weight of our packs. We still have a long way to go and we will not reach our destination until some time tomorrow. We must decide on five essential items for our packs. We have to leave the rest behind.

This is an important decision! What shall we take? What will we need the most?

Through class discussion, eliminate the items that students think they could do without for the rest of the trip. Come to a consensus of five essential items, then continue the story.

Now, to cross the bridge! Our hearts are pounding with fear. Will we all make it?

The wind blows. The bridge sways. It creaks and cracks with our weight. It seems to take forever for all of us to cross. As the last person steps onto solid ground, we cheer and jump for joy.

We know that when we get back to school, no one will believe what we have been through. Now complete your activity sheets.

The Adventure on Rugged Rock Pass

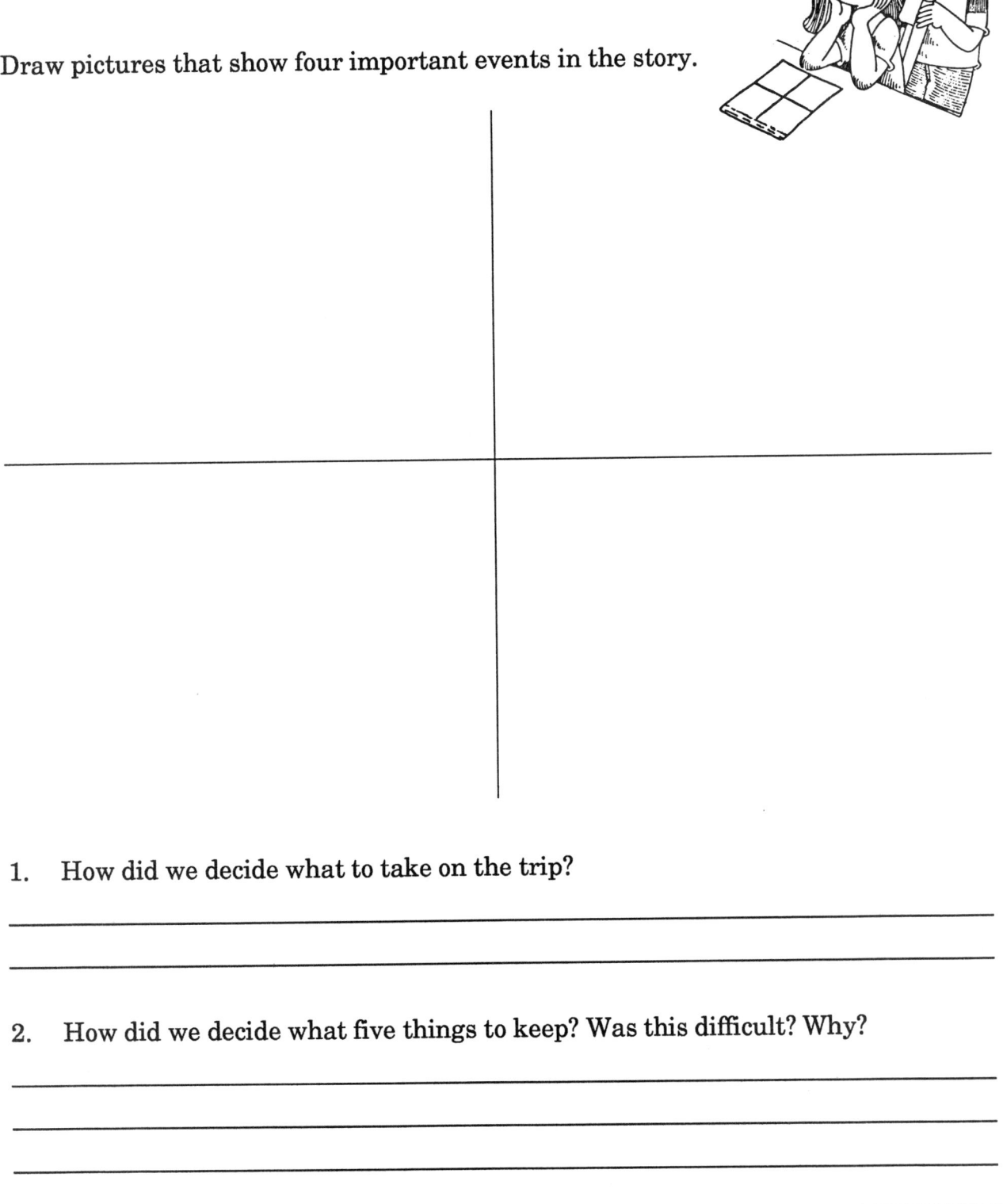

Draw pictures that show four important events in the story.

1. How did we decide what to take on the trip?
___
___

2. How did we decide what five things to keep? Was this difficult? Why?
___
___
___
___

Surviving in the Mountains

Objective   Students will learn that working as a group often produces a higher rate of accuracy than working individually.

Materials   Two copies for each student of worksheet provided at the end of this activity

Procedure   Read to the students the following account of an ill-fated weekend outing:

A friend stops by your house on a weekend morning in the fall. He suggests that you come along on a day-long drive in the mountains because he wants to try out his new Jeep. You think that this would be fun and put on some jeans, a sweatshirt, and tennis shoes. Later that afternoon you are on a narrow trail in a remote part of the mountains. A snowstorm starts up and soon the going gets harder and harder. You can hardly see because of the snow. The Jeep starts sliding and plunges down a steep ravine. You are thrown out of the car. Stunned, you pick yourself up and make your way to the overturned jeep. You find that your friend has been killed, while you have suffered only a few scratches. You guess that you must be 30 or 40 miles from civilization.

Remembering that you saw a cabin off the trail earlier, you slowly make your way to it. When you find it, you are relieved to see that it has a woodburning fireplace and is well-stocked with about a week's supply of food. It has no telephone and you realize that, since it is obviously a summer cabin, no one will be coming to it for several months and you cannot hope to be rescued. Nobody knows where to start looking for you. When the snow stops, you decide to try to make it back to a town. You know that it will probably take you about 3 days to get there. This means that you must pack your supply of food and gear carefully.

Give students a list of some of the items available in the cabin, and their weight. Have them decide individually what they must take, being careful not to exceed 40 pounds total weight. You may want to assign the sheet for homework. Instruct students not to consult each other or discuss the assignment with one another.

To score the individual answer sheets, mark off each item that is marked incorrectly as well as those left blank when they should have been marked. Total these points to get the individual's overall score. The lower the score, the more accurate the students' answers. Explain that while many items are debatable, the items thought to be most crucial have been selected.

After they turn it in, hand out the second copy of the survival items. Ask them to form groups, or assign groups to work with each other. Appoint a recorder. This time they are to come to an agreement (consensus) with their group members as to which items to take along. Make sure they understand that they are not to change their minds if they are not convinced, just to avoid conflict. They should try to understand the suggestions of other members, but not come to a decision by majority rule. They should try to get everyone in the group to completely agree on the choices. After the groups have come as close to consensus as possible, ask the recorder to mark the one copy of the sheet with the group's answers.

Hand the individual work sheets back to the students. Ask, through a show of hands, which students arrived at their answers through consensus. Ask students to compare working individually to working in groups.

Cooperative Survival Simulation Activities

Handout for "... Mountains"

A.	_____	wool hat (1/2 lb.)
B.	_____	saucepan to melt snow for drinking water (1/2 lb.)
C.	_____	50 feet of 1/8" rope (2 lbs.)
D.	_____	heavy wool mittens (1/2 lb.)
E.	_____	axe (8 lbs.)
F.	_____	pack frame and bag (6 lbs.)
G.	_____	heavy wool jacket with hood (3 lb.)
H.	_____	fire-starting kit with matches (1/2 lb.)
I.	_____	gasoline camp stove and fuel (10 lbs.)
J.	_____	plastic canteen filled with water (2 **lbs.**)
K.	_____	150 feet of 7/16" rope (8 lbs.)
L.	_____	large can of beef stew (5 lbs.)
M.	_____	rock-climbing gear, including rock hammer, pitons, etc. (10 lbs.)
N.	_____	folding camp saw (1 lb.)
O.	_____	five two-pound cans of soup and vegetables (10 lbs.)
P.	_____	boxes of high protein dry cereal (2 lbs. total)
Q.	_____	plastic tarp (2 lbs.)
R.	_____	air mattress (1 lb.)
S.	_____	canvas tent (10 lbs.)
T.	_____	high-top hunting boots (6 lbs.)
U.	_____	snow shoes (5 lbs.)
V.	_____	down-filled jacket without hood (1 lb.)
W.	_____	knife with can opener (1/2 lb.)
X.	_____	downhill skis, bindings, poles (10 lbs.)
Y.	_____	sleeping bag (5 lbs.)
Z.	_____	first aid kit with splints & other equipment for setting bones (4 lbs.)
AA.	_____	heavy wool pants (1 lb.)
BB.	_____	first aid kit without splints, etc. (1 lb.)

Answers for Surviving in the Mountains

A. 1/2 lb.

B. 1 lb.

C. 2 lb.

D. 1/2 lb.

F. 6 lbs.

H. 1/2 lb.

J. 2 lbs.

N. 1 lb.

P. 2 lbs.

Q. 2 lbs.

R. 1 lbs.

T. 6 lbs.

U. 5 lbs.

V. 1 lbs.

W. 1/2 lb.

AA. 1 lbs.

BB. 1 lb.

Rescue Plans

Objective Students will cooperate as small groups to devise a rescue strategy for various hypothetical situations.

Materials Situation cards, resource cards

Procedure Divide the class into groups of six to eight students each. Place the packs of situation cards and resource cards on a table. Each group sends a member to the table. The person draws one situation card and six resource cards. The person returns to his group. The teacher signals all groups to begin a 10-minute period when they must think up a rescue plan for a group placed in that situation with only those resources available. After the time limit, ask each group to tell what their situation was, what their resources were, and to share their plan.

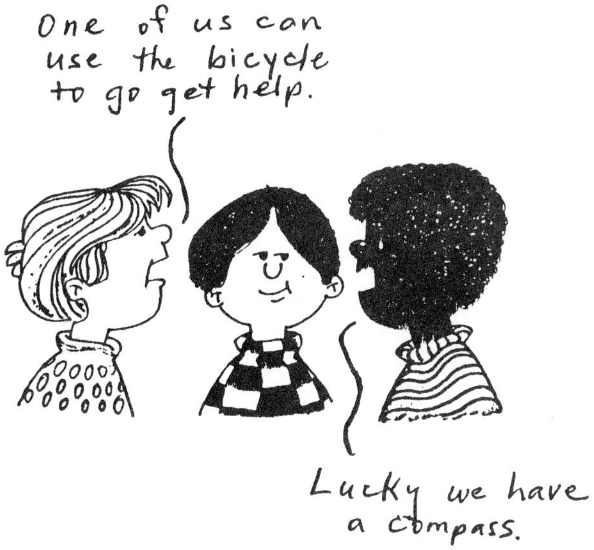
One of us can use the bicycle to go get help.
Lucky we have a compass.

Rescue Resource Cards

Compass	Pocket knife
Aluminum foil	Magazine
Four quarters	Marking pens
Fishing line	Kitchen matches
Transistor radio	Candles
Bicycle	Bottle of Coke
Rubber bands	Basketball

Rescue Situation Cards

Your car runs out of gas in the desert.	Your group is caught in a snowstorm while hiking in the mountains.
Your group is accidentally locked in the city zoo after hours.	During a power failure, your group is caught in an elevator between floors.
Your van breaks down in a small village in South America.	Your boat washes ashore on a small deserted island.
Your group becomes separated from the main group while on a safari in Africa.	Your group is accidentally locked in an abandoned warehouse.

Cooperative Puzzle-Solving Activities

The Great Puzzle Payoff . . . . 223 - 239
Four Corner Puzzle 241
Solving Puzzles Cooperatively . . . . 242 - 251
Group Cooperation Puzzle . . . . 253 - 255
The String Puzzle 257

Conclude each of these activities with debriefing exercises found in the Introduction and/or on page 183.

The Great Puzzle Payoff

Objective Students will cooperate in small groups to assemble a puzzle.

Materials Seven puzzle packages (7 manila envelopes, 70 small envelopes, 7 copies of each puzzle), play money, pieces of cardboard 8-1/2" x 11"

Procedure Before class, the teacher needs to prepare the puzzle packages, duplicate the play money, and cut it apart ($8,000 in $50's and $100's). One large manila envelope should contain 10 cut-up nursery rhymes (each in a small envelope) and one piece of cardboard.

Divide the class into groups of four students. Explain that the groups will work cooperatively to solve Nursery Rhyme puzzles. Each group will compete for play money and the group with the most money will be the winner.

Give each group a puzzle package. On a given signal, each group will select an envelope from the package. Ask them to arrange the puzzle pieces on the piece of cardboard, so that the pieces correctly show the nursery rhyme. When it is completed, one student from each group takes the puzzle to the teacher. The group then receives $100. The puzzle pieces are returned to the envelope and a new envelope is selected. Repeat the activity until the time expires. Each group works at its own pace.

Ask each group to tally the total amount of dollars they have earned. The group with the largest amount wins the game. Discuss with the class the following questions: "How did your group solve the puzzles quickly? What did you learn about working in a small group?"

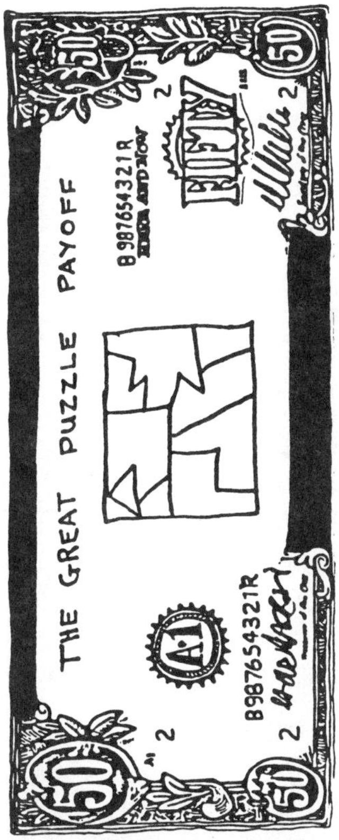
THE GREAT PUZZLE PAYOFF
FIFTY
B987654321R
50

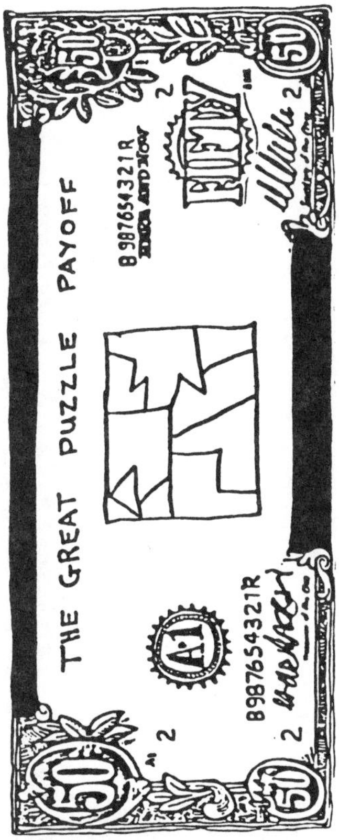
THE GREAT PUZZLE PAYOFF
FIFTY
B987654321R
50

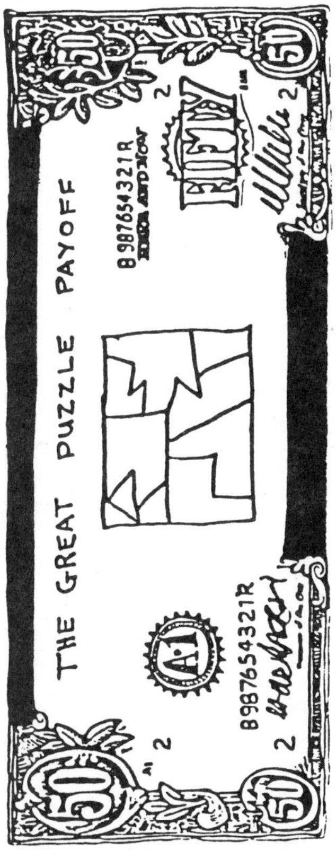
THE GREAT PUZZLE PAYOFF
FIFTY
B987654321R
50

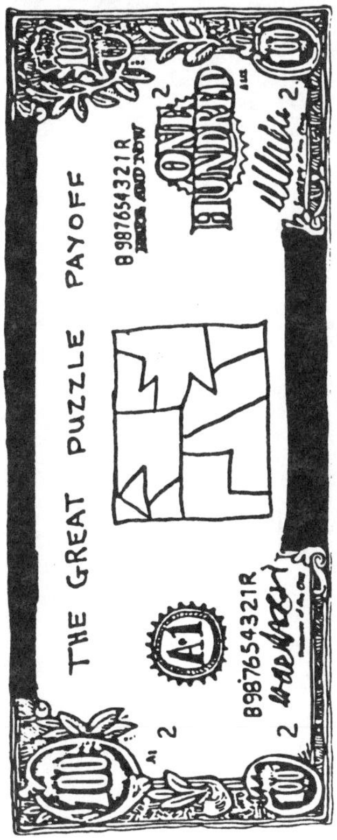
THE GREAT PUZZLE PAYOFF
ONE HUNDRED
B987654321R
100

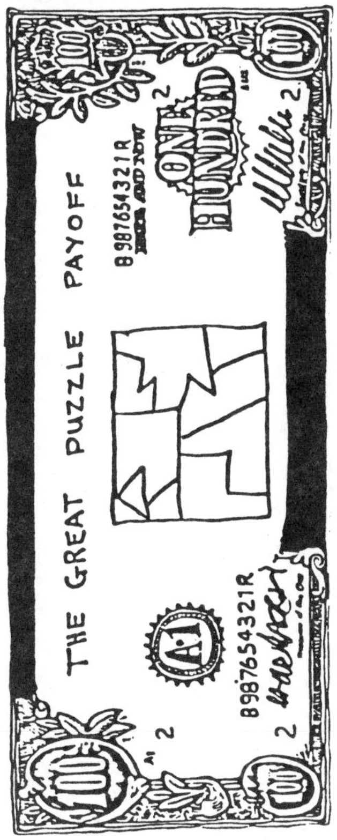
THE GREAT PUZZLE PAYOFF
ONE HUNDRED
B987654321R
100

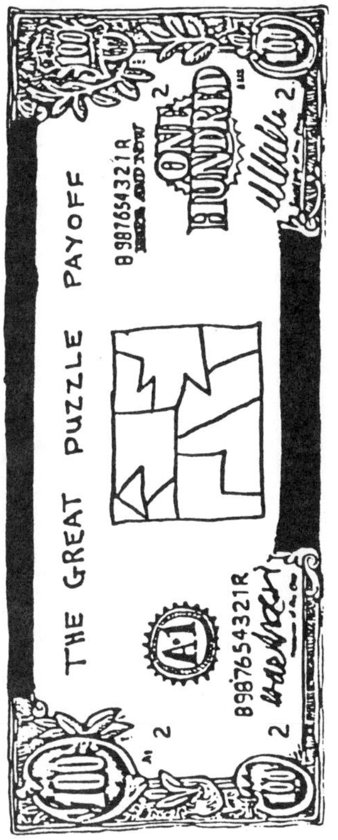
THE GREAT PUZZLE PAYOFF
ONE HUNDRED
B987654321R
100

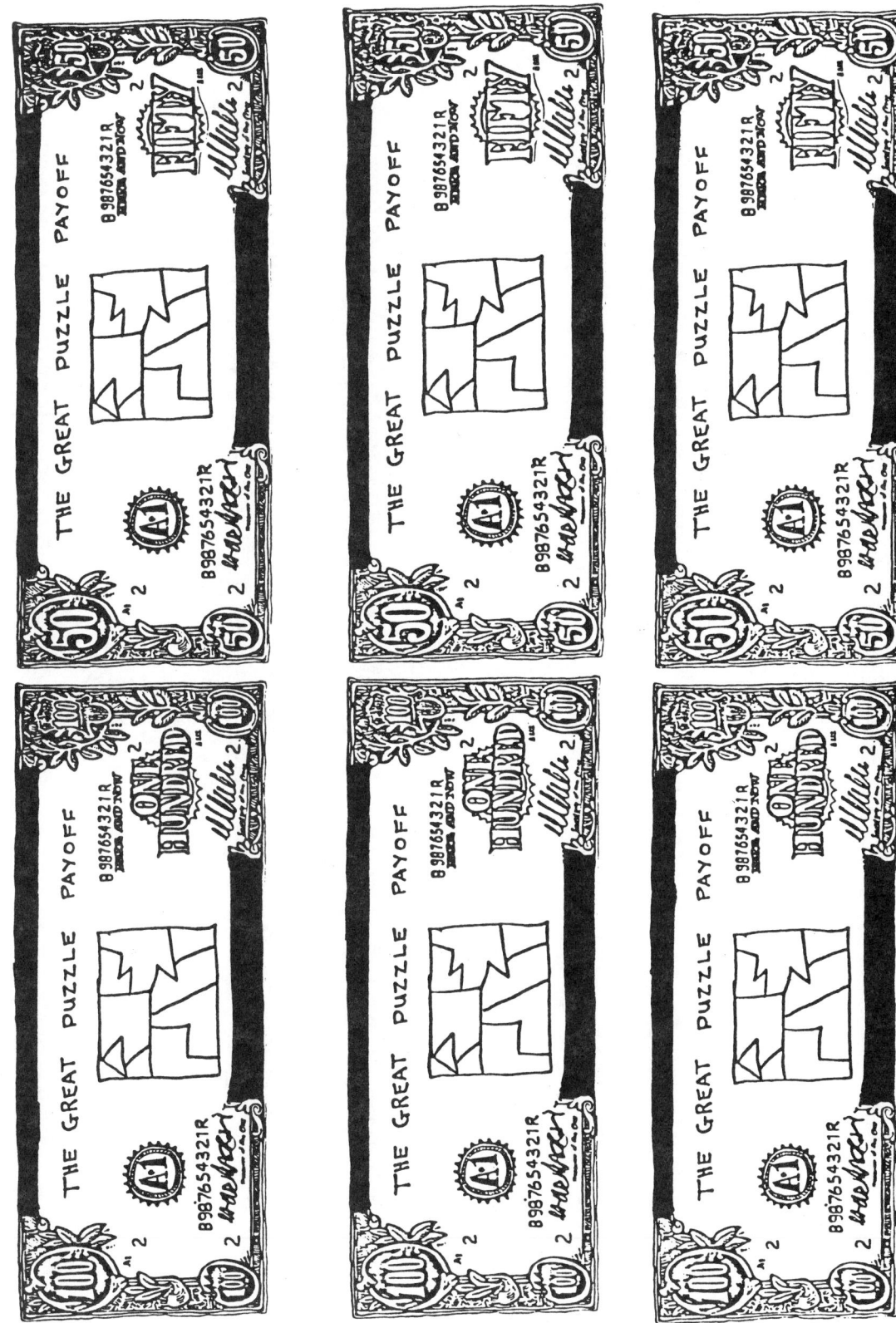

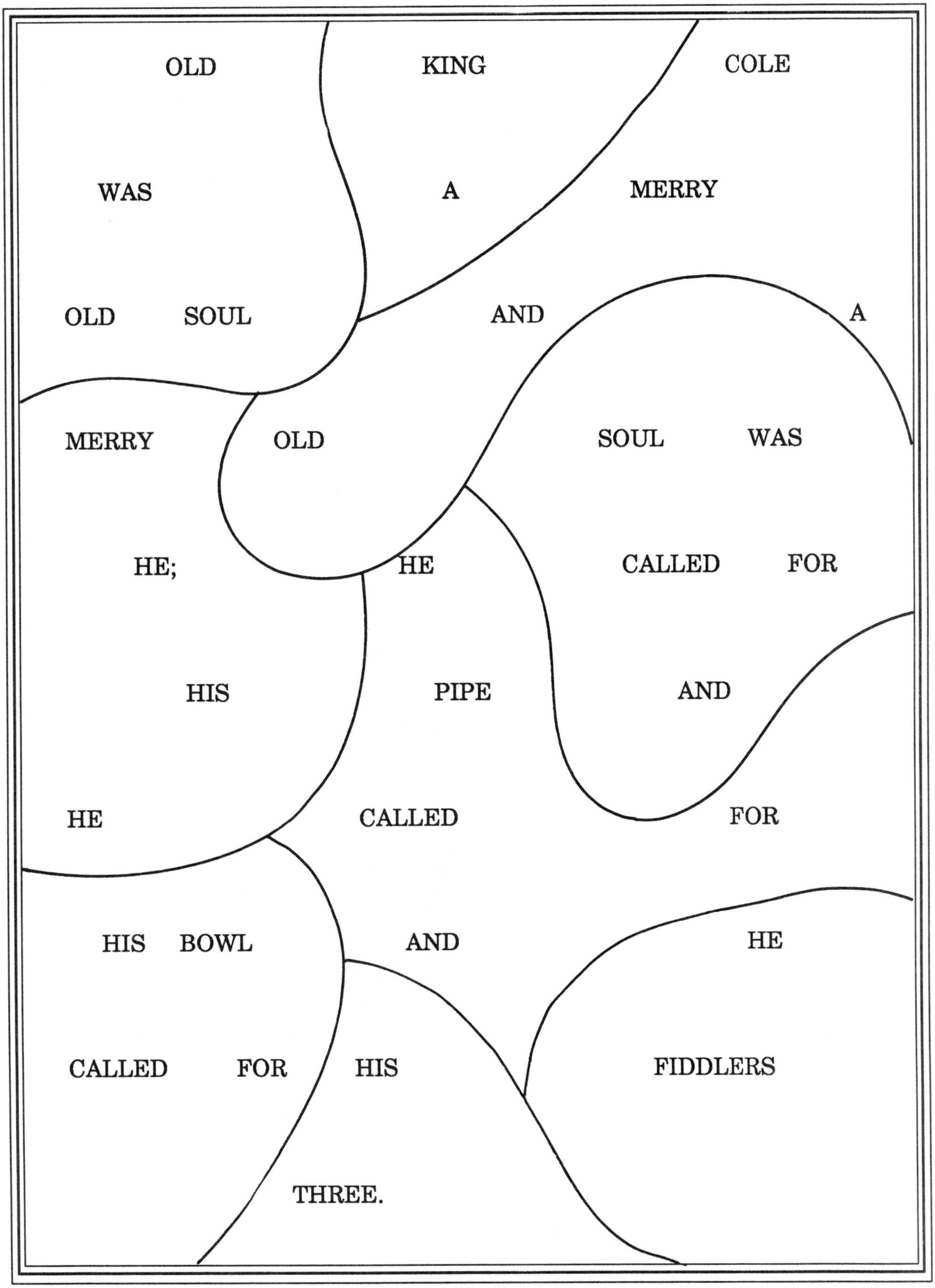
OLD KING COLE
WAS A MERRY
OLD SOUL AND A
MERRY OLD SOUL WAS
HE; HE CALLED FOR
HIS PIPE AND
HE CALLED FOR
HIS BOWL AND HE
CALLED FOR HIS FIDDLERS
THREE.

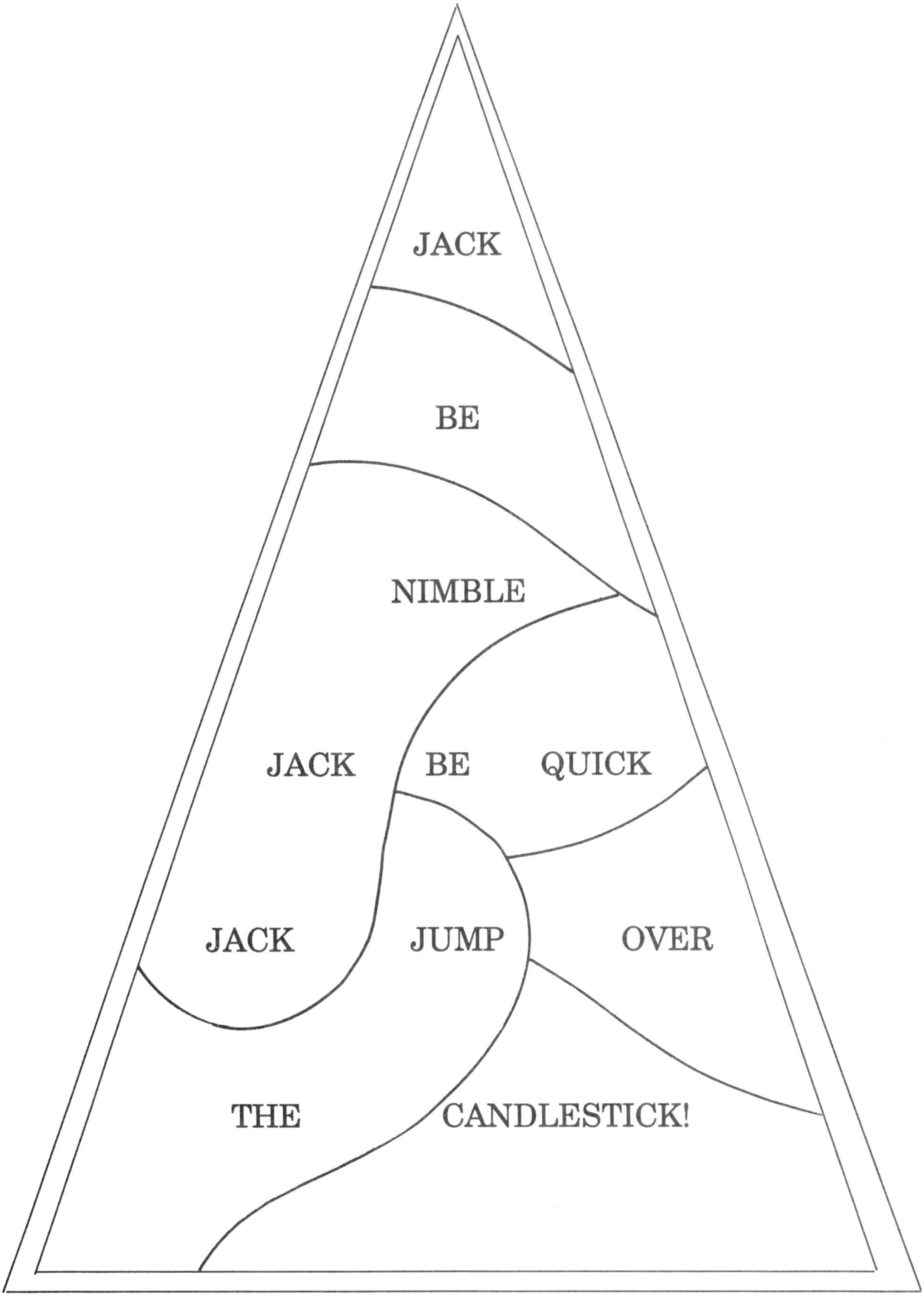
JACK
BE
NIMBLE
JACK
BE
QUICK
JACK
JUMP
OVER
THE
CANDLESTICK!

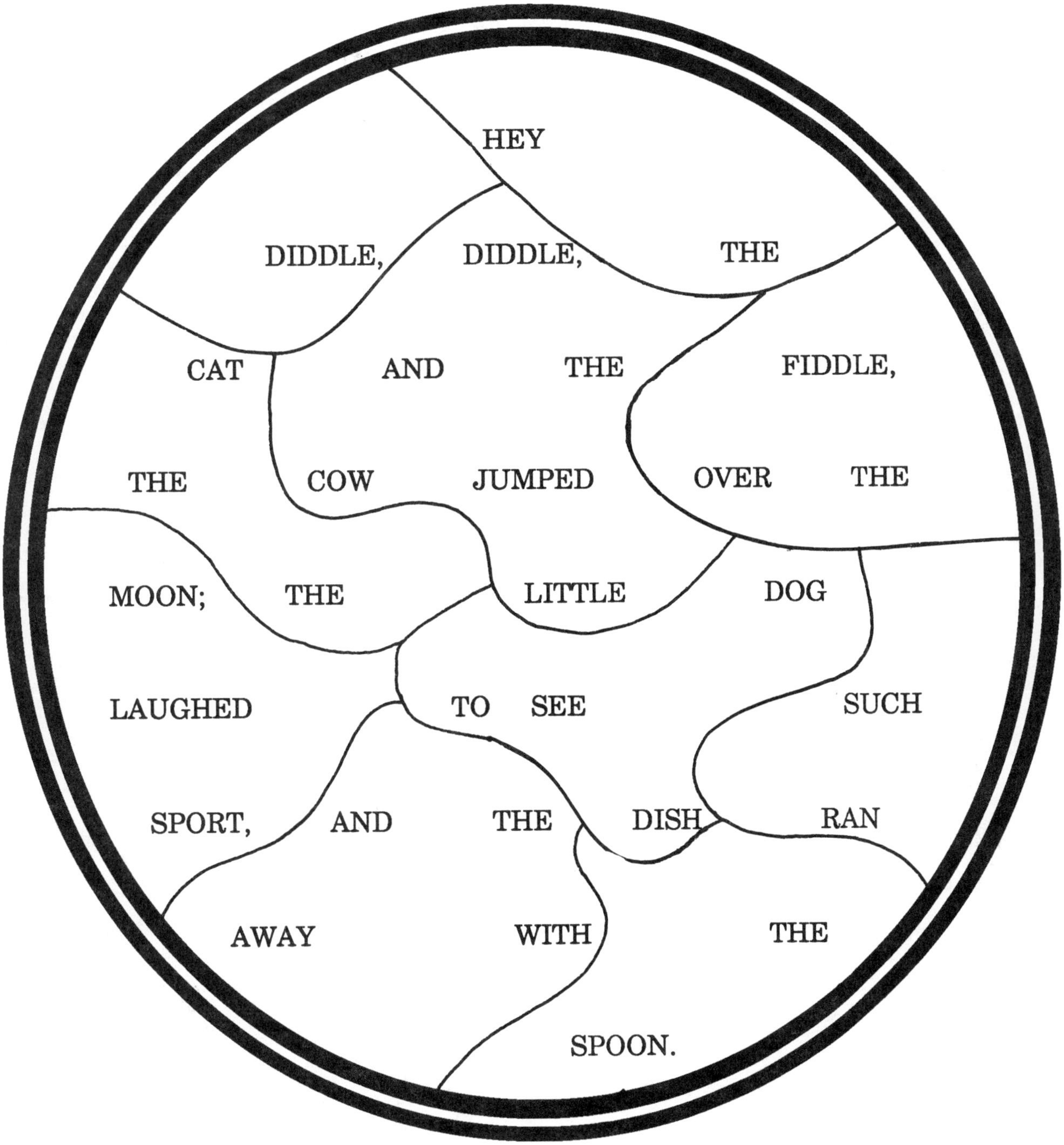
HEY
DIDDLE,
DIDDLE,
THE
CAT
AND
THE
FIDDLE,
THE
COW
JUMPED
OVER
THE
MOON;
THE
LITTLE
DOG
LAUGHED
TO
SEE
SUCH
SPORT,
AND
THE
DISH
RAN
AWAY
WITH
THE
SPOON.

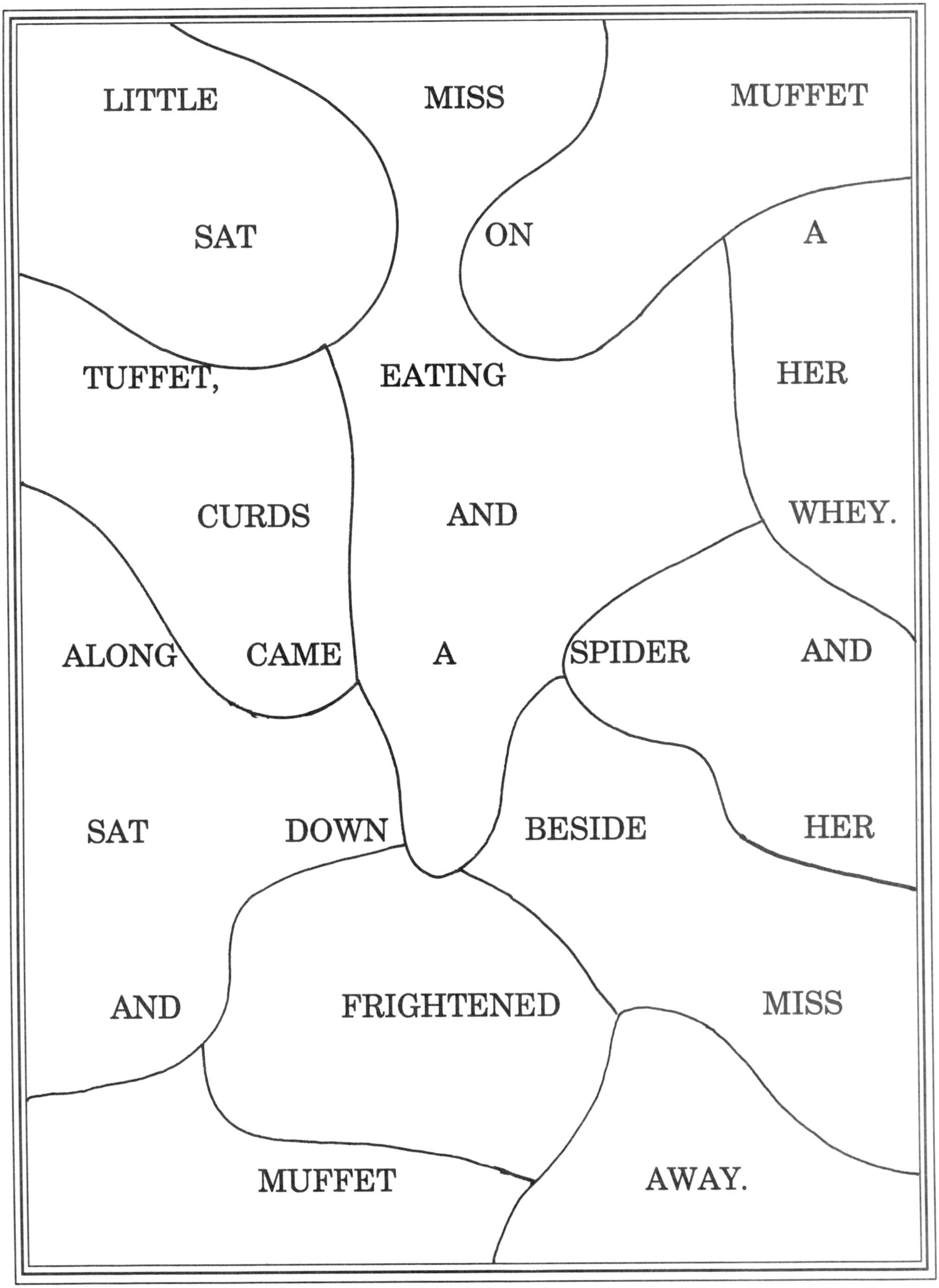
LITTLE
MISS
MUFFET
SAT
ON
A
TUFFET,
EATING
HER
CURDS
AND
WHEY.
ALONG
CAME
A
SPIDER
AND
SAT
DOWN
BESIDE
HER
AND
FRIGHTENED
MISS
MUFFET
AWAY.

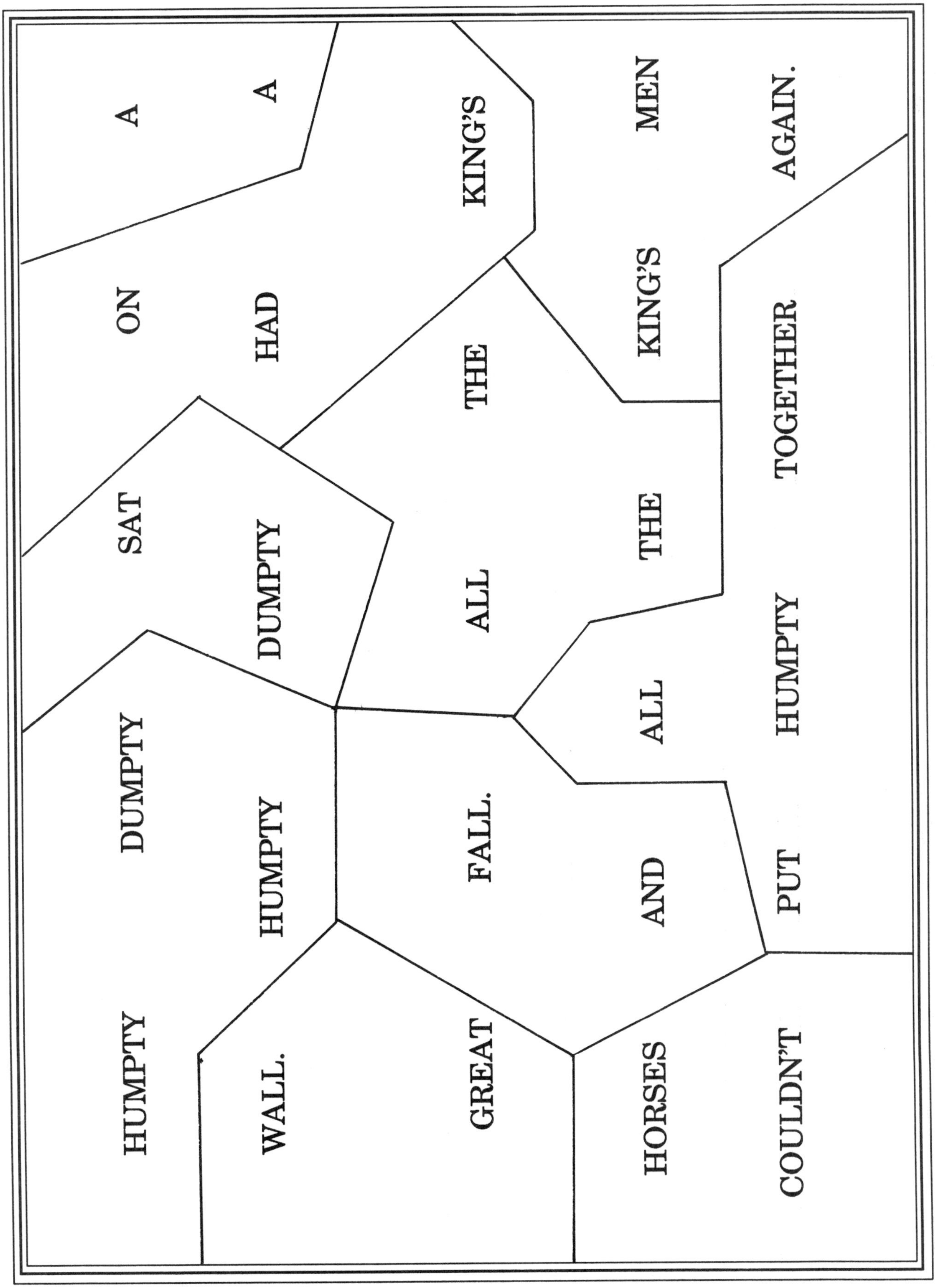
HUMPTY DUMPTY SAT ON A
WALL. HUMPTY DUMPTY HAD A
GREAT FALL. ALL THE KING'S
HORSES AND ALL THE KING'S MEN
COULDN'T PUT HUMPTY TOGETHER AGAIN.

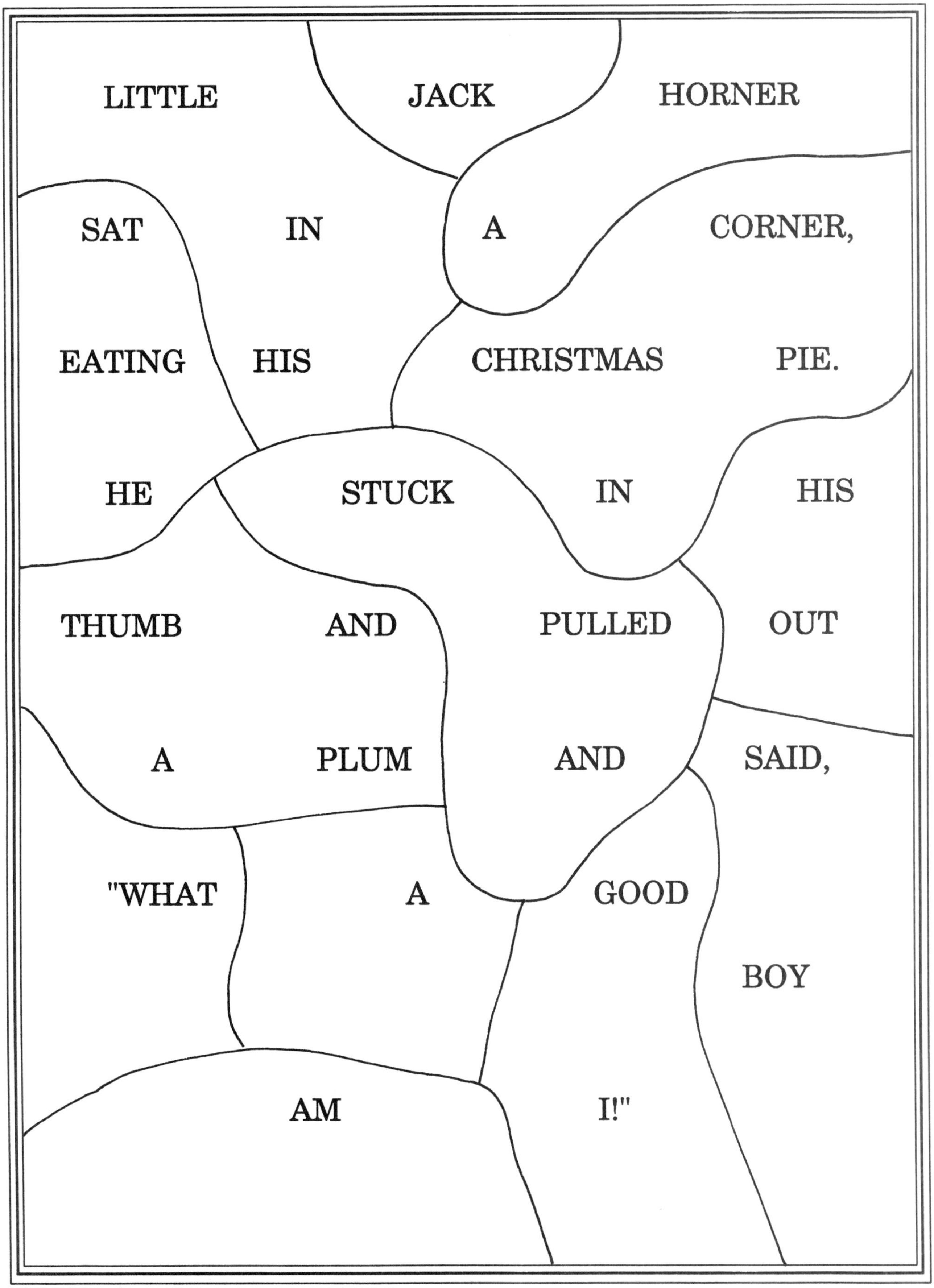
LITTLE
JACK
HORNER
SAT
IN
A
CORNER,
EATING
HIS
CHRISTMAS
PIE.
HE
STUCK
IN
HIS
THUMB
AND
PULLED
OUT
A
PLUM
AND
SAID,
"WHAT
A
GOOD
BOY
AM
I!"

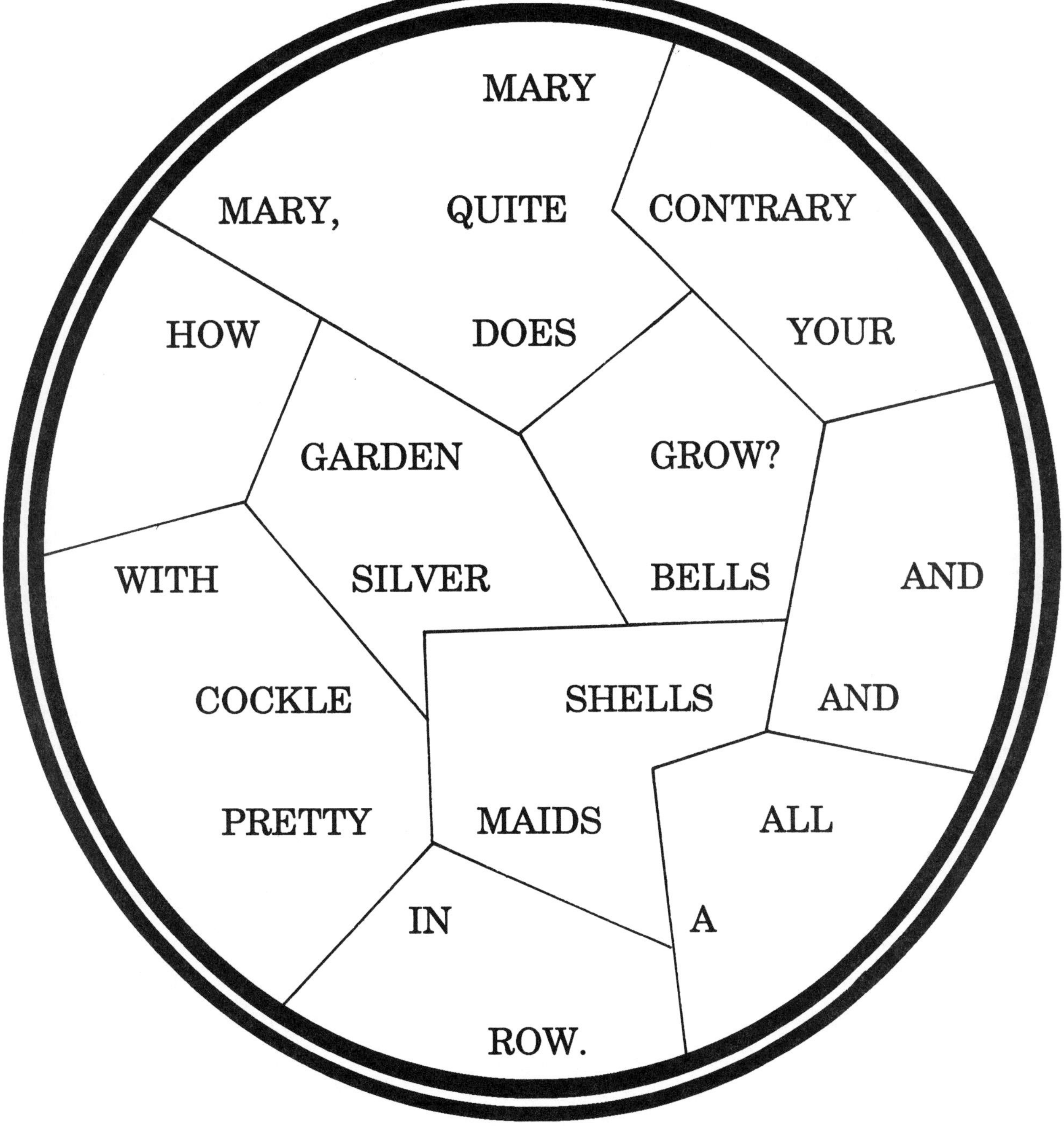
MARY
MARY,
QUITE
CONTRARY
HOW
DOES
YOUR
GARDEN
GROW?
WITH
SILVER
BELLS
AND
COCKLE
SHELLS
AND
PRETTY
MAIDS
ALL
IN
A
ROW.

Four Corner Puzzle

Objective Students will cooperate in small groups to complete a puzzle.

Strategy Cooperation puzzle-solving activity

Materials Four simple commercial jigsaw puzzles with pieces marked on the back for identification (a's, b's, etc.), mixed and divided into four boxes

Procedure Divide class into four groups, sending each group to a corner of the room. Each group receives a box with some of the pieces of each of the four puzzles so that all pieces are distributed. The teacher announces only that the task is to complete the puzzles. (The teacher should refuse to elaborate or answer questions about this.) In order to complete the task, players from each group may meet in the "giving" area (a space designated in the middle of the room). No player may carry more than one piece of a puzzle from a member of any other group. When a piece is offered, it may be taken or rejected. Pieces may only be given. The task ends when the puzzles are finished.

During this activity, you may have to remind students several times to offer pieces to one another. Also, they cannot take a puzzle piece unless it is offered to them.

Refrain from saying anything about competition or cooperation during the task. This is a good subject for the post-task discussion. Below are other topics for discussion:

- Who felt that they were in competition to be the first to be finished?
- Was there a winner and/or loser?
- Could it be said that the last to be finished was the real winner?
- What strategies were developed for completing the task?

Solving Puzzles Cooperatively

Objective   Students will cooperate in small groups to solve a puzzle.

Materials   Puzzles made from tagboard or construction paper, puzzle patterns, envelopes

Procedure   Make copies of the puzzles following this activity on tagboard or construction paper. You will need a set of five puzzles for each group of five students. Cut each puzzle into quarters, so that each puzzle piece will be a square. Place all 20 puzzle pieces into an envelope for each group. Divide the class into groups of five and give each group an envelope of puzzle pieces.

Read to the students the following rules for putting the puzzles together:

1. **The task of your group is to make five puzzles from the pieces of paper in the envelope given to you.**
2. **Each of you must take four pieces from the envelope without looking into it.**
3. **Once you have begun to construct your puzzle, you'll probably find out that you don't have all the pieces you need. You will probably have some of the pieces that belong to other people.**
4. **You can give only one of your pieces away at a time. You cannot take a piece of someone else's puzzle or ask them in any way (verbally or nonverbally) for a piece of their puzzle.**

Explain to students that this exercise is meant to show them the importance of cooperation and sharing. When all groups are finished with their puzzles, ask students about the methods they used to solve their puzzles. Reinforce students for any positive behaviors you observed that were examples of cooperation.

Tree

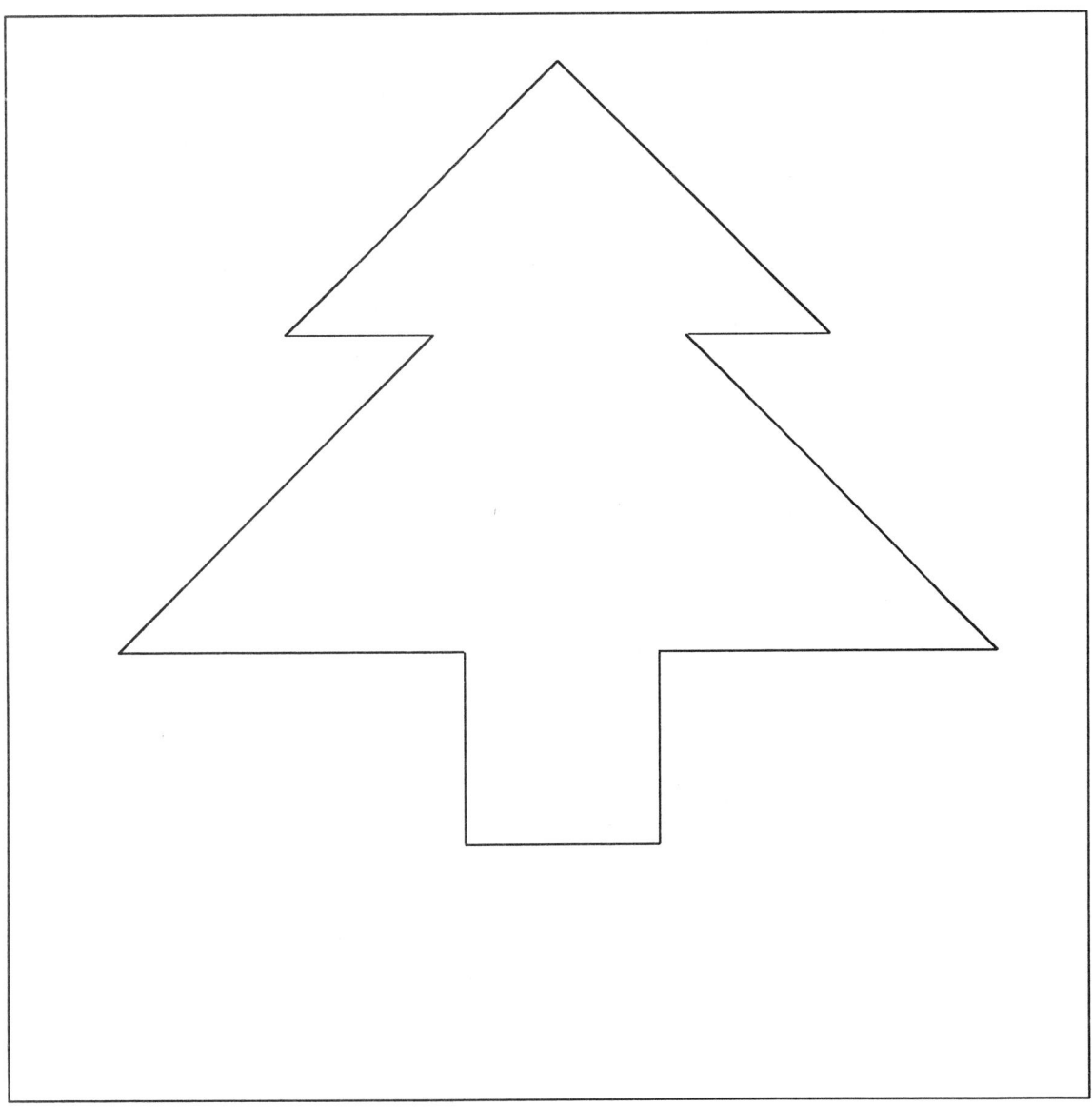

Person

Chair

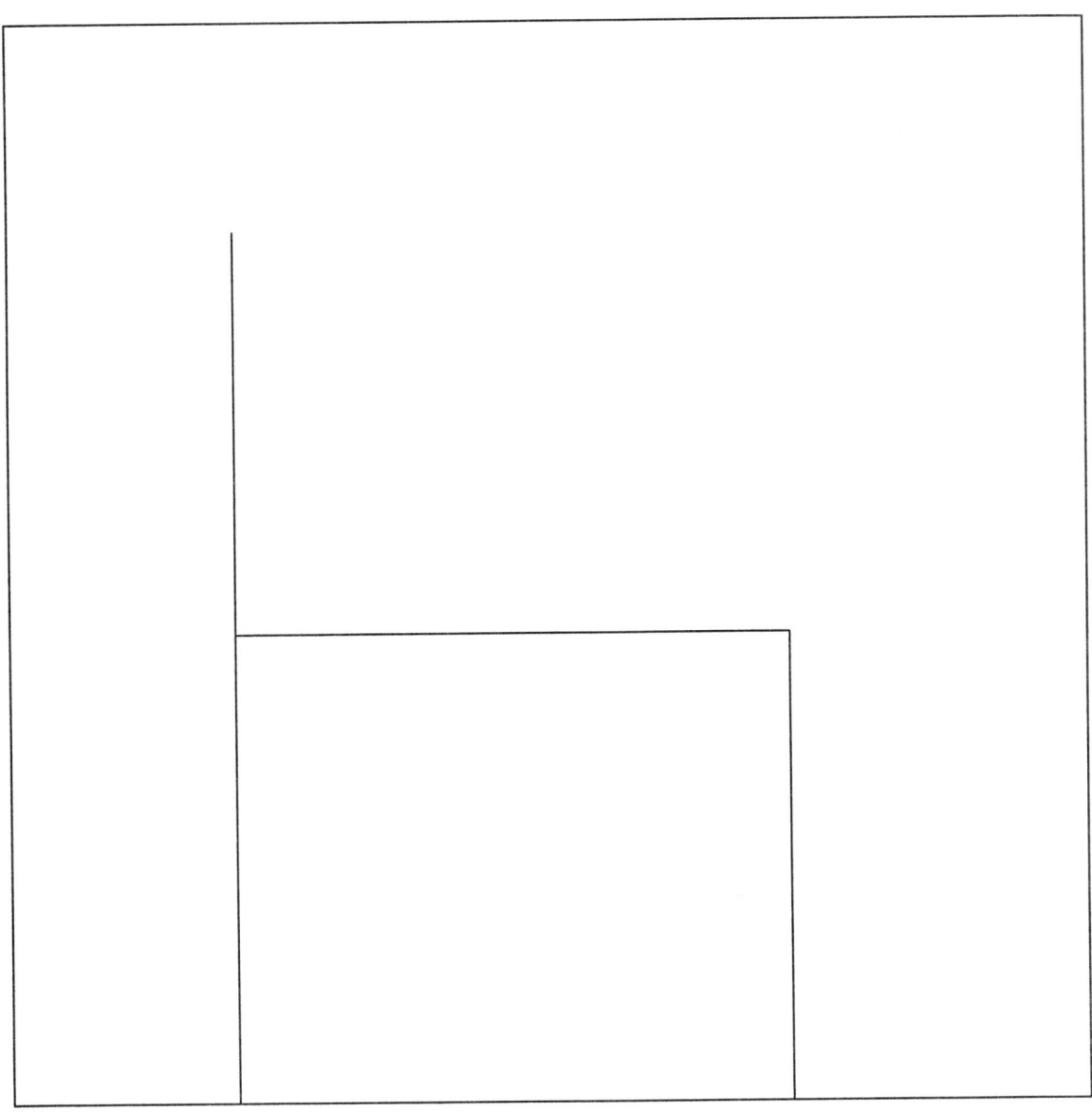

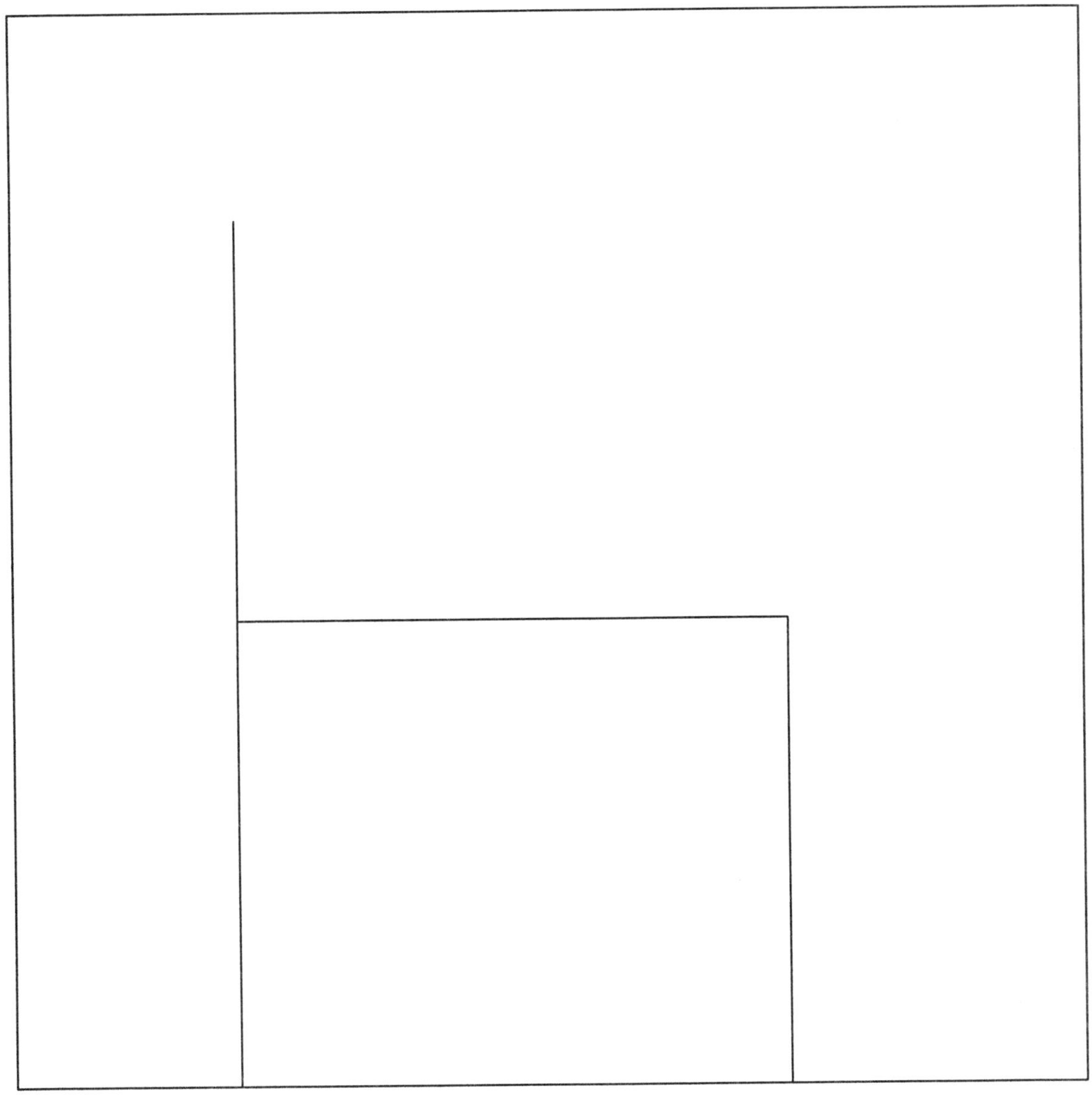

Inverted Y

Z

Group Cooperation Puzzle

Objective Students will cooperate in small groups to solve a puzzle.

Materials Tagboard or construction paper, envelopes, puzzle pattern

Procedure Before class, prepare a set of squares and an instruction sheet for each five students. A set consists of five envelopes containing pieces of stiff paper cut into patterns that will form five 6" x 6" squares, as shown on the puzzle pattern. Several individual combinations will be possible, but only one total combination. Cut each square into the parts "a" through "j" and lightly pencil in the letters. Then mark the envelopes "A" through "E" and distribute the pieces thus: Envelope A, pieces i, h, e; B, pieces a, a, a, c; C, pieces a, j; D, pieces d, f; and E, pieces g, b, f, c.

Erase the small letters from the pieces and write instead the envelope letters "A" through "E," so that the pieces can be easily returned for reuse.

Divide the class into groups of five and seat each group at a table equipped with a set of five envelopes and an instruction sheet. Ask that the envelopes be opened only on a signal from you.

The object of this activity is for each group to put together their puzzles by forming five squares of equal size. The task is not completed until everyone in the group has a perfect square and all the squares are the same size.

The following rules should be followed during the activity.

1. No talking
2. No eye signals
3. No hand signals

4. They must each construct one square directly in front of them.
5. They may not take a puzzle piece away from someone.

Tell students to open their envelopes and begin putting the puzzles together. Remind them that the key to the game is cooperation. When all or most of the groups have finished, call time. Questions for discussion might be,

1. Did people in your group seem to help each other?
2. Did you notice any people in your group not helping?
3. How did others in your group react when someone finished his square?
4. Did you notice anything else about the way people in your group acted during this activity?
5. What were your feelings if you finished your square and then began to realize that you would have to break it up and give away a piece?
6. How did you feel about the person who was slow at seeing the solution? If you were that person, how did you feel?
7. Did you see anybody completing his/her square, then sitting back to watch the others?
8. Did anybody give away all the pieces, receiving none in return?
9. Did a person receive many pieces and pass on only a few or none?
10. Was anybody having trouble following the rules, having to help, take or direct?
11. Did anybody make a large square or two or more of his own, with few pieces left for anyone else?

Materials for "Group Coop. Puzzle"

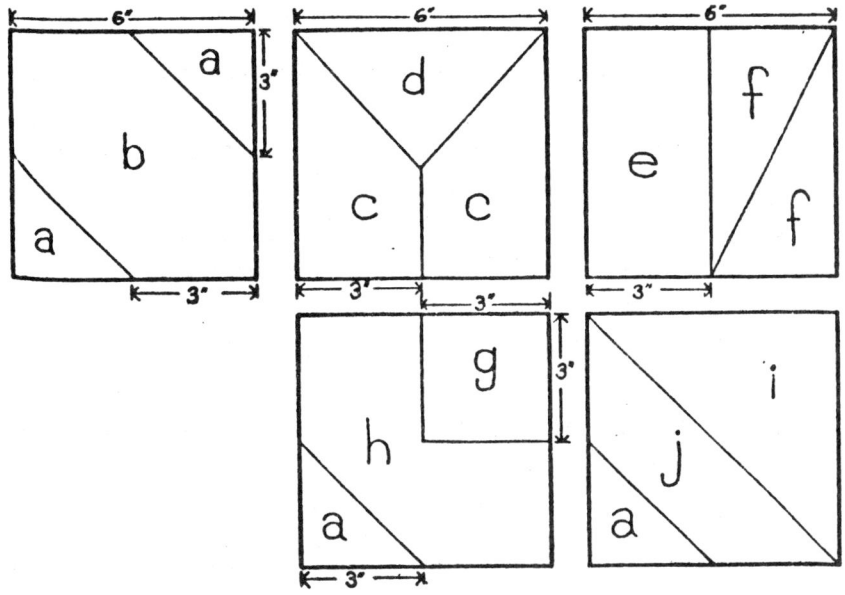

Cooperative Puzzle-Solving Activities   Primary/Intermediate Level

The String Puzzle*

Objective Students will cooperate in pairs to solve a puzzle.

Materials A 3-foot piece of string for each player.

Procedure Divide students into pairs and tie one end of the string to a student's left wrist and the other end to his right wrist. Then take a second piece of string and loop it through the other student's tied arms and tie one end of the second piece to the partner's left wrist and the other to his right wrist. The two students are now locked together and their goal is to become unlocked without breaking or removing the string.

<u>Solution:</u> There is only one solution to this puzzle and that is to have one of the pair slide his string between his partner's wrist and string and then loop it around the partner's hand.

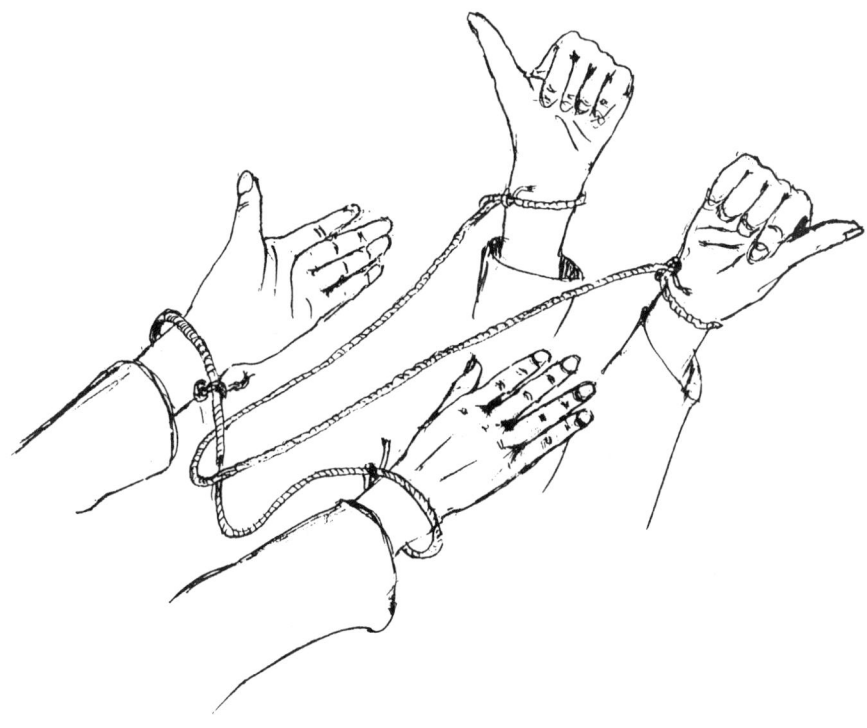

*   J. Wilt and B. Watson, *Relationship Builders*, 1978.

Cooperative Free Time and Recess Activities

Cooperative Checkers 262
Cooperative Three Deep 262
Blanket Toss 262
Pan Pong 263
Cooperative Jacks 263
Cooperative Jump Rope 263
Center Throw 263
Bouncing Ball Series 264
Equality 264
Bat Ball . . . . 264 - 265
Cooperative Shuffleboard 265
Human Checkers 265
Eight Feet Up 265
Circle of Hands 266

Conclude each of these activities with debriefing exercises found in the Introduction and/or on page 183.

Free Time and Recess Activities

Objective Students will play the following games through cooperative efforts.

Materials As indicated

Procedure In cooperative games everybody cooperates, everybody wins, and nobody loses. Children play with one another rather than against one another. These games eliminate the fear and the feeling of failure. They also reaffirm a child's confidence in himself or herself as an acceptable and worthy person. In most games (new or old) this reaffirmation is left to chance or awarded to just one winner. In cooperative games it is designed into the games.

Although the games have been played cooperatively in many cultures for centuries, there are very few games being played in our culture today that are designed specifically so that all players strive toward one common, mutually desirable goal. Genuine cooperative games with no losers are extremely rare in the Western world. Their rediscovery is something we can look forward to and gain from.

Select from the following games ones that are appropriate for your class.

Cooperative Checkers

This game differs from the regular game of checkers in that there is no jumping or moving backwards, and no checkers are removed. The two players aim to exchange all the black checkers and all the red checkers so that they are all on opposite sides of the board from where they started. The game is won if both players' checkers are moved to the last open position on the opposite side of the board at the same time. Therefore the players must cooperate with one another to make it easy for the other person to move his/her checkers.

The same game can be played with Chinese checkers, the goal being for all players to reach the opposite section at the same time.

Cooperative Three Deep

Students form a double circle, with each player in the outer circle standing behind a player in the inner circle. One player stands in the center of the circle. The center player throws a ball to any player in the inner circle. Immediately upon releasing the ball, the center player runs and stands behind someone in the outer circle. This person must run to the center in time to catch the ball that, in the meantime, has been thrown by the person in the inner circle to someone in the outer circle. The new center player catches the ball thrown by the person in the outer circle, and now throws the ball to another player in the inner circle, runs and takes a position behind a player in the outer circle, and so the game continues, with players coordinating their movements so that the new center player gets back in time to catch the ball.

Blanket Toss

Cut a hole in a large sheet or blanket big enough for a balloon to fall through. The players each hold a corner of the blanket and stretch it out. Place balloons of different sizes on the blanket or sheet and have the players toss them in the air by jerking the sheet. The object of the game is to get all the balloons to fall through the hole. The players may want to time themselves to see if their skill in working together has improved.

Pan Pong

Each player has a pan (a deep pan would probably be best for younger students). Players bounce a ball out of their pan into the pan of the next player. The purpose is to see how long the players can keep bouncing the ball into the next pan in one bounce. He/she can keep bouncing the ball until the transfer has been made.

Cooperative Jacks

The game is played in the traditional way, except that the first player will pick up the jacks one at a time, then hands jacks and ball to the next player. This one throws the jacks and picks them up two at a time. The next player picks up three at a time, and so on. If the player makes a mistake (touches a jack or misses the ball), his group has to begin over again. The game is won when the group has progressed to sixes. For younger children it may work best to eliminate the ball and just have them pick up the appropriate number in succession.

Cooperative Jump Rope

Two players turn the rope. The other players line up to jump. The first player jumps once, runs out, and quickly takes the place of one of the players turning the rope. The player who had been turning runs to the end of the line. Meanwhile, the second player jumps two times, runs out, and takes the other end of the rope. The player who had been turning runs to the end of the line. The third player jumps three times and runs out to take the end of the rope, etc. If someone misses, the next player begins all over again, jumping once.

Center Throw

Players form a circle with one player standing in the middle. This player throws the ball to a person in the circle, and then quickly runs to stand beside another player. This player takes the place of the person in the middle of the circle, trying to be there in time to catch the ball being thrown into the middle by the player in the circle.

Bouncing Ball Series

Players form a circle. The first player bounces a ball once over to the next player, who immediately catches the ball and bounces it two times. The next player catches the ball on the second bounce and bounces it to the next player on the third bounce, etc. If a mistake is made, the next player begins all over again.

A variation is to bounce as described once around the circle until the ball comes back to the one who started the game. This player bounces the ball one more time than the preceding player. But the next player starts over again at one. This prevents the bouncing from reaching such high numbers that the other players have to wait too long for their turns.

Equality

The goal of this card game is for each player to end with the same number of points. The cards are dealt out equally to the players. The first player leads any card and the other players follow suit. If they cannot follow suit, they may throw any other card. The player who has thrown the highest card (ace is the highest, with king, queen, jack, 10, etc. following) takes the pile, or "trick." The player who wins the trick places face up on the table any ace, 2, 3, 4, or 5 that was in the trick. All cards higher than 5 that were in the trick do not count and are discarded. This player now leads a card and the play proceeds in like manner. All the players attempt to follow suit or discard in such a way as to give the trick to the player who needs points to make all scores equal. The scoring system is as follows: aces count one point each, twos count two points each, threes count three each, fours count four each, and fives count five each. The total number of points is 60. At the end of the game, each player's score must be the same. Thus, to get the goal score, divide 60 by the number of players.

Bat Ball

The goal of this game is for the players to score more points than are credited to the game. The game scores a point every time the ball hits the ground. The players score a point every time the batted ball is caught without touching the ground. Players form a more or less complete circle around the batter, at a distance suitable for pitching and catching. Anyone who catches or recovers the ball may either pitch to the batter or throw the ball to another player who is in a better position to pitch. Each player takes a turn at batting from one to five times. Positions are rotated at the convenience and will of the players. They may choose a regular or a variable rotation.

Cooperative Shuffleboard

You may use a regular shuffleboard court by merely changing some of the numbers to minus. The goal of the game is to have players place their shots so that the team score will total exactly 15 when all discs have been used.

Human Checkers

For this activity you will need 24 large pieces each of red and black construction paper. Tape the construction paper on the floor in the form of a checkerboard. Divide students into red and black "teams" and have them make a headband out of a strip of red or black construction paper. Also, have some of the students (or all) make crowns out of the red and black paper.

Position the players on the board and play checkers using the rules for a regular game. The one exception will be that all moves must be agreed upon by the players of the same color.

When someone becomes a king, he/she will put on a crown and then can move as if he/she were a king in a regular game.

Eight Feet Up

Put students of similar height into groups of four. Have all members of each group lie on their backs with their feet in the air and their heels touching. Place a pie pan on the bottom of each group's feet. The groups must balance the pie pan while each group member takes off his shoes, one at a time. Students will need to interact with each other in order to coordinate this activity and not let the pie pan fall. Tell girls to wear pants rather than skirts or dresses the day you are planning to do this activity.

A Circle of Hands

Divide the class into groups of 8 to 10 students. Have each group form a closed circle, shoulder to shoulder. Ask students to stretch out both hands to the center of the circle and take a different classmate's hand in each one of theirs. A tangle of arms and hands should result. The goal of the game is for each group to attempt to untangle itself and form a circle without breaking hand contact. The end circle should have students holding hands in a normal side-by-side position.

Working Cooperatively on Academic Tasks

Cooperating on Math Activities . . . . 271 - 275
Cooperating on Language Arts Activities . . . . 277 - 293
Cooperating on Social Studies Activities . . . . 295 - 301
General Cooperation Strategies . . . . 303 - 305
Interdisciplinary Activities . . . . 307 - 308

Conclude each of these activities with debriefing exercises found in the Introduction and/or on page 183.

Section C

Working Cooperatively on Academic Tasks

Changing a collection of individual students into a productive working unit in which members cooperate on academic tasks means students must develop new skills and attitudes. It takes a lot of practice for students to learn to work together.

One of the best ways to help students begin to work together academically is to give them problem-solving activities that are challenging and that call for group decisions. Many assignments traditionally given to students to complete individually can be used to enhance cooperation skills as well as skill in a particular subject area. It's helpful to find assignments where students can see the advantage of pooling their thoughts and efforts. It is also helpful to find assignments that all students will be able to grasp sufficiently to make a contribution to their group. For instance, many math textbooks have challenging math puzzles or story problems that would be appropriate for students to work on in groups.

After making sure students understand clearly the directions for the academic activity they are to do together, it may also be helpful to review the guidelines for cooperative group work from time to time. Briefly go over the cooperation behaviors taught in previous lessons. It's a good idea to select one student from the group to monitor or observe group cooperation behavior using one of the cooperation rating scales found in the introduction. Explain that their rating scores will be collected at the end of the activity. When you collect them, you can use them as an opportunity to praise students who have demonstrated positive behavior.

Once groups get started, it is helpful if you circulate among them. Sometimes a group has a question that no one can answer, or may get bogged down and need your help. You will quickly need to determine whether the difficulty is in students' understanding of the activity itself or with the way the students are handling their roles in the group. It may be that no one is taking some of the necessary participant roles of giving ideas or asking questions. Perhaps no one is assuming the helper role of summarizing, encouraging others to get involved, or keeping everyone on the subject. By modeling for students some of these roles, you can show them what it is they need to do on their own.

If students are stuck on the problem, you need to help them restate what they know so far and suggest another way for them to approach the activity. If they're pursuing an erroneous idea, you need to point out the inconsistency in their thinking.

When debriefing at the end of the activity, it is important to discuss both content and process issues. When groups have finished exploring a problem, for instance, ask students to describe the approach they took to sharing the work. Ask students how they went about getting the job done by asking the following questions:

- Did you lose much time getting organized?
- How did you prevent everyone from talking at once?
- Was the assignment divided equally or did several of you collaborate on each item?
- Was one person in your group chosen to write everything down or was this task shared?

By listening to one another, students can gain new perspectives on ways to work cooperatively and can arrive at their own principles of cooperative behavior without you having to tell them how to organize for maximum group effectiveness on every task.

During critiquing, have students use the "Sentence Starters for Promoting Thinking" in the Appendix. For example,

- I learned . . .
- I felt that . . .
- I was surprised . . .
- It would have been better if . . .
- Next time . . .

The following is an assortment of academic activities in traditional subject areas which lend themselves to cooperative learning. Some of the activities utilize the learning structure of competition as well as cooperation by having cooperation groups compete with one another. This is a low-risk way to use competition since success and failure are shared by an entire group, not a single person. Activities for primary grades are given first, followed by those for intermediate grades.

Cooperating on Math Activities*

Objective Students will cooperate on learning tasks in the area of mathematics.

Materials None

Procedure *A good problem to give groups is the following math activity. This requires that each group find all the ways it can to write the numbers 1 to 25 as the sum of consecutive numbers. For younger students, finding the consecutive sums for the numbers from 1 to 15 may be sufficient. For students who work quickly or for gifted students, the task can be extended to include higher numbers.*

Say the following to students:

Today we are going to work together on some math activities.

By working with others you'll be able to see how several brains working to solve a problem are better than one.

Here's what I'd like you to do: We're going to work with the numbers 1 through 25.

I'd like you to take each number and think of the numbers that add up to it.

For instance, if you take number 3, the numbers 1 + 2 add up to 3.

If you take the number 5, the numbers 2 + 3 add up to 5.

The hard part of this problem is that I'd like you to find only consecutive numbers that add up to each number from 1 to 25.

---

* M. Burns, "Groups of Four: Solving the Management Problem," *Learning*, Sept. 1981, pp. 49-50.

For instance, if you take the number 9, you will find that 4 + 5 = 9. 4 and 5 are also consecutive, that is, one follows the other.

5 + 4 also equals 9, but 5 + 4 are not consecutive. There is another set of consecutive numbers that also equals 9.

Can anyone guess what it is? (Allow for student response)

Right, 2 + 3 + 4 equals 9 also, and these are consecutive numbers.

Some numbers won't work, such as 2 and 4. There aren't any consecutive numbers that add up to 2 and 4 because 1 + 1 isn't consecutive and 3 + 1 or 1 + 3 or 2 + 2 aren't consecutive numbers.

See if you can discover certain patterns for numbers that won't work. Also try to find patterns for numbers that do work.

Write down the patterns you find, but experiment with the pattern to make sure you are right.

For example, you may decide that all even numbers are impossible.

But what about 1 + 2 + 3? The sum of these numbers is 6, so saying that even numbers don't work is incorrect.

Now see what patterns you can find by putting your heads together.

Put everyone's brain to work.

Let's see who can be the first group to get done.

When groups have finished exploring the problem, summarize the results for the entire class. Post the recording sheets so that everyone can see them. Ask the class to look at differences and similarities in the organizational methods of recording. Some groups divide up the numbers so that one person does 1 to 6, another does 7 through 12, and so on. Other groups just work on whatever numbers each individual wants, and add their findings to a group chart. Some groups have one person do all the recording; others share that job among the members.

Recording systems differ also. Some groups list the numbers from 1 to 25 and write the sums next to each. Others organize the numbers by how many different sums they found for each, recording all those that could be written in only one way in one column, those that could be written in two ways in another, and so on.

Who Gets the Candy Bars?

Write the following situation on the board or give students a copy of it.

Five friends walk up to a candy machine and everyone decides they want a candy bar. All candies cost 20 cents. The machine does not give change back and only takes the exact amount needed for a purchase. There is no other way to obtain change except from the five friends.

   a. Mitzi has a quarter and a nickel.
   b. Lisa has two dimes and two nickels.
   c. Christopher has three nickels.
   d. Emmy has two dimes.
   e. Matt has no money.

Divide the class into groups of five. Have each group get together and come up with answers to these questions:

1. How many candy bars can be purchased?
2. Which children will get to have candy?
3. If any change is left, what should be done with it?

Mythical Budget

Explain to the students what constitutes a family budget. Each team must make up a budget for a mythical family, including all factors in running a home, taking emergency situations into account. Each team reports to the class and the class then votes on the best presentation.

Musical Problems

Make different cards containing math stories or number problems. Hand a number of cards to each team and ask them to cover up the cards so no one can read what is on them. The co-leaders pass one card to each team member. Begin the music and have students pass the cards to each other in a designated pattern, still face down. When you lift the needle off the phonograph, the passing stops and the students are allowed to read what is on their cards. Students from the same group may help each other as they solve the problem. Give one student in the group the answers to the problems. Have students check with the person who has the answers as they complete the problems. Have the group tally the points earned by individual members. The group with the most points earned wins. You may wish to set a time limit.

Cooperating on Language Arts Activities

Objective Students will cooperate in small groups on learning tasks in the area of language arts.

Materials Varied

Rhyming Activity*

Distribute ditto sheets with rhymes to the groups. These can be found in most primary reading workbooks. Have group members read the rhymes together and fill in the blanks with the appropriate word. When everyone is done, call on a student to read one of the completed rhymes. If he is able to read the rhyme, the group gets one point, and if he is able to fill in the blank correctly, the group gets an additional point. If one or more of the other groups have a different word in the blank that could also be correct, they may read their rhyme and get the same amount of points.

Alternate between groups and record the points earned on the board. The group with the most points wins. Rhymes might be something like this:

> Matt and Nat
> Play with a _____.
> Mouse, mouse,
> Get out of my _____.

Phonics Activity*

Divide the class into groups and give each group two words on a piece of paper. Each student on the team tries to form another word by changing the initial sound of the word only.

> Example: sat: mat, hat, gnat, bat
> heat: meat, seat, treat, beat

---

* M. Burns, "Groups of Four: Solving the Management Problem," *Learning*, September 1981.

The group with the most words wins. All groups must have the same two words at one time.

Alphabet Activity*

Go over the alphabet and discuss alphabetical order with the class. Divide the class into groups and give each group a list of dictionary guide words along with a list of words to find in the dictionary. Ask each group to find the numbers of the pages in the dictionary on which they found the words. The first group to finish the exercise wins.

Spelling Tic-Tac-Toe*

Have students do this activity when reviewing spelling words, so that there is not a high incidence of failure. Mark off a large tic-tac-toe on the floor with tape. It should be about 6 feet square. If there are more than two groups involved, you may want to make several squares so that several games can go on simultaneously.

Ditto off spelling words and cut the paper up into pieces containing several words. Put them in a container for random drawing. Label groups either A or B and establish a leader for each group.

Have group A choose a word from the list he drew for the opposing group B. The leader of group B can designate who is to spell the word, or students may volunteer. Everyone must get a turn before anyone is allowed to spell a word again. If the word is spelled correctly, the student stands in the tic-tac-toe box to help win the game for his group. X's and O's can be cut from construction paper to help keep track of who is who.

If a word is missed, the group loses a turn. The student who missed the word must copy it down for further study. You may want to give each

---

* M. Burns, "Groups of Four: Solving the Management Problem," *Learning*, September 1981.

student a vocabulary list from which the words were taken so he/she can study them until it is time for him/her to take their turn.

Haiku Poetry*

Explain to the class that Haiku poetry is a Japanese form of poetry which consist of 17 syllables. The first line must have 5 syllables, the second 7, and the last 5 again. Its theme revolves around the emotions or nature.

Example: In the setting sun
           A seagull dipped its golden wings
           As if to greet me.

Have groups form huddles and work on creating their own Haikus. The results can be read to the class, displayed on the bulletin board, or made into a book for classroom display.

Homographs, Homophones, Homonyms*

Give words to the different groups and have them give the definition of the words. Then have them decide which words are homographs, homophones, and homonyms. The group to complete their list correctly first wins.

Creative Writing and Vocabulary Development*

Each group makes a list of 10 words they feel will be unfamiliar to the other students. They may use dictionaries, a thesaurus, books, parents, or other adults. This can also be a homework assignment, with each student preparing five words and their definitions they can bring to class the next day. Then the group can decide on which 10 words they want to use. They then give their list to another group and group members individually, or as a group write a story using these words. If done

---

* M. Burns, "Groups of Four: Solving the Management Problem," *Learning*, September 1981.

individually, the group can get together and decide which story will be chosen to represent them. The story is then read to the rest of the class.

Vocabulary and Classification Skills Activity*

Divide the class into groups. Each group is to draw a 5" x 5" grid large enough for a word to fit in each 1" square. You may want to draw an example on the board. Together with the students, decide on five categories for which they are to find words. Examples could be foods, movie stars, cars, colors, things you find in school, etc. Write the categories on the left side of the grid, one for each row. Then decide on five letters, which you write above each column. The students are to find words that begin with these letters and fit in the right category. You might suggest to older students that they try to find words that they think will not be chosen by other students. A point could be earned for each word that is unique. For younger students one category might be enough. You can suggest that they try to find pictures in magazines of things filling the category and paste them in the boxes.

From Words to Story*

Divide the class into groups of four or five. Have each group select any five unrelated words. The groups are then to make up a story or play using these five words. After a set time, have each group tell or act out its story.

Finish a Story**

Divide the class into groups of four or five. Read a fairy tale or a story to the entire class, either finishing it or ending before the conclusion. Have each group work on a different ending or write a conclusion to the story. After a period of time, have the groups act out the entire story, incorporating their endings.

---

*   M. Burns, "Groups of Four: Solving the Management Problem," *Learning*, September 1981.

** J. Wilt, and B. Watson, *Relationship Builders*, 1978.

Shared Stories

Ask students to write a number of nouns and verbs on slips of paper and put them into a box. Suggest that they pick words that would be good for stories. Divide the class into groups of two or three and allow each group to draw several words from the box. They will then write a story together, based on the words they drew. You may also wish to have students brainstorm an adjective and adverb list and use it along with the nouns and verbs in writing a story.

Noun Suggestions	Verb Suggestions	Adjective Suggestions
elephant	ran	interesting
girl	swam	white
boy	remembered	beautiful
octopus	helped	intelligent
bicycle	traveled	big
ice cream	sang	gigantic
balloons	painted	happy
spaceship	disappeared	huge
Martian	discovered	scary
guitar	suspected	

Proverb Pantomime*

The teacher pantomimes a familiar proverb or saying and the groups try to figure out what it is. Each group takes turns pantomiming a saying or proverb. Groups may take several days to pantomime these sayings or proverbs; they don't all have to do it in one day. The other groups try to guess what proverb is being acted out. For example,

A stitch in time saves nine.
A bird in the hand is worth two in the bush
A rolling stone gathers no moss
Many hands makes light
Slow and steady wins the race.

---

* M. Burns, "Groups of Four: Solving the Management Problem," *Learning*, September 1981.

Relay Game*

This may be used for sentence construction review, vocabulary review, warm-up at the beginning of the period, etc. The teacher prepares his or her own review or uses already available material. The group members, each in turn, are given a sentence or a word to complete or write out at the board. As soon as a group member returns to his or her group, another goes to the board. Allowance needs to be made for groups that have more members than others.

Vocabulary Lists*

The lists are divided among groups. The leader assigns words to individual members. Groups then present the words to others with their usage, receiving a point for each correct word. Groups quiz each other on the words.

Vocabulary Building*

The groups huddle to study vocabulary words and to put them in sentences. The sentences are handed to the teacher who uses them in a fast vocabulary drill exercise.

Spelling Bee

Groups huddle to study their words and to prepare sentences incorporating the words. The groups challenge other teams with their sentences by using them for oral fill-ins, asking the other groups to use the word in a sentence or asking for spelling, definition, and use in sentences, or in another way the class and teacher wish to run the cooperative competition.

---

* M. Burns, "Groups of Four: Solving the Management Problem," *Learning*, September 1981.

Cooperative Commercial

In this activity, students are asked to work cooperatively to plan and later perform a skit (short play). Divide students into small groups of three or four. Each group needs to decide what "ZIP," the product name, stands for -- for example, it could be dog food, laundry soap, toothpaste, cereal, cleanser, a soft drink, chewing gum, a computer game, etc. The groups plan a 1-minute skit/commercial for selling their product. All group members must play a part in the skit. Examples of types of commercials are interviews, demonstrations, testimonials, jingles or songs, comparisons, and panel discussions.

Tell the students that they have 15 minutes to plan and practice their skit and that the skit may be no longer than 2 minutes in length. Ask students to present their skit.

Putting on a Mini-play

Each group selects a young children's book from the library. The group then works out a dramatization (script acting, narration, puppets, video tape, etc.) and presents it to a younger class. Group members should also make any costumes or scenery necessary.

Radio Show

Each group is responsible for creating a particular part of a radio broadcast -- news, weather, music, contests, comedy routines, etc.

Parts are then be put together to form a complete radio show. This could be put on tape to become part of a listening center. Shows could be modern or concerned with a particular time in history, such as the Roaring Twenties or World War II.

Word Meaning Challenge

Each group finds 10 unusual words in the dictionary and formulates questions incorporating the words which can be answered yes or no.

Example: Would you eat a friar for dinner?

Groups would then exchange questions and answer them, giving reasons for any "no" answer: "No, I wouldn't eat a friar for dinner because I am not a hungry cannibal."

Encyclopedia articles might also be used.

Grammar Rules

Each group would be responsible for dramatizing one or more rules of grammar in such a manner as to make them memorable.

Example: A short vowel in the middle of a three-letter word becomes long when a final "e" is added.

Groups could costume or shape themselves to represent a particular letter: vowel could squat down when "short," silent "e" could come out with a gag on his/her mouth, short vowel could stretch out on floor or stand on chair to become "long."

Directions

Each group writes explicit, step-by-step directions for a simple activity: putting on a shoe, brushing teeth, etc. Each member reads directions to another group.

Directions must be followed to the letter; i.e., all prior knowledge of how the activity is done should be forgotten so that group members do only what they are told to do and how they are told to do it.

Paper folding and/or cutting to end up with a particular figure is easier in that there is no prior knowledge of the product, but the directions are very difficult to write.

Another possibility would be to have an object hidden somewhere on the school grounds and write directions on a "Treasure Map" for the other group to follow.

Writing a Book

Each group writes and illustrates (hand-drawn or magazine pictures) a book for younger grades. The book should have an attractive cover, index, glossary, typed pages (by students themselves), a title page; i.e., everything necessary for a real book. The book should also be bound- contacting the pages, then sewing or stapling together. The group does a dramatization of the book to interest readers and/or make an accompanying tape (with sound effects and background music). The book is presented to the library with a tape, if one was made, to be cataloged.

Library Hunt

Each group goes to the library at different times to select 10 books (reference and shelf) about which they are to devise questions. Questions must be formed so that only one book would be the correct answer. For example, "What is a book about horse racing written by Mary Calhoun?"

When all groups have completed their questions, they trade and go on a Library Hunt, each group trying to find the correct book to answer the questions.

Music

Each group selects a well-known song and writes their own words to it to sing for the class. Or, groups could make up a completely original song, make their own instruments and costumes, and be part of a class talent show. Poetry or Haiku written by team members could be put to music.

Weaving Words Into a Story

Objective Students will cooperate in small groups to analyze and evaluate their class.

Materials Student handout

Procedure Divide the class into small groups. Pass out worksheets and read the instructions to the students. Give them 15 minutes to write their paragraphs. Ask students to figure out their scores. Share the scores and ask for volunteers to read their paragraphs.

Ask the students the following questions: Which words were easiest to use? Hardest to use? Why? Comment on the paragraphs read by students: How were they similar? Different? What kind of group is this class? Which paragraph best describes the class as a group?

Weaving Words Into a Story

Name _____

You are to write a paragraph about our class that makes sense. Below is a list of words. Try to use as many of these words in your paragraph as you can. You may use a word from this list up to three times. You will receive one point every time you use a word from the list below, which means you can get a total of three points for each word listed below. To help in scoring, every time you use a word from the list, underline it in your paragraph.

WORD LIST

cooperative	worst	kind	participate
never	listen	ideas	success
together	problem	proud	like
frustrated	noisy	happy	friend
group	leader	helpful	unkind

A Story About a Trip

Objective Students will cooperate in pairs or trios to write a story about a trip.

Materials Student handout "A Story about a Trip"

Procedure Divide students into pairs or trios. Tell the students to imagine that they are going on an exciting trip, and then write a story about it. Ideas about trips could be a trip to Disneyland, a boat trip, a trip in a hot air balloon, a camping trip, etc. They can use the back of the student handout, if they need more space.

Cooperating on Language Arts Activities　　　Handout for "A Story About a Trip"
Page 293

A Story About a Trip

Cooperating on Social Studies Activities

Objective Students will cooperate in small groups on learning tasks in the area of social studies

Materials Varied, "Group Report" form

Procedure Select the following activities that would be appropriate for your class:

Group Scrapbook*

Give each group a stack of magazines, scissors, paste, and a scrapbook. Assign a subject they are to look for in their magazines, for example, subjects discussed in social studies for which suitable pictures can be found in popular magazines. When pictures are found for the particular subjects, the group pastes them in its scrapbook. Captions related to the unit of study can be printed under each picture. The group scrapbooks may then be displayed for other class members to see.

Creation of Country through Map Skills*

Tell the class that each group will be creating its own country. Review map skills with them. Then have the groups get together individually to create a country, draw a map, and make a relief map of it. When they are finished, have them exchange maps with other teams. They are to analyze the maps and countries according to correct location, longitude, latitude, etc. You can also use this procedure to create the fictitious country's government, economy, history, etc.

Outline Map*

Give each group a large outline map and a sheet of numbered tasks to be done. Have the groups decide who will do what and find the necessary references. When the map is finished, one member of the group will place the map on the bulletin board and the other group will evaluate it following guidelines set up by the other students and teacher.

* M. Burns, "Groups of Four: Solving the Management Problem," *Learning*, September 1981.

Example: Map of Washington
1. Color Puget Sound blue.
2. Color the Olympics gray.
3. Color the Strait of Juan de Fuca red.

You can also have the group decide on symbols or pictures for forests, mountains, population, climate, etc.

The Thirteen Colonies*

Each group is assigned or selects a colony to study. They research the colony and then make a lesson plan on how they are going to teach the rest of the class about their colony. They may write a play with the information gathered and they may use additional media, such as slides, maps, drawings, photographs, etc., and prepare a quiz. After the presentations, the class takes the quiz. Points can be given by the other groups for the lesson itself and for the team's ability to cooperate on the project.

News Events*

Each group is assigned a certain news category for the week, such as miscellaneous, county, state, world, local, etc. Each group member is responsible for an article within this category. The group then selects the best article for presentation to the class. The group may have an editor or an assistant editor to select the best article, or the team can vote by a show of hands after an open discussion. A set of questions on the article is also prepared for the class.

In the case of a tie or when two students bring in the same article, one may be selected to do the presentation, and the other may do one at a later date.

The other groups judge the article by the subject, presentation, interest, and questions. The judging groups may also ask questions.

---

*   M. Burns, "Groups of Four: Solving the Management Problem," *Learning,* September 1981.

After all the presentations have been made, the points are called out to the scorekeeper, who tallies them on the board. The group with the highest total of points wins for the day. You may choose to set a time limit for the selection and preparation part of the activity.

Time Capsule

Ask students to imagine what it would be like if 100 or 500 years from now someone dug up the remains of their school building and found a time capsule they had stored there. What could they include in a time capsule that would really show something about life in this community this year? Students can bring things from home and find pictures in magazines and newspapers.

Students should be placed in several groups and given sufficient time to construct a time capsule. Remind them that space is limited, but they may assume the capsule will be stored in a way that everything will be kept in perfect condition.

Groups should share the items they chose with one another. Students may wish to bury their time capsules and indicate the year they are to be opened on a marker. Three-pound coffee containers, ice cream containers, or plastic buckets from restaurant suppliers may be used for the time capsules.

Suggested items for a time capsule:

- Newspaper and magazine articles showing current events
- Small items of clothing
- Item of jewelry popular with young people
- Examples of modern advertising showing products in common use, i.e., Kentucky Fried Chicken box
- Penny candy
- Election buttons or program bumper stickers
- Photos from magazines

- Novelty items or toys, i.e., glow-in-the-dark silly putty
- Recipes
- Pamphlets showing modern products, such as video games
- Records
- Cosmetics, especially those that tend to be common

Creating a Symbol for an Organization

Decide in advance the subject to be symbolized. It could be a symbol for the school, a club, a political party, a country, a city, etc. Divide the class into groups of four or five and give each group a poster-size sheet of paper and crayons or colored chalks. Give the class about 20 minutes to create a pictorial symbol of the chosen subject. You may want to show them examples of symbols on flags, coats of arms, and seals to give them ideas.

Group Report

Have students work in groups to prepare a 10-minute presentation for the rest of the class on a topic of their own choosing or a topic they have selected from a list of options prepared by the teacher. Explain that they will need to do the following:

1. Choose a speaker.
2. Prepare handout material such as outlines, summaries, or topics for discussion, etc.
3. Put together a visual presentation (charts, diagrams, slides, pictures, etc.).
4. Prepare an audio presentation (to go with visuals -- records, background music, scripts, tapes, sound effects, etc.).
5. Write a short quiz for the class to take based on the materials presented.
6. Select someone to grade the quiz and give results.
7. Select someone to lead a class discussion following the program.

Have them complete the handout "Preparing our Presentation" that follows this section.

Reporting on Countries or States

Each group selects a foreign country (or state) they would like to visit. Compile information including location, size, population, climate, products, dress, religion, food, etc. Resource people should also be found and used whenever possible.

Make a travel folder that would entice other people to want to visit. Presentation to class could include bringing in a resource person to speak to the class, preparing food for the class to taste, dressing in national costume, playing music of the country, etc. -- almost anything other than just reading a report to the class.

Historic Events

Each group selects or is assigned a particular event important in history. Research should include what precipitated the event, who was involved, and what its consequences were in the development of the nation.

Present the research to the class in an interesting way: dramatization, puppets, murals, etc.

Occupations

Discuss the various occupations of parents and other people in the community. Make a list.

Have each group select one occupation that interests them. They will then research it, including necessity and contribution to society, educational or experiential background required, means or chances for advancement, salary, etc. If possible, group members should be allowed to spend some time "on the job" with a resource person. Then they should present their findings.

Group Report
Preparing our Presentation

Steps in preparing a presentation:

Topic your group picked _____

Who is speaking? _____

Who prepares "hand-out" material? _____

Who prepares visuals? _____

Who prepares audios? _____

Who makes the test? _____

Who scores the test? _____

Who runs the discussion? _____

When will your presentation be given? _____

How long will it be? _____

How will your topic be presented? _____
_____
_____

Did you pick a project leader? _____

If yes, how? _____
_____

Does everyone have an equal workload? _____

Are all members pleased with their jobs? _____
_____
_____
_____

General Cooperation Strategies

Objective Students will cooperate in small groups on learning tasks in many academic areas.

Materials Varied

Procedure Select the following activities that would be appropriate for your class:

Studying a Unit

Each group is assigned a section or unit to study. An evaluation sheet is passed out to each member of all groups. The groups are graded on the basis of the evaluation sheet. Points to be evaluated should be discussed before the groups prepare their reports so they will know what will be expected of them. Reports may be given by one member of the group selected by the teacher, the leader, or the consensus of the group members. A written report may or may not be required. If it is, each member should be represented in the report for an individual grade. The group as a whole should be evaluated for points on the entire written report, as well as on the oral report.

Quiz Squares*

This game can be played at any time, especially when reviewing some particular subject such as social studies, English, science, etc. Make up a long list of questions and answers. Also prepare nine posters with "X" on one side and "O" on the other. Form a panel of nine students. Have three sit on the floor, three sit in chairs behind them, and the last three stand behind the students in chairs. Give each student a poster. The rest of the students are the contestants and are divided into two groups.

---

* J. Wilt, and B. Watson, *Relationship Builders*, 1978.

Assign one of these groups to be the "O's" and the other the "X's." The leader asks the "X" group to pick a square. The group decides who they want to answer the question. The panel member questioned gives an answer and the "X" group decides to agree or disagree. The leader gives the answer. If the group chose correctly, the panel member holds up an "O." The group alternates guesses as the game of tic-tac-toe becomes the object. Remind groups to make sure that all students get a turn.

Quiz Makers and Takers

Each group prepares a quiz for another group. The group taking the quiz is graded for knowledge of the materials, and the group making the quiz is graded for accuracy and wording of the questions. A variation could be for each group to prepare a quiz and hand it to the teacher. The teacher then takes parts of each quiz and prepares a class quiz.

Cumulative Score*

Randomly select a group and direct a question to it. If the correct answer is given, the group earns a point. If the group is unable to answer, or if an incorrect answer is given, go on to the next group for two points. A question may be worth up to four points. If the correct answer hasn't been given by that time, the teacher gives the answer and a new question is asked. Later during the period the teacher may ask the same question again. A variation is that the questions are arranged in sets ranging from easy to difficult. The team members may be chosen by number to answer.

---

* G.A. Poirier, *Students as Partners in Team Learning*, 1970.

Group Editing

In group editing, members learn that by working with and helping others, they can often produce better results than they can by working alone.

Step 1: Each member works alone on an assigned problem for a prescribed period of time and then writes a solution.

Step 2: B and C switch and edit each others' paper. D and E do the same. A circulates and discusses with each member the reasons for any proposed changes.

Step 3: B and C confer and produce a common written solution. D and E do the same. A oversees the process, helping when necessary.

Step 4: Another switch: B and C together edit D's and E's solution and vice versa.

Step 5: The whole group working together produces a common solution.

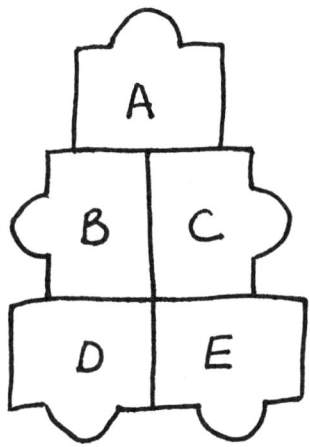

Interdisciplinary Activities

Game Show

Have groups watch various TV game shows and decide on one they liked. They then reproduce the show, write a take-off on it, or create their own show by using collective ideas. Then groups present to the class.

The game could be based on a specific subject area being studied or could be just for fun.

Questions

Each group selects a particular "thing" to be, researches it in such a way that each group member is responsible for knowledge in a certain area, then challenges the class or another group to guess their identity by asking 20 or fewer "yes-no" answer questions.

Depending on what is being studied at the time, the "thing" could be

Presidents	Mythical characters	Teacher
States	Story characters	Students
Countries	Disney characters	Movie Stars
Historic figures	Sports figures	Etc.

Cooking

Each group selects a simple recipe and plans a cooking-tasting demonstration for the class. Afterwards, "just for fun," groups make up their own "ridiculous recipes." Make up names (Worm Waffles, Crocodile Cream Cookies, Tortoise Tarts), write the recipes, illustrate, and combine into a class cookbook.

Holidays

Each group selects a little-known holiday (one other than Christmas, Thanksgiving, etc.) and researches it to find why we celebrate it, why on that particular day, who was responsible for it, who it is commemorating, when it was declared a holiday, and how it is supposed to be celebrated. Presentation to the class should include any special rituals and a visual.

Inventing a Machine

Each group invents a machine to do something no machine does at present. Example: a banana split maker, an elephant washer. It may be completely fantastic or really useful.

The groups construct the machine out of boxes and junk, or choose to be the machine parts themselves by repeating specific movements in conjunction with each other. This lends itself particularly to musical accompaniment.

Other groups either guess what was being done or are told in advance so as to evaluate the product.

Perfect School

Each group designs what they consider to be the perfect school. Groups draw up plans for the entire building, its location, type of rooms, furniture, AV materials, books, teachers, students, and schedule.

The only stipulation (to prevent all-day recesses) is that students must learn as much or more than they do today and it cannot be done by magic (pouring liquid knowledge into their ears).

Crazy Zoo

Each group creates a zoo filled with "never before seen" animals. The groups plan physical structures, rearranging the room, creating imaginary animals (sock puppets or paper bag masks), and writing a tour guide for visitors, giving location and description of each animal. A group member then leads the class on a tour of the group's "zoo."

Teacher for a Day

Each group is assigned a particular lesson to present to the class. Group members are each responsible for a portion of the presentation. They introduce the subject, explain it, prepare necessary materials for class use, are resource people, make and evaluate assignments.

Bibliography

Burns, M. (1981, September). Groups of Four: Solving the Management Problem. *Learning*.

Calgary Board of Education. (1982). *Family Life and Sex Education Curriculum*. Calgary, Alberta, Canada.

Cartledge, G. & J.F. Milburn. (1980). *Teaching Social Skills to Children: Innovative Approaches*. Elmsford, N.Y.: Pergamon Press, Inc.

Casteel, J. Doyle. (1978). *Learning to Think and Choose*. Santa Monica, CA: Goodyear Publishing Co., Inc.

Daniel, B. & Charlie Daniel. (1980). *Strain Your Brain*. The Learning Works.

Glatthorn, A. *Write On: A Scenario for Poetry*. Mimeographed learning packet.

Hawley, Robert C. & Isabel L. Hawley. (1975). *Human Values in the Classroom*. New York City: Hart Publishing Co., Inc.

Herberholz, B. (1980, November). Double Value: Visual Images/Verbal Reinforcement. *Arts & Activities*.

Johnson, David W. & Frank P. Johnson. (1975). *Learning Together and Alone*. Englewood Cliffs, N.J.: Prentice Hall, Inc.

Martin, K., M. Black, & C. Wolter. (1980). *It's Up To Me*. Glendale, CA: Project Focus.

Poirier, Gerard A. (1970). *Students as Partners in Team Learning*. Berkeley, CA: Center of Team Learning.

Saulnier, L. & Tersa Simard. (1973). *Personal Growth and Interpersonal Relations*. Englewood Cliffs, N.J.: Prentice Hall, Inc.

Stanford, Gene. (1977). *Developing Effective Classroom Groups.* New York City, NY: Hart Publishing Company, Inc.

Stanish, B. (1982). *Connecting Rainbows.* Benton Harbor, MI: Patterson Printing Co.

Wilt, J. & Bill Watson. (1978). *Relationship Builders.* Waco, TX: WORD Educational Products Division.

Books for Students About Cooperation With Others

Beim, Lorraine & Jerrold. (1945). *Two is a Team.* New York: Harcourt, Brace & World.

Slobodkin, Louis. (1956). *One is good but Two are Better.* New York: Vanguard.

Lionni, Leo. (1967). *Frederick.* New York: Pantheon.

Appendix

Sentence Starters for Promoting Thinking

I LEARNED...

I WAS SURPRISED...

I REALIZED THAT...

I HOPE THAT...

I CHANGED MY MIND ABOUT...

I WONDER...

I'M STILL CONFUSED ABOUT . . .

NEXT TIME . . .

I LIKED...

I DIDN'T LIKE...

WHAT PUZZLES ME IS . . .

THE BIG IDEAS SEEM TO BE . . .

ANOTHER POINT OF VIEW IS . . .

I'VE GOT IT! YOU MEAN . . .

A QUESTION I HAVE IS . . .

A WAY TO USE THIS IDEA IS . . .

THIS IS SIMILAR TO WHAT I KNOW ABOUT . . .

I'D LIKE TO TALK MORE ABOUT . . .

THIS REMINDS ME OF . . .

THIS IS SORT OF LIKE . . .

THE MAIN IDEA SEEMS TO BE...

IF THIS IS TRUE...

IF YOU LOOK AT IT IN A DIFFERENT WAY...

THIS COULD BE HELPFUL WHEN...

I COULD USE THIS WHEN . . .

WHAT I NEED TO KNOW IS . . .

ANOTHER WAY YOU COULD SAY IT IS . . .

THIS IS JUST LIKE . . .

IT WOULD HAVE BEEN BETTER IF ...

IT FELT GOOD WHEN ...